THE RICE QUEEN DIARIES

THE RICE QUEEN DIARIES

a memoir

Daniel Gawthrop

ARSENAL PULP PRESS

VANCOUVER

THE RICE QUEEN DIARIES
Copyright © 2005 by Daniel Gawthrop

ARSENAL PULP PRESS
341 Water Street, Suite 200
Vancouver, BC
Canada V6B 1B8
arsenalpulp.com

The publisher gratefully acknowledges the support of the Canada Council for the Arts and the
British Columbia Arts Council for its publishing program, and the Government of Canada
through the Book Publishing Industry Development Program for its publishing activities.

Text and cover design by Shyla Seller
Cover painting by Nhan duc Nguyen
All photographs and illustrations courtesy of the author, except for page 43 photo courtesy of
Walter Quan and page 89 photo courtesy of Thai Van Tran
Film still on page 33 from *Chinese Characters* by Richard Fung, reproduced with permission

This is a work of non-fiction, but some names have been changed to protect individuals' privacy.
Efforts have been made to locate copyright holders of source material wherever possible. The
publisher welcomes hearing from any copyright holders of material used in this book who have
not been contacted.

Printed and bound in Canada

Library and Archives Canada Cataloguing in Publication

Gawthrop, Daniel, 1963-
     The rice queen diaries / by Daniel Gawthrop.

Includes bibliographical references.
ISBN 1-55152-189-X

     1. Gawthrop, Daniel, 1963- 2. Gay men—Canada—Biography. 3. Gay
men—Asia. 4. Asians. I. Title.

HQ75.8.G39A3 2005   306.76'62'092   C2005-903688-5

for
Saw Aung Htwe Nyunt Lay

Contents

A man lives not only his personal life, as an individual, but also, consciously or unconsciously, the life of his epoch and his contemporaries.
– Thomas Mann

Truthful contact between nations and lovers can only be the result of heroic effort. Those who prefer to bypass the work involved will remain in a world of surfaces, misperceptions running rampant.
– David Henry Hwang

Preface

ONE NIGHT IN SAIGON DURING THE SPRING OF 2000, I was browsing through a silk boutique near the Rex Hotel when I spotted the perfect kimono: one of those shiny, reversible gowns with the Chinese-style embroidery and fancy dragon design on the back. I thought it was charmingly flamboyant – the kind you'd wear lounging about in the study with a gin martini – so I bought it. Back home in the West, my fellow Caucasians offered a more sobering assessment of that gown. "It's a smoking jacket," smiled a friend, "like the one that dreadful Rice Queen wore in *The Year of Living Dangerously*."

Later, when I happened to be watching a rented video of the 1982 film, it struck me that Wally O'Sullivan – the character my friend was referring to, a middle-aged correspondent for the *Sydney Herald* – never *once* appears in a kimono. Had my friend confused him with a similar character from another film? Perhaps. But it's more likely that two fleeting hints of Wally's sexuality – his tender caress of a young Indonesian waiter serving him a late-night drink, and a scene in which he's accused by the film's protagonist/narrator of "using boys for pleasure" – had provided enough stereotypical coding to peg him as a "dreadful Rice Queen." A kimono would have completed the caricature.

The term "Rice Queen" is a product of contemporary western gay vernacular. It refers to a man, usually Caucasian, who is sexually attracted to men of Far East – including Southeast – Asian origins. Like his heterosexual equivalent, the Rice Queen is drawn to youthful, androgynous features typical of the "Oriental" look: smooth brown skin, black hair, and broad faces with high cheekbones, elongated ("slanted") eyes, and porcelain-perfect lips. Along with the physical attraction is an obsession with all things Asian: from cuisine and home decor to history, culture, religion, and spirituality. Many Rice Queens, after travelling to the Far East, return with planeloads of Asian knick-knacks.

Where does this attraction come from? How is it that sexual preference can be limited to – or, at least, dominated by – a certain racial (stereo)type? For some white men, the appeal is transgressive: Asian guys are a turn-on because their boyish looks, regardless of their actual age, allow for paedophilic fantasies that can be acted upon with exhilarating results – but without breaking the law. For others, the appeal is rooted in culturally determined, essentialist notions of Asian passivity or femininity. Asian guys are seen as more "gentle" or agreeable than white guys, so an interracial match is seen as complimentary. (Again, in either case the same can be said of "Rice Kings" – straight white men attracted to Asian women.)

Not surprisingly, "Rice Queen" is heavily burdened with political baggage. It's most often a pejorative label that denotes ethnic fetishism and a preference for relationships based on inequality. Those saddled with the label are often charged with neo-colonial racism. The stereotypical Rice Queen is middle-aged or older, wealthy, and overweight; his Asian lover is young, sleek, feminine, servile, and passive in bed. What makes the Rice Queen more notorious than other cultural fetishists named after food groups – "Curry Queens" for lovers of South Asians, "Salsa Queens" (Latin Americans), "Chocolate Queens" (Africans), "Potato Queens" (Europeans) – is the dubious legacy of "Yellow Fever" in the Orient. In no other hemisphere, it seems, does imperial dominance-as-sexual-metaphor carry such heavy symbolic weight: Imaginary Occidental power in the Far East is typically embraced through the fetishization of smaller bodies and the essentialist notion of the inscrutable Asian whore.

In 1978, Edward Said's *Orientalism*[1] prompted fierce academic and literary debates about racism, cultural Darwinism, and western imperialism in the nineteenth and twentieth centuries. Said argued that the West, in the course of establishing its dominion over the non-Caucasian, non-Christian East, invented the idea of "The Orient" and an entire corporate and institutional mindset for "making statements about it, authorizing views of it, describing it, by teaching it, settling it, ruling over it." Said's "Orient" was confined geographically to the Middle East of Palestine, Egypt, Syria, and Arabia – the "near Orient," in relation to western Europe. But for North

1. New York: Random House, 1978.

American readers, who tend to equate "the Orient" with the Far East, the western triumphalism Said was describing could also be seen in the Pacific Rim. Orientalism was alive and well in the development of modern China during the opium wars; the colonial history of Burma, Indochina, and the Philippines; the post-World War II administration of Japan; the Cold War politics of Korea; and the tourist economy of Thailand, to name a few.

Nowhere is the mentality of essentialist Orientalism more evident than in the treatment of Far East Asians as sex objects. Western literary references to Oriental or Far East Asian beauty typically focus on the "beguiling," the "sensual," and the "mysterious." Such attractiveness is often depicted as a powerful, even dangerous erotic force the white western male is incapable of resisting. Consider the following passage by W.P. Kinsella, from a short story many readers have interpreted as a thinly veiled ode to the author's erstwhile girlfriend, the former teen prostitute-turned-novelist/poet Evelyn Lau:

> He stared at her beautiful peach-colored skin, her small,
> delicate Asian eyes, and was overwhelmed with love....
> Lloyd leaned over and kissed her right earlobe. It was as
> soft as a peach.[2]

If it were possible to compile an image bank of my own sexual history, the volume of couplings with East Asians would far outnumber those featuring any other ethnic group – my own included. Over the decade and a half that encapsulates the following narrative, I fell under the spell of countless "Orientals" with dark eyes, lean brown bodies, smooth skin, and "inscrutable" charm. But unlike the stereotype, I was not – at least, by most Rice Queen standards – considered a "UFO": ugly, fat, and old. I was attracted to men of all races and was *not* an obsessive collector of all things Far East Asian, an expert in Far East Asian languages, or an adherent of Far East Asian religion. So, what kind of Rice Queen would *that* make me?

Whatever the case, it wasn't long into my erotic life before I felt the glare of disapproval from a critique that saw "Yellow Fever" desire as politically suspect. Radical feminists like bell hooks accused white men attracted to non-whites of "commodifying Otherness." Eric C. Wat argued that not

---

2. W.P. Kinsella, "Lonesome Polecat." *Canadian Author,* Winter 1998.

enough Rice Queens were aware "that their desire, when based on fantasies and stereotypes, shares the same source of [sic] a bigot's hatred."[3] And Song Cho lamented Rice Queens' reduction of gay Asians to "boy toys" for their "predatory consumption," even describing one Toronto bar as a "hunting ground" where Rice Queens "cruised looking for their prey."[4]

I didn't see myself as a "predator" or my attraction to Far East Asian men as anything to be ashamed about. Human reality is too complicated to be reduced to competing stereotypes or social orthodoxies, and people develop sexual tastes, preferences, and habits for reasons that defy prejudice. On the other hand, the fact that a Rice Queen discourse existed – and that anecdotal evidence raised questions of motivation I found disturbingly familiar – was a compelling enough argument to put my own history of desire under the microscope. But how to share the results of such a probe?

It wouldn't be easy. Since the early 1980s, the discourse that began with Edward Said has set the standard by which all writing about race, sex, and culture is to be taken seriously as post-colonial thinking. At the same time, the increasing number of Far East Asian cultural critics obtaining tenure in the western academe has ensured that sins of literary racism – facile stereotyping, appropriation of voice – get pounced upon immediately, the offenders exposed as "reactionary." One unfortunate consequence of all the vigilance has been a literary chilling effect: depictions of interracial desire that are not simply narratives of objectification (see the Kinsella passage quoted earlier) often adhere to a "multicult" school of writing whose expression is so cautious and freighted with euphemism that it seems almost crafted by committee.

Anti-Orientalism doesn't go far enough to account for layers of complexity in human relationships that obscure what might on the surface seem concrete political "truths" about interracial contact. Even video artist Richard Fung, a respected critic of Orientalism, conceded as much in his groundbreaking (and unforgettably titled) 1991 essay, "Looking for My Penis: The Eroticized Asian in Gay Video Porn."[5] Fung argued that several

---

3. "Preserving the Paradox: Stories from a Gay-Loh." *Asian-American Sexualities: Dimensions of the Gay and Lesbian Experience*, edited by Russell Leong (New York: Routledge, 1996).

4. Introduction. *Rice: Explorations into Gay Asian Culture & Politics* (Toronto: Queer Press, 1998).

5. First published in *How Do I Look?: Queer Film and Video*, edited by Bad Object-Choices (Seattle: Bay Press, 1991).

questions of sex and ethnicity could not be confined to the usual discourses of power. Chiefly:

> How and to what extent is desire articulated in terms of race as opposed to body type or other attributes? To what extent is sexual attraction exclusive and/or changeable, and can it be consciously programmed? These questions are all politically loaded, as they parallel and impact the debates between essentialists and social constructionists on the nature of homosexuality itself. They are also emotionally charged, in that sexual choice involving race has been a basis for moral judgement.

Fung was asking some of the same questions about sex and race that I'd been pondering as a white male. However, the negative stigma of the RQ label had cowed me into silence. (As Fung's partner, Tim McCaskell, once said: "Smart rice queens learn to keep their mouths shut.") In the end, the only way to break through that silence was to adopt the Rice Queen label, temporarily, as a kind of experiment: to embark on a physical, emotional, and intellectual journey of Rice Queendom that would deconstruct and, hopefully, demystify the label. To do so, I would have to begin by reaching back to my earliest perceptions of race and culture, recall the growing sense of awareness of all things erotic (and how they often intersect with the exotic), and then – accounting for my adult experiences – navigate the heady politics of ethnic fetishism and cross-cultural confusion as I stumbled my way through a succession of Asian partners.

There is no way of doing this without describing at least *some* sex. As with most literary depictions of lovemaking, the physical details are often less relevant than the lessons learned. In the story that follows, the lessons become more significant once the Narrator crosses the Pacific Ocean. In recounting the exotic East, many western correspondents downplay their own amorous adventures – and whatever challenges to their assumptions may result – in the guise of maintaining some heroic omniscience or objectivity. This book is an attempt to offer a more nuanced, human dimension to the discourse.

Imprinting

Sex comes to us in different ways; it alters us; and I suppose in the
end we carry the nature of our experiences on our faces.

– V.S. Naipaul, *Half a Life*

I
Skeletons

Deep in the Fraser Canyon, nestled in a mountain range about ninety minutes east of Vancouver on the Trans-Canada highway, is a riverside logging town called Hope. To outsiders, it was once best known as an ideal shooting location for low-budget Hollywood fare. Hope was where Sylvester Stallone began his *Rambo* franchise with the filming of *First Blood*. A few years later, it still had a few things in common with the fictional, Anytown U.S.A. it portrayed in that film. Hope in the late 1980s was the kind of place where only drifters took solitary walks along the highway and loners were regarded with suspicion; where everyone was on a first-name basis with the mayor and the local sheriff; and where no one seemed offended by the sight of a teenaged boy walking around wearing a baseball cap that read: "AIDS: Kills Fags Dead." During the first few months of 1989, this was the place I called home.

At twenty-five, I was beginning my writing career as the reporter/ photographer for Hope's weekly community newspaper. One day, I was assigned to cover a performance by a visiting dance troupe from Vancouver. Kokoro Dance, appearing at the local high school as part of a provincial tour, had caused quite a stir with its new production. "Rage," a symbolic re-enactment of Japanese internment during World War II, had special resonance in this part of British Columbia: a few weeks after the Japanese attack on Pearl Harbor, some 26,000 Japanese-Canadian residents of Vancouver Island and the Lower Mainland had been stripped of their homes and possessions and sent to internment camps from the Fraser Valley to the Kootenays. One of those camps was located on a former cattle farm just outside Hope. So it wasn't hard to build tension for this show.

As the lights went down in the school gymnasium, a brief silence was followed by the pounding of taiko drums. The presence of the drummers – each wearing a bandana and a loose-fitting pair of fishermen's trousers – was gradually revealed by a fade-in follow spot. After entering the gym, they began circling the centre of the basketball court. Then they retreated, and a lone figure appeared in their midst. Slowly the crouching body unfolded until the audience could see that this muscular, bald-headed man – covered in talcum powder and wearing nothing but a loin cloth – was bound to the floor by a web of ropes.

Not long before the performance, the federal government officially apologized to all Japanese Canadians for the miscarriage of justice that had led to internment forty-seven years earlier. It also reached a redress settlement of $12 million, or $21,000 for each internment camp survivor, plus community legacy funding. "Rage" was asking its young audience members – most of them white and all of them born more than a generation after the war – to come to grips with a dark chapter in the nation's history, part of which had occurred a few kilometres down the road. The message? We were all implicated – if not in the event itself, then by our collective responsibility never to allow such things to happen again.

For me, "Rage" was a sobering reminder of something I too had learned about in high school. *Yellow Peril. The Enemy Within. Japs Out!* Stories of deprivation, pain, and ostracism that had left their imprint on tens of thousands of people who had built their lives on North American soil and played a part in building our still young country – only to be banished for the colour of their skin. Stories revealed in Joy Kogawa's *Obasan* and Ken Adachi's *The Enemy That Never Was*. In university, I had bemoaned the injustice and held strong opinions about the "racists" who carried it out. It didn't matter that times had been different, or that the "racists" represented a large proportion of the Canadian public. I just knew, with the smug self-righteousness of youth, that I wouldn't have condoned such a policy.

Three years after seeing "Rage," I was handed a scrapbook that had once belonged to my uncle. After his death, it was passed on to my father, his only brother. But Dad had never discussed its contents in detail, and the first time I'd flipped through it I hadn't bothered to read the faded news clippings inside. The rest of the contents – an assortment of photographs, telegrams and greeting cards – seemed mostly concerned with long-lost relatives I'd never met. But now, turning the pages until I found my grandfather's obituary from the *Victoria Times*, I decided to read every word.

More than twelve column inches in length, the obit was accompanied by a large portrait photograph and a subhead describing Granddad as a "widely known" civil servant for the provincial government. It said that Granddad was once the regional director of development for the old Trade and Industry ministry, an expert on unemployment and rehabilitation who had held important posts in the relief government during the Depression. It went on to say he had worked on flood rehabilitation in the Fraser Valley and with the Doukhobors after the loss of their mortgaged communal lands. And then it said this: "During [the] Second World War, he was loaned to the federal government to organise reception centres for 26,000 Japanese ordered to quit BC's coastlands...."

So, there it was: my grandfather, an English immigrant whose claim to Canadian citizenship was more recent than that of many Japanese immigrants, had been one of the "racists" I had condemned in my student days. Was it possible to feel betrayal from new information about an old event? Guilt by association for something that happened in my family long before my birth? I felt both. Why hadn't I been told? My father said I had – but that I must have been too young for the information to register. Now here it was, five decades after Pearl Harbor – and I was only *just* learning of my blood connection to Yellow Peril.

Flipping through the rest of the scrapbook, I gazed deeply into each photo of Granddad – reading his face, looking for clues, trying to find answers in between the wrinkles. The most striking image was an official government portrait taken not long before Granddad's death. In it, my father's father is dressed in a black wool jacket and a fedora, its brim resting high on his brow. A Commonwealth pin is attached to his lapel, and his tie is loosely fastened to his white shirt. He sits casually for the session – his left hand in his pocket, his right hand dangling a cigarette. Knowing roughly when the photo was taken, I found it hard not to see his face as a mask of the burdens he had carried until that moment.

Like Roland Barthes in *Camera Lucida* gazing at the photo of a condemned would-be assassin just before his execution, I saw catastrophe in this portrait. Granddad may have been nothing more than a cog in the wheel of Japanese internment – a low-level bureaucrat "just following orders." But at the moment this photo was taken, World War II had come and gone. How did he feel about the camps? Did he ever think about internment? Or was it merely an unpleasant consequence of *real politik*, a bad dream to be stored away in the subconscious? How often did Japanese Canadians pass him on the street? How would he have felt when they did? I would never know.

∞

While pondering these questions, I was struck by an unsettling irony: two generations after J.T. Gawthrop had helped round up a group of East Asians to "quit BC's coastlands," I, his grandson, had begun targeting East Asians for special welcome to those very same coastlands. Since moving to Vancouver shortly after seeing "Rage," I'd found that an increasing number of notches on my bedpost had been delivered by handsome young pan-Asian men – not infrequently Japanese. Why, just the other night after visiting the Club baths, I had brought home Yukio – a tall, slender androgyne in his early twenties who had feathery long hair and a twenty-six-inch waist.

We had passed each other twice in the Club's shadowy labyrinth, both times turning around for another look. In the second instance Yukio stroked my palm with his fingers as he passed by. White guys never did that. Then he followed me into a telephone booth-sized cubicle where our towels fell to the floor and our naked bodies met. As I watched his tongue run a trail down my abdomen, a white bandana with red-and-black calligraphy suddenly appeared around his forehead. Visions of a samurai warrior began dancing in my brain.

Later we felt our way to the back of a dark room where other strangers were having sex. I sat down on a bench against the back wall. Yukio, facing me, stepped onto the bench, planted his feet around my hips, and stood up straight, his boner quivering a few inches above my face. Then, leaning against the wall by his forearms as he bowed his head, his long sweaty hair matting his brow and covering his eyes, he began to lower himself. His body folded into a crouch as he wrapped an arm around my neck, and I grabbed his waist with both hands to help him down. As the crack of his ass reached the tip of my erection, it occurred to me that Yukio might want to "bareback" – a cause for some concern, since my better judgement was disappearing by the second. But then he produced a condom, seemingly from nowhere, rolling it onto me just fast enough to maintain some illusion of spontaneity.

Having signaled his desire to be penetrated, Yukio had shattered the samurai warrior fantasy and replaced it with visions of a fully clothed Tokyo urbanite in a starched white shirt and black tie. Ah yes, Yukio: faithful torchbearer of a workaholic culture. Yukio, getting his thick black hair all messy while rushing to meet deadlines for his bottom line-chasing capitalist slavemasters. Yukio, bowing to company guests before getting drunk and inappropriate over sake. Yukio, eyeing the vice-president in the men's room and then going down on him in a cubicle. Yukio, right here with me now, bouncing on my lap in a western sauna....

Who or what was he thinking about?

When I invited him to my apartment, he accepted. We had sex once more on the couch before going to bed, and again in the morning a few moments after waking up. I didn't know it yet, but Yukio would return to Vancouver only a month later, at Christmas, and again the following Christmas. He would call on the phone each time to invite himself over, then spend the night with his legs wrapped around my neck before disappearing for another year. With each passing Christmas I would begin to associate the festive season at least partly with the memory of his perfect lovemaking.

And yet, I knew next to nothing about him. I knew he was born and raised in Tokyo and now lived in Brussels. I knew he worked as an accountant while collecting the final credits for a Master's in business administration. And I knew he had a western boyfriend, who he'd leave back at the hotel while he came over to my place to get fucked. But other than these few facts, Yukio was a complete mystery. Nor, for that matter, did I know much more about the other young Asian men I'd had sex with than my grandfather must have known about the anonymous Asian faces he'd sent packing to the internment camps.

Why was I so attracted to Far East Asians, rather than repelled by them, as Granddad's generation had been? In making these young men a part of my universe, I had altered the family narrative from a politics of Yellow Peril to one of Yellow Fever; from Asian Invasion to Asian Persuasion, in two generations. How had this happened? Closing the scrapbook, I went to the bathroom and looked in the mirror. There was no denying the power of genetics. The traces of Granddad could be found in the eyes, the mouth, the jawline, and the puffy cheeks. With the exception of a few trendy Asian habits (shirts made in Hong Kong, a preference for stir-fries), everything about me screamed Rule Britannia.

The old man may have died a decade before I was born, but we were connected. Could I have made the same choices, had I been in Granddad's position? Instead of cruising young Japanese guys like Yukio and licking every inch of them, could I have torn apart their families? Repossessed their homes? Sold off their belongings and sent them to camps in the Fraser Valley and points east? Could I have dumped them in poorly heated wooden shacks in the middle of winter, only to forget about them for the next four years? There was no way of knowing. But if I went far enough back in my own history, perhaps I could learn just how and why this peculiar desire for Far East Asian men had ever risen to the surface.

II
Echoes

ONE HOT AFTERNOON IN JUNE OF 1969, near the bottom of a forested ravine that leads to the seashore at Departure Bay in Nanaimo, I got my first lesson in suburban racism. I was on a field trip with my kindergarten classmates, and we had almost completed the half-hour walk downhill from the school to a long stretch of sand just north of the ferry terminal, when I noticed something sticking out of the trees near the bottom of the trail. It was the rusty, severed hull of an abandoned boat covered in blackberry vines, with a tangle of metal cables at its base. An eerie sight, its pointy hull aimed out at the sky like a leaning tombstone.

"What's that?" I asked no one in particular.

"It's a Jap gunboat," said a classmate.

"Huh?" I had no idea what a "Jap" was.

"The Japs tried to beat us in the war," he continued, "but one of our guys shot this gunboat and killed the Japs, so they lost the war."

Then he poked through a porthole with a stick.

"Wow," he said. "A dead Jap. He must have burned to death."

Eager to catch my first glimpse of human remains, I peeked through the hole and stared at the ugly mass of moldy, yellow pus. *So*, my five-year-old brain thought, *this is what the charred and petrified corpse of a defeated 'Jap' looks like*. It didn't strike me as odd that the remains had somehow failed to decompose in temperate conditions. (But then, I also had no idea that the "war" my classmate was referring to had ended twenty-four years earlier and that "Jap" gunboats had never come close to Nanaimo.) Instead, for some time afterward I would assume that decomposing Japanese remains resembled a flowering species of rainforest fungus. That's what I was actually observing through the porthole of an abandoned fishing boat, growing at the end of a mossy log my classmate had convinced me was a decaying torso. Since "Jap" was a category of Other, I would also assume that Caucasian remains couldn't possibly be so ... *yucky*.

∞

Nanaimo, British Columbia, the town where I was born and raised, got its name from the aboriginal Coast Salish word *Sney-Ny-Mous*, which translates roughly as "place of the black rock." Like most seaside communities in the Pacific Northwest that were colonized by Europeans in the eighteenth and nineteenth centuries, Nanaimo began as a trading post whose social and economic development was fueled by the export potential of its primary staples: coal, timber, and fish. As with most New World trading posts, the influence of aboriginal culture on the surrounding area began to evaporate the moment white people decided it was a nice place to live.

Indigenous culture in Nanaimo was gradually replaced by a homogenous but vaguely defined white pioneer society whose prevailing wisdom was grounded in the Darwinist prerogatives of British imperialism. This new, transplanted reality expressed itself through a Lockean liberal view of private property and a redemptionist Christian view of "progress" and "morality." Like many other pioneer towns, it was a more welcoming place for traders, explorers, accountants, and real estate speculators than painters, musicians, philosophers, or poets. Inward-looking, pedestrian, and driven by the acquisitive goals of material contentment, Nanaimo would be governed by this pioneer mentality for at least the first hundred years of its history as an incorporated city.

By the end of the twentieth century, Nanaimo was British Columbia's "Harbour City": a picturesque little town with postcard waterfront views and a thriving real estate market. It boasted a degree-granting post-secondary college, a booming population of young families, a healthy tourism industry, a half-decent arts centre, and the distinction of being the hometown of international jazz superstar Diana Krall. Back in the 1970s, when I was growing up, the town was known chiefly for three things: the Nanaimo Bar, a three-layered, chocolate, nutty confectionery that mothers in England used to send their coal mining sons to cheer them up; the "Full Nanaimo," a men's fashion trend begun by the city's car salesmen and Rotarians which typically combined a powder-blue polyester jacket with white lapels, black shirt, white tie, clashing polyester pants, and white shoes; and the annual Nanaimo-Vancouver bathtub race, a summer festival event in which amateur daredevils riding bathtubs fitted with outboard motors and a pair of water skis sped across the Georgia Strait to Kitsilano Beach, where they would stagger up the shore on wobbly legs to ring a bell and win a cash prize.

The unofficial mascot of the bathtub race was the town's colourful and long-serving mayor, Frank Ney, a walking tourist attraction who enjoyed dressing up in pirate suits for civic events and spouting lines from Robert Louis Stevenson. When asked why the city spent so much money promoting the bathtub race, boxing matches, and Barnum and Bailey circuses instead of cultural events – this was before the city had an arts centre – Ney's usual response was: "The people prefer corn to culture." Of course, it's unlikely that "the people" he was referring to included any of the town's non-white residents. But then, why would it? The local native folks had been pushed to the town margins long before the first bathtub race, cordoned off from everyone else by the uniquely Canadian apartheid of the reservation system. The Japanese had been pretty quiet since internment, while the Chinese were still recovering from the loss of Chinatown, a thriving neighbourhood in the south end that had burned to the ground in 1960. So, whether or not *those* people "preferred corn to culture" was rather beside the point.

The house I grew up in was located in a middle-class suburb where the lawns were kept trimmed and most of the residents were white. There were one or two Chinese or Japanese kids at my school, but I never went to their homes after class. I did on occasion visit the townhouse of a South Asian classmate, a Fijian whose grandmother's peculiar body scent – a combination of incense, jasmine, and Indian spices from the curry dishes she made for us – literally provided my first whiff of the exotic. But the closest I came to contact with Far East Asians was an outing to a Chinese or Japanese restaurant, or a trip to the corner grocer across the street from the junior high school.

During the fall of 1973, a large colour poster of a Chinese action movie star found its way onto my bedroom wall – replacing one of a whitebread American TV star. Bobby Sherman's twinkling eyes and over-whitened teeth on TV's *Here Come the Brides* had once captivated me, but now his wholesome and fully clothed image seemed bland next to Bruce Lee's primal, threatening, half-naked image. On the poster, the famous kung fu artist wore nothing but a loose-fitting pair of black cotton sweatpants. He was suspended in the air, in a full-extension scissor-kick – his face a mask of determination, his rippling torso an immaculate display of perfection. I couldn't believe he was dead.

The world's hottest non-white action star was only five-foot-seven and 140 pounds, but he seemed like a giant. Bruce Lee had an oddly un-Hollywood sort of charisma – his good friend, the basketball legend Kareem

Abdul Jabbar, likened it to that of a renegade Daoist priest. For a short time after his death, I would try to capture some of his magic by dabbling in the martial arts. But karate and kung fu were too violent, so I opted for judo. At first, I enjoyed it. Those white outfits were pretty cool, and I liked the feeling of bare feet on vinyl mats – even the smell of group sweat after a solid hour of practice. I also enjoyed the grace of a perfectly executed throw … except when it happened to me. Gradually my interest in judo began to fade with each thud on the floor as I suffered one humiliating defeat after another. At age ten, I was still too young to realize that I didn't want to *be* Bruce Lee so much as *have* him.

Three years later, when the local cinema held a Bruce Lee festival, I went to see *Fists of Fury*. While my school chums *ooh*-ed and *ahh*-ed over Bruce's acrobatic moves, I quietly *ooh*-ed and *ahh*-ed at the sight of his glistening chest. I didn't care if he beat up all the bad guys or even if he won in the end. I only wished the camera would close in more often on those beautiful, sand dollar nipples.

∞

During the fall of 1978, I was a Grade Nine "junior boy" at a pseudo-Victorian private boys school where the sport of rugby was an institution in itself – part of God's plan to make little Rudyard Kiplings of us all. I was too small for rugby – my physical development lagged behind that of my age-mates – and I lacked the Darwinian instinct our schoolmasters insisted was part of becoming a man. One day, during scrimmage, I was tackled by two opponents and had the wind knocked out of me. Slowly I got up, dusted myself off, and informed the phys ed teacher that I was quitting.

"You can't quit," he said, incredulous. "This is rugby. You have to play."

"No, I don't," I said. "I can play soccer on the Chopper Squad."

The teacher was stunned. Like the Queen, or the study of Latin, rugby was one of those things we weren't supposed to question – and here I was, pissing on it by *volunteering* to join a group of loser non-athletes on the lower field.

The "Chopper Squad" was a pejorative label for an unfortunate group of nerds who, during the fall term when rugby was the only competitive sport, were sentenced to a recreational game of soccer. Demotion to its ranks was reserved for a particular class of athletic rejects that included science geeks and budding potheads. Its membership was dominated by recent immigrants from China, boys considered too delicate or feminine to play a manly bloodsport like rugby. A demotion to the Chopper Squad was greeted by most boys with a *chop-chop* gesture of both hands – implying that you belonged with the "Chinks" if you couldn't play rugby. (Of course, some Chinese boys played rugby quite well. But their ascension to the First or Second Fifteen was typically regarded as a biological accident.)

Unsurprisingly, the Choppers were the subject of ridicule. Far away from the real athletes, they played a casual, non-competitive, no-rules game of soccer. With limited supervision and no refereeing, they were free to fumble away and bump into each other like the sad participants of a Monty Python "Twit of the Year" contest. All that was required of the Chinese boys and their white loser teammates was to kick the ball around until the session was over and it was time to return to math class – where, of course, their real talents lay.

For all my pride at having rebelled against the system, I arrived for my first day with the Choppers secretly hoping that our attempts at athleticism would go unnoticed by visiting parents, school officials, and fellow students. I was one of only five or six white boys on the squad that fall, and – like the others – was unfamiliar with the experience of marginalia: whether it was choice, delayed physical development, or lack of ability, I now belonged to the "Others" category for the first time. Most of the Choppers were much more visible as "Other" than I was, but they never complained about their second-class status as athletes. The Chinese soccer players were all good sports, never whining about discrimination or the racist pedagogy of the "Chopper Squad" label itself.

I learned from their example. Soon I began to appreciate the simple joy of playing soccer: connecting shoe with ball, hitting a teammate with a good pass, sliding in the mud, scoring a goal. The longer I played with them, the more these Chinese boys with their horn-rimmed glasses and bowl-style haircuts shed their nerdy images and transformed into physical beings. Simply by breaking a sweat, messing up their hair, and exposing more of their flesh than I was used to seeing, these boys became something other than math geniuses. They had bodies as well.

III
Initiations

In Yukio Mishima's autobiographical novel, *Confessions of a Mask* (1949), the first-person narrator struggles to comprehend the irrepressible urges of homosexuality in his life. Such desire he regards, if not as an illness, then as an unfortunate component of his creative temperament – which also happens to encompass Augustinian predeterminism, narcissism, sado-masochism, nostalgic ultra-nationalism, and an insatiable death fetish. Mishima's transgressive vision of the erotic explored a sensibility seldom, if ever, seen in Japanese literature before *Confessions*: that of an "invert" who describes his desires matter-of-factly as if every other Japanese male has at some time had those very same desires.

The narrator's earliest memory of male beauty occurs at age four, when he spots his first "night soil man" – a "ladler of excrement" who captivates him with his "handsome ruddy cheeks and shining eyes ... [the] dirty roll of cloth around his head for a sweatband ... [and] dark blue cotton trousers of the close-fitting kind called 'thigh-pullers'."[1] Eight years later, while exploring his father's vast library, he locates the heart of his erotic sensibility. Flipping through an Italian museum guidebook, he finds a reproduction of Guido Reni's "St. Sebastian" image that hangs in the collection of the Palazzo Rosso in Genoa. The painting shows a handsome, naked youth bound to the trunk of a tree, his crossed hands above him tied by the wrists, his left armpit and right side pierced by arrows. The image inspires the narrator's first orgasm, right there in his father's study. Mishima cites German sexologist Magnus Hirschfeld to describe the St. Sebastian image in terms we might today regard as classic gay iconography. He argues that the sight of a muscular, god-like youth in a state of total defeat satisfies the kinky, voyeuristic fantasies of dominance and submission that all "inverts" supposedly share. "In the overwhelming majority of cases of inversion," the narrator argues, "the inverted and the sadistic impulses are inextricably entangled...."[2]

In the autumn of 1978, I began Grade Ten and turned fifteen having yet to

1. Yukio Mishima, *Confessions of a Mask* (New York: New Directions, 1958).
2. *Ibid.*

reach puberty. Stealing glances in the shower room, I was shocked to find that most of my boarding school classmates and several of the new Grade Nines had physically eclipsed me over the summer. Boys with bald peckers only months earlier had all sprouted pubic hair and now had big cocks and balls; fellow sopranos in the church choir had graduated to baritone – leaving me, still squeaking, on the lower pew. Even some of the Grade Eights appeared to have reached manhood, and this was bad news. A thirteen-year-old boy in the full flowering of adolescence was, in the eyes of a late bloomer, traumatic to behold: an object of both envy (his body had no logical right to be more advanced), and desire (I wanted a closer look at the fruits of his good fortune but knew my curiosity would never be satisfied unless I made an advance, which was risky). Hiding my shame, I put up my defenses in gym class – never once raising a basketball above my head when shirtless (lest I expose my hairless armpits), always undressing with a towel around my waist, and facing the wall in the showers. As for sex, an event I had witnessed the previous year had only reinforced my physical insecurities in relation to other people.

During Grade Nine, I lived in the junior dorm: a single room with two paper-thin dividers creating three units, each with two double bunk beds. The units were entered from the adjoining hallway, from which we could gaze out into the forest through ceiling-to-floor plate-glass windows. Mine was the third unit, at the end of the hall. One night after "lights out," a group of Grade Twelve prefects entered the junior dorm with flashlights, all snorts and giggles, looking for mischief. Seconds later, I heard the sound of a sleeping bag zipper being pulled open with a single tug, then a startled voice, a struggle of kicking arms and legs, and finally the sleeping bag being stripped away.

Oh, goody, I thought, recognizing the voice. *It's Jackson.* Rising from my bed, I snuck across the second room and hid behind the first divider. Soon I could see what was going on without even looking behind it: the prefects had lit several candles, turning the window opposite Jackson's unit into a mirror.

Rumour had it that some of the junior boys had already suffered indignities at the hands of these prefects. But since the unfortunate few tended to be tight-lipped afterwards about what had transpired, the exact nature of the initiation ritual was shrouded in mystery. It was anyone's guess who would be targeted next and what their "punishment" would be. Jackson, the victim on this night, was the first Asian boy to be targeted, and the Grade

Twelves had chosen well. Jackson was a Poor Little Rich Boy from West Vancouver: a bully who picked on defenceless Grade Eights, a smart ass who made obscene gestures behind the teacher's back, a troublemaker who always seemed to avoid punishment, and a braggart who claimed to have deflowered several girls. The notion of someone like Jackson being humiliated through initiation rites struck me as such profound poetic justice that I couldn't help eavesdropping on his misfortune.

"C'mon, get his legs!" hissed one of the prefects. Jackson whimpered as another pulled off his cotton undies. As flickering candles cast the entire scene on the hallway window, the purpose of the ritual became clear: the Grade Twelves, all four of them upper-middle class Wasps, wanted to see what hot, dripping candle wax looked like on Chinese balls....

One of Yukio Mishima's favourite tropes of "inverted" sexuality was the raw, anarchic sensuality of the unharnessed rebel. In *Confessions of a Mask*, this trope finds its ultimate expression in a boy named Omi, a classmate of the narrator's during second year of middle school. When we first meet Omi, he has just been expelled from the dormitory for an undisclosed discretion. At age fourteen, he surpasses every one of his classmates in physique, is the "special favourite" of the drillmaster and the gymnastics instructor, and is said to have "already had lots of girls." The muscles of his shoulders and chest are "that sort which can be spied out even beneath a blue-serge uniform." And his features?

> Something about his face gave one the sensation of abundant blood coursing richly throughout his body. It was a round face, with haughty cheekbones rising from swarthy cheeks, lips that seemed to have been sewn into a fine line, sturdy jaws, and a broad but well-shaped and not too prominent nose. These features were the clothing for an untamed soul.[3]

3. *Ibid.*

Late in the spring, the narrator is left breathless when Omi demonstrates pull-ups on the exercise bar during an outdoor session of gym class. Taking off his T-shirt, Omi leaves "nothing but a dazzlingly white, sleeveless undershirt to cover his chest"; the tank top on his "swarthy skin" is like plaster of Paris, "carved in relief, showing the bold contours of his chest and its two nipples."

When he leaps up and grabs onto the iron bar, hanging by two strong arms "worthy of being tattooed with anchors," his classmates gasp in wonder – less at his show of strength than at the big, black bushes revealed in his armpits:

> This was probably the first time we had seen such an opulence of hair; it seemed almost prodigal, like some luxuriant growth of troublesome summer weeds.... Those two black thickets gleamed glossily, bathed in sunlight, and the surprising whiteness of his skin there was like white sand peeping through.[4]

I had seen Jackson in the shower. At fourteen, his lean brown body had lost all its baby fat. His torso was V-shaped, and he had the firmest, roundest pair of buns in all of Grade Nine. His skin was smooth all over, except for two manly patches of armpit moss and a thick, black bush of pubic hair – that all-important badge of manhood I'd begun to obsess about but which would not appear on my own body for another year. Jackson also defied a racist stereotype about Chinese males by possessing a larger-than-average cock.

That night, I was the only boy in the junior dorm curious enough to investigate what was happening to him. At first I couldn't see his struggling figure on the bed as the older boys surrounded him. But once they broke down his resistance and moved back a little, his naked, supine body became visible in the window's reflection. One of the prefects, leaning over him while the others pinned him down, lit another candle, and began dripping wax all over Jackson's smooth brown chest: first his nipples, then a trail down his abdomen. Eventually Jackson let out a high-pitched squeal, cracking a voice that had long since changed to a baritone. Finally the two Grade Twelves who

4. *Ibid.*

had been holding his arms and legs let go and began rubbing the wax that was already congealing around his belly. As the prefect with the candle continued pouring onto Jackson's thighs, the hands of the other boys gradually made their way south as they began rubbing circles with the still-liquid wax. Finally, all four of them moved close together, surrounding Jackson and blocking my view. Nothing was said. The room grew silent.

Minutes earlier, the prospect of lying naked and vulnerable before a juiced-up quartet of sadistic Grade Twelves had seemed frightening. But now I wished it was me in Jackson's place. His tormentors were all handsome Adonis figures – varsity rowers with tanned skin and muscular bodies. And, far from hurting Jackson, it appeared they were doing something to give him pleasure. Jackson's breathing grew heavier, turning into a gentle moan and accelerating in speed, until … silence. What had they *done* to him? Finally, standing it no more, I peeked behind the divider. The Grade Twelves were hovering quietly around Jackson, wiping off his body with a towel, and helping him pull his undies back on. Then they sat on his bed, lit cigarettes, and passed them around. Jackson was *laughing* with them – sharing their jokes and their smokes. A few minutes later, they tucked him in and left. Soon Jackson and his roommates – who must have seen the whole thing – were snoring.

In *Confessions of a Mask*, the narrator recalls that late spring day in the outdoor gym class, and the vision of Omi on the exercise bar. He remembers the young beauty's "close affinity with St. Sebastian," and how the sight of a semi-nude Omi had given him a hard-on. And yet, for all the similarities to Guido Reni's vanquished hero, Omi's tactile presence as a living, breathing human being – as opposed to a work of art – had created a troublesome new emotion for the narrator. Omi's very existence, his "sheer extravagant abundance of life-force" and physical perfection, was itself a bitter reproach of the narrator's imperfection, and that of his classmates:

> They were overwhelmed by the feeling he gave of having
> too much life, by the feeling of purposeless violence that
> can be explained only as life existing for its own sake, by
> his type of ill-humoured, unconcerned exuberance….

> Here I was, looking upon the naked body I had so longed
> to see, and the shock of seeing it had unexpectedly
> unleashed an emotion within me that was the opposite
> of joy. It was jealousy…. It was jealousy fierce enough to
> make me voluntarily forswear my love of Omi.[5]

It was a complex jealousy, to be sure. For while the narrator "tossed (his) love for Omi onto the rubbish heap of neglected riddles, never once searching deeply for its meaning," he also spent hours in the mirror gazing into his own armpits, where "there was only the faintest promise of buds that might yet blossom." Mishima was twenty-four years of age when he wrote these words in 1949, a decade removed from the fictional events of *Confessions*. At the time, he was addressing a mostly Japanese audience. But forty years after the adolescent trauma of Mishima's imaginary fourteen-year-old in pre-World War II imperial Japan, an actual fourteen-year-old in North America witnessed similar perfection in another boy's precocious manhood, was jealous of it, couldn't fathom his own imperfection in the face of it, and made a fetish of the armpit just as Mishima's narrator had done.

As Jackson's hazing was in progress, I envied the fact that he had been deemed worthy of such an exotic and intimate ritual. Within days I would also resent the new-found maturity it inspired in him: seemingly overnight, Jackson abandoned the obnoxious behaviour that had turned some of his classmates against him. Perhaps having one's balls hot-waxed and then being jerked off by four Grade Twelves was merely Pavlovian psychology at work: punishment as the route to humility. Jackson's hazing, far from scarring him, seemed to have awakened him.

Looking back on it now, I'm struck by a number of things that didn't occur to my fourteen-year-old self. As a lapsed Catholic, I can't help but see Jackson's initiation as a metaphor of confirmation – with candle wax on the balls replacing ashes on the forehead, and the initiate's own youthful cum replacing the priestly sprinkling of holy water. But more important than the sacrament, I think, was the shifting power dynamic in that room. Until

5. *Ibid.*

Jackson's hazing, I had never seen ethnicity treated as an altar at which to worship – or, from Jackson's point of view, *be* worshipped. But that's exactly what happened that night, when the subject of an ostensibly demeaning ritual was transformed from victim into angel. Jackson's difference – his *Chinese-ness* – had at first been an object of teasing. But that same difference, revealed under candlelight, became so powerful in its naked beauty that not even the prefects – hotblooded, macho jocks that they were – could deny it. Each had been transformed by the experience. I knew this, watching from behind the divider, as surely as Jackson, staring into their faces, must have known it. And at that moment he must have discovered a new kind of power in himself, something whose importance for the rest of his life would be worth all the embarrassment he may have suffered during those ten breathtaking minutes in 1977.

IV
Hongcouver

IN THE LATE SPRING OF 1989, I moved to Vancouver. My first apartment in the West End was on the bottom floor of a wafer-thin, thirty-one-storey high-rise overlooking the beach at English Bay. Known throughout the gay community as "Vaseline Towers," this building, located about fifteen minutes from the nightclubs on Davie Street, was notorious in the 1970s for its high proportion of single male tenants and the marathon orgies of sodomitical excess that allegedly took place there. Worthy of its phallic nickname, "Vaseline Towers" was the tallest protuberance in a West End cluttered with high-rise apartments. Flying past these buildings on the descent into Coal Harbour, one was reminded of a similar view entering Hong Kong. Skyscrapers weren't all the two cities had in common.

Among the crowds of shoppers and students and business types who filled the sidewalks of Robson and Davie were scores of handsome young pan-Asian men – men whose moussed-up black hair, high cheekbones, and rose-petal lips seemed exotic to a recent transplant from white suburbia. Some of these men clearly had money to burn on fitness club memberships, spa treatments, and exotic facial creams. Some had a fashion sense that rivaled the top houses of Paris or Milan. And some – regardless of beauty, wealth, or fashion sense – enjoyed making eye contact with white guys. Some would end up between my sheets at Vaseline Towers, helping me contribute to the building's legendary reputation. This joining of Asian and Caucasian bodies, which was happening all over the city, was the inevitable result of long-forgotten events.

The first Chinese to land in what is now British Columbia were mere pawns of cheap labour in the service of white European expansionism. The five dozen artisans who disembarked in Nootka Sound in 1788 as passengers of the British sea captain John Meares were there to help set up a fur trading post and establish British sovereignty. It would be another seventy years before the Chinese began arriving in large numbers, their exodus prompted by the 1847 flood of the Yangtzee and the Taiping Rebellion of 1850–64 which between them killed more than twenty million. In 1858, when gold was discovered in Barkerville, the first Chinese immigrants to Canada came from San Francisco.

The history of Canada's west coast over the century that followed provides a lengthy docket of racist and xenophobic offenses against Far East Asian people. Despite the fact that some 10,000 Cantonese labourers helped complete the Canadian Pacific Railway – and fifteen percent of them lost their lives due to accident or disease while on the job – the Chinese were suddenly prevented from voting in provincial elections. Then the federal government stepped in with laws excluding Chinese (or "Asiatic") immigrants and a Chinese "head tax" that was doubled from $50 to $100 in 1901 and quintupled to $500 two years later. Anti-Chinese hate literature was as commonplace as "diversity" literature is today. As for Japanese-Canadians, they found out soon after December 7, 1941 just what their adopted country thought of them.

By Vancouver's centennial in 1986, all this had changed. Chinese, Japanese, and other citizens of Far East Asian ancestry were now a celebrated part of the Canadian mosaic. In May of that year, the provincial government staged a multi-billion-dollar world trade fair and science exhibition, Expo '86, that promised to "Invite the World." Among the multitudes that converged on the city over that long hot summer, Far East Asians numbered among the highest. The Chinese, in particular, liked what they saw in Vancouver's housing market, clean environment, safe streets and abundant investment opportunities. Many visitors from Hong Kong, anticipating rough times after the Chinese handover in just over a decade, decided to raise their families in the New World.

It didn't take them long to make their presence known. With Mandarin- and Cantonese-speaking entrepreneurs using their Expo visits to score property development contracts, *feng shui* – the ancient Chinese belief that balance and harmony in physical surroundings can determine health, prosperity, and good luck – soon began to compete with scale and view as the city's dominant design priority. The Bank of Hong Kong even flew in a *feng shui* expert before opening its Vancouver headquarters, paying him $300,000 to redesign the interior. (A pendulum was placed in the main foyer "because the building itself had been placed incorrectly on the site according to *feng shui* principles.")[1] In the art world, East Asian faces began

1. Elspeth Sage, Introduction, *Feng Shui: Wind & Water* catalogue (Vancouver: On Edge, Locus +, 1994).

appearing on local stages and in film and video productions.

But it wasn't all multicultural bliss. After the Expo lands were sold to Hong Hong billionaire Li Ka-Shing for next to nothing, all-Asian shopping malls began sprouting up in nearby Richmond, where most of the households were Chinese. In the neighbourhood of Kerrisdale, Asian property owners offended environmentalists by chopping down old-growth trees to make way for their large new houses, called "monster homes" in the press. In East Vancouver and Chinatown, Asian gang activity was suddenly a hot news item. And so were the "astronaut parents": middle-class couples from Hong Kong who bought houses on the West Side and then hired nannies to attend to their "satellite kids" while they flew back and forth between Vancouver and Hong Kong.

Yes, the tables had turned in the 200 years since those humble Chinese artisans landed in Nootka Sound with Captain Meares. Far from being slaves of white colonial rule, these "Fresh Off the Boat" (FOB) Chinese were richer than many white residents whose families had been in Vancouver for generations. Richer, too, than many long-term Chinese residents. Some of the new immigrants had homes in the upper-crust neighbourhoods of Shaughnessy and West Vancouver. Some had part or full ownership in overseas property development firms. Some had staffs of 500. And some had teenaged offspring who sulked when they got a Mazda Miata, instead of a Jaguar or a BMW, for their birthday. This was the city that greeted me in the summer of 1989: a place becoming known as "Hongcouver."

Moving to the city had seemed the best way to come out of the closet after a decade of sexual hibernation. During the summer of 1979, my departure from boarding school had coincided with the long-awaited onset of puberty. Along with the physical changes came the simultaneously thrilling and horrifying realization that occurs to most gay males at precisely the same adolescent moment: the awareness that each sighting of a beautiful boy triggers an immediate internal excitement, and a sense of longing that can neither be suppressed nor extinguished. I didn't know what to do about such knowledge. And so, a few months before my sixteenth birthday, a combination of Catholic guilt and small-town paranoia conspired to ensure that I would squander the prime years of sexual development in a self-loathing quest to be "normal."

It wasn't until my early twenties that I began taking the first awkward steps toward embracing my sexuality: coming out to friends and family, pining after hopelessly hetero hunks at university, not averting my eyes from the cashier when I bought homo porn at the corner grocery, and, if chaperoned by a "sister," stepping into a gay bar. Throughout this period, Far East Asians barely registered on my internal erotic database; almost everyone I had privately worshipped since Jackson had been white. The fact that my private mental archive was so skewed in favour of androgynous white boys can be attributed to the selective racism of mass media: the young studs of *Hot Male Review*, or Hollywood pin-ups like River Phoenix and Christopher (*Blue Lagoon*) Atkins, were churned out by marketing wizards who believed that most North American consumers would *not* find Asians sexy. To this point, the most striking images of Asian male beauty I had seen were the leftist heroes of a slide show about the Philippines I attended at university just before the fall of the Marcos regime. Those smiling, bare-chested young cadres from the New People's Army sure seemed a refreshing departure from all that formulaic white beefcake served up daily by the powers that be.

By the time I was twenty-five and living in Hope, the disconnect between mind and body was becoming too much. My closet was getting crowded. One day I found myself ogling the son of an aboriginal band chief during a traditional ceremony on native land I was invited to attend as the town's only newspaper reporter. The proximity of so much slippery, naked male flesh in a steaming sweat lodge – especially that of "Jonathan," a lean and smoulderingly handsome nineteen-year-old – distracted me from the solemnity of the occasion. Pent-up emotions and blue balls were threatening to compromise my objective distance as an earnest young representative of the fifth estate. I had to move to the city. So when the *Vancouver Sun* offered me a summer internship a few weeks later, I packed my bags.

Having left behind a life of dull suburban closetry in Nanaimo and Hope, I was excited by the prospect of living in a multicultural city. And I couldn't make sense of alarmist news reports that saw an upsurge in Chinese immigration as some kind of "Asian invasion." As a newcomer, perhaps I was bound to be more open-minded than, say, a sixth-generation Kerrisdale Wasp seeing his *lebensraum* disappear. But the Vancouver I moved to in 1989 seemed a far more interesting place than the whitebread cultural backwater it must have been in the 1950s. In time, I too would develop my own prejudices about certain Asian immigrants – those who, shortly after becoming Canadian citizens, would use the privilege to vote for homophobic, anti-abortionist politicians whose values more closely mirrored their own "traditional" ones. But for now, fascination was all that mattered. *Gee*, I thought one night, as I wandered through a sea of Chinese faces on Robson, *if this be an "Asian invasion," by all means, bring it on….*

∞

By the time I moved into Vaseline Towers, the hedonistic abandon I had missed out on during the glory days of gay liberation had been replaced by a funereal dirge. As more young men succumbed to the plague, city apartment vacancies caused by AIDS-related deaths had begun to outnumber those related to geriatric deaths and nearly equalled the student turnover rate. There may have been optimism by the end of the 1980s that sero-conversions had "plateaued" in the gay community. But the devastation AIDS had wrought after only six years of traceable infections had overwhelmed the city. As a freshly uncloseted, HIV-negative twenty-five-year-old, I had not only never lost a loved one to AIDS but didn't know a single person living with the virus. Since I wanted to keep it that way, one of the first things I did was visit the Persons With AIDS Society library and check out a copy of the latest edition of *Safer Sex Guidelines*. Memorizing the document, I carefully noted which activities the country's foremost HIV experts considered high, medium, or low risk. Then, on a warm Friday night in early June, I set out to find companions.

Amid the throngs of gay white pedestrians on Davie Street was a sprinkling of young East Asians. Reaching the queue outside Celebrities, one of the city's more popular gay clubs, I spotted a Chinese guy in his mid-twenties. A few inches shorter than me, he was wearing a black silk shirt and blue jeans that tugged on his firm, round ass. He saw me joining the queue, turned around, and introduced himself. Taking me by the hand, "Carmen" led me into the club and straight to the dance floor where we nuzzled cheek to cheek to the pounding of Madonna's "Vogue." A sense of euphoria took over. Skin-to-skin contact with someone like Carmen – his whiff of cologne mixed with the warmth of his young male sweat – was exactly what I needed. After fifteen minutes, we left Celebrities and took a taxi to my apartment.

Moments after we sat down on my living room couch, Carmen planted his tongue in my mouth. I was still wondering if it might be rude to go for his pants right away when he shoved his hand down mine. Unzipping his jeans, I caught my first glimpse of those tiny cotton briefs I would come to recognize as the undergarment of choice for multitudes of gay Asian men. This little white thong, which I would begin to call the "Pebbles and Bam-Bam Bondage Diaper," suggested infantile innocence and passive enslavement. But Carmen was twenty-five, like me, and anything but passive. To him, the slinky bikini was merely a cocktease – a hint of the real action, which he began by pulling my head into his crotch.

Minutes later, our clothes on the floor and our bodies entwined at opposite ends, I found myself gazing up at a pair of perfectly round, hairless buns with a smooth, unshaven crevice. Until this moment, I had been led by Christian televangelists and right-wing newspaper columnists to believe that this part of the anatomy – especially a man's – was a filthy place; a cesspool of afflictions and the root of all evil. But Carmen's didn't seem filthy at all; on the contrary, its scent was so sweet he might have dusted it with lavender. As for the "evil," I suppose that was the pleasure he derived from whatever my tongue did to it. In the end, his lack of inhibition in climaxing all over my couch and pillow was enough to send me over the edge: in the end, the evidence of my delirium could be found on Carmen's ass, the pillow, the couch, the carpet, and that day's edition of the *Vancouver Sun*, which lay draped over the coffee table.

Yellow Fever

A youth may have a thorn or two, but he is like the first plum blossom of the new year exuding an indescribable fragrance.

– Ihara Saikaku, *The Great Mirror of Male Love*

V
Fascination

Bill proudly exhibited his treasure trove.

Sometimes, when I think of my connection to Asian men, I'm reminded of Yoshio and Billy, a pair of fictional schoolboys who become the best of buddies not despite but *because of* the differences that attract them to each other. Their story is contained in a children's book published in 1937, *Yoshio: A Japanese Boy in Canada*. In the foreword, author Helen Dickson said she wrote *Yoshio* "to promote friendly feeling between Canadian and Japanese children."[1] The irony seems tragic now, given the distinctly *unfriendly* feeling that would sour Japanese-Canadians on their second home just four years later. But the story's message of tolerance makes a lot of sense today: racism is learned behaviour acquired from adults, and there's a kind of purity in the innocence of childhood friendships that transcends the harsher realities of nation building.

Yoshio chronicles the adventures of a little Japanese boy growing up in Vancouver in the 1930s. When the story begins, Yoshio – the son of a cod fisherman – is six years old and beginning his first day at school. As a recent immigrant, he's having a rough time. He can't speak English, so he doesn't understand what's going on. Other children make fun of him, and he's taunted by the school bully. But soon he is "rescued" by a handsome blond boy named Billy Peters. Billy, a year older than Yoshio, is a sort of boy-next-door Everyman who represents the best of white liberalism. "Greatly impressed by the strength and command of his rescuer," Yoshio adopts Billy as his best friend. The story goes on to explore the two boys' adventures together, reinforcing the idea that it's okay for white people to befriend or love East Asians. It's a quaint story, hard not to appreciate for its homoerotic charm. In one of the illustrations, the two friends are seen on the beach where the white boy shows off his secret stash of seashore collectibles ("Bill proudly exhibits his treasure trove") while his Japanese playmate looks on in wonder.

In the early days of my sex life, it wasn't just Asians who stirred my lust. After Carmen, I enjoyed the caresses of several white boys. These included an

1. Helen Dickson, *Yoshio: A Japanese Boy in Canada* (London: Thomas Nelson and Sons, 1937).

eighteen-year-old redhead who seduced me on the phone while I was trying to reach a friend living in his co-op house; a twenty-seven-year-old yuppie who took me home from a cruising area known as the "Fruit Loop"; a sports organizer I met for coffee to discuss the Gay Games; a bisexual broadcasting technician I met at Celebrities; a tall, brown-eyed actor; and a short, blond-haired architecture student. I was catching up for lost time: I *had* to sample the menu.

But the longer I lived in the West End, the more East Asian guys I ended up with. Pondering the reasons for this, I came up with the usual checklist of fetishes: smooth skin, "almond" eyes, shiny black hair, sleek bodies, and youthfulness. But it was more than just physical. My desires were motivated as much by a need for knowledge as a need for release. I wanted to understand my lovers – if only to learn more about myself. What I knew so far was that the factor of youthfulness in East Asian guys awakened memories of Jackson, which in turn reminded me of my own arrested development and how I both resented and worshipped Jackson for his beauty. So all that smooth brown skin, all those firm round buns and boyish faces, had become a potent elixir of nostalgic eroticism and wish fulfillment fantasies. All that other stuff – the stereotypes of passivity, good manners, "traditional values," inscrutability – was merely a challenge, an invitation to strip away layers.

East Asian men who had integrated into Western ways were often less attractive than those who hadn't. The former were less conflicted about their sexuality. The transgressive aspect of homo sex (especially if committed with a white guy) and the fear of disappointing the family with disclosure of queerness were less inhibiting for the Canadian-born or the integrated immigrant than for the recent arrival. For me, it was far more exciting to watch a Chinese boy strip off his thong if he still regarded queerness as a cultural taboo. For the tension caused by his impending violation was that much greater and his orgasm that much better, the theory went, than if he felt no anxiety about what he was doing. The liberation resulting from the encounter made sex with him all the hotter, proving that obstacles to sex and romance such as culture and religion are often the aphrodisiac that guarantee their occurrence. "The gratification is incomparable," the great filmmaker Luis Bunuel once said, "because it is always colored by the sweet secret sense of sin."[2]

2. Luis Bunuel, *My Last Sigh* (New York: Knopf, 1983).

In a pan-Asian metropolis like Vancouver, it wasn't all that great a leap from mild interest in Asian men to a chronic case of Yellow Fever. There were simply too many hot and available guys in the city who happened to be Chinese, Japanese, Filipino, Vietnamese, or whatever, for sex not to occur often. Some argued it was all a matter of statistical odds. "Most analysis of the 'rice queen' looks for an explanation in the inner-most psychology of the individual and its relation to the public fantasies and discourses of imperialism and colonialism," writes Tim McCaskell, in an essay exploring the meaning of Yellow Fever in the North American metropolis.[3] "The rice queen can be better explained with reference to a racialized economy produced in the sexual marketplace of the gay community and its effects on patterns of individual couplings and ultimately on individual tastes."

McCaskell argues that the sheer volume of sexual couplings in the gay world creates clearly visible patterns of desire after repeated couplings. Likening the urban gay metropolis to a sexual marketplace, McCaskell divides large North American cities into white and Asian gay male populations. Most white guys, he says, embrace "dominant ideas of beauty" and are attracted to other whites; most Asian guys are also mainly attracted to whites (or at least were when he wrote this essay). "That means," says McCaskell, "that those white guys who like Asians are in a buyer's market."

Somewhere in Vancouver, tucked away in a storage locker in some dusty old liquor box, is a steno pad with the word "Partners" scribbled on the cover. Inside is a sex log I kept in the early nineties, when the life of the body was still new and each encounter bristled with meaning. Much of its contents are too trite, naïve, or pornographic to include here, but a few moments of clarity stand out. And so, from the first hundred or so adventures I recorded before losing count, I offer you….

> Jason (Taiwanese). Poor little rich boy from Taipei, 26.
> Very hot to trot. Spotted him staring one night from the
> window of Pastamelli's on Denman. But he was with a

3. "Towards a Sexual Economy of Rice Queenliness: Lust, Power and Racism." *Rice: Explorations into Gay Asian Culture & Politics*, edited by Song Cho (Toronto: Queer Press, 1998).

white guy, so I stepped outside and locked up the bike. He smiled. An hour later, coming back for the bike, there's a piece of yellow paper rolled neatly around the crossbar with adhesive tape. Thinking it's a parking ticket (those anal city police!), I open it and read the black felt scrawl: "I saw you in Pastamelli's. I want to meet you. J." And a number….

Jason represents the most radical example of political dissonance in my sex life. This was not one of those James Carville-meets-Mary Matlin, "opposites attract" sort of romances. Without the physical turn-on, we wouldn't have spent more than two minutes together. Jason, whose father owned a global convenience store chain, was somewhat to the right of Atilla the Hun. In his view, panhandlers were not the unfortunate victims of a failing economy but a threat to small business; the best response to political protesters was a fire hose. Such opinions were perhaps not unusual in Taiwan, where the "Asian Way" did not preclude police brutality. But in a dope-smoking, libertarian, hippie-socialist enclave of the Pacific Northwest, they were rather extreme.

When I first spotted him in the pasta bar, Jason was wearing a multi-coloured leather jacket with a Number "8" on the back and black designer jeans that showed off his hot ass. He had high cheekbones, and lines around his pouty lips. Taking his note off my bike, I called him. He was having dessert somewhere else with the same friend he'd been with at Pastamelli's. Twenty minutes later, he arrived at Vaseline Towers in a shiny, black Volkswagen Rabbit. He took me for a drive around Stanley Park, and then stopped the car around the corner from Prospect Point.

Jason had moved to Vancouver a few years earlier and was working in sales at a luxury retailer downtown. He was glad to be away from Taipei, and from a father so desperate to have him back in the family fold that he'd offered him millions of dollars to leave his decadent life of sodomy in the West. That was more than enough money for a significant upgrade on the Rabbit – to say nothing of a new luxury condo, or perhaps an estate in West Vancouver, to replace the modest, two-storey townhouse that Daddy had set him up in, along with a regular allowance. But Jason's father was holding out to see what his son would do, and the offer would be withdrawn immediately if Jason did anything stupid – like, say, shacking up with a white western faggot.

Like many children of the rich, Jason had no interest in politics. So it was surprising to learn that one of his previous lovers had been a well-known human rights activist. This man, who would later die of AIDS, was a passionate crusader for Third World development issues. Jason could barely stifle a yawn for the poor and oppressed, but he and the activist had enjoyed a brief period of stellar sex. Contemplating my own imminent romp in the sack with him, I was less concerned about Jason's HIV status than by the political implications of shagging an apolitical label queen.

Parked in the middle of Stanley Park after midnight, listening to a recent immigrant complain about the Canadian welfare and taxation system, I suddenly felt the urge to grab Jason by his thick black hair, pull his head toward mine, and force my tongue down his throat. We necked for a while, and then drove back to my apartment where he stripped down to the same Pebbles-and-Bam-Bam jockstrap that had looked so good on Carmen. Jason's thick brown thighs and bubble-shaped buns were clearly the product of a platinum gym membership. His pubic hair was trimmed into a neat, adolescent-size patch. But he was bathed in so much cologne that it was hard to chew on his nipples, or lick a trail down his six-pack abdomen, without my tongue tasting like it had dabbed a hundred stamps.

Over the next two days, we did everything in bed – almost. When I asked Jason why he didn't want to fuck, he said he was holding out until he knew I was boyfriend material.

"But we'll never be boyfriends," I said. "We've got nothing in common."

Jason burst into tears. "You're just using me!"

I shrugged, guilty as charged. And yet: two weeks after saying he never wanted to see me again he was on the phone, inviting me to his place as if I *hadn't* torn his heart into pieces. Jason's townhouse was lined with white shag carpets and lots of mirrors. Barbell weights littered the floors, and a little white poodle – a silly, annoying yapper – followed his master everywhere.

Jason led me to the bedroom, drew the blinds, and stripped down to a clean white thong. Then he put on some music – Enigma's "The Principles of Lust" – and pulled off my pants. Leading me to a squeaky wooden chair, he grabbed a condom from the night table, unrolled it on me, pulled off his thong, and planted himself. Soon he was rocking insistently on my lap. On the stereo, a Yoko Ono-like voice, accompanied by pseudo Gregorian chants, whispered what sounded like *Dis-moi!* Jason sighed and splashed all over me;

I exploded inside him. Seeing me to the door, he seemed in a much better mood. Perhaps being "used" wasn't so bad after all. For my part, I was glad to know that my positions on public health care and education needn't be compromised as a result of having fucked an unapologetic capitalist.

∞

Nino (Filipino): Very horny, about 23. Got cruisey in Celebrities one night as I was handing out condoms for the AIDS walkathon. Slipped him my phone number along with a condom; he called two nights later.

Nino showed up at my doorstep carrying his car stereo, which he proceeded to plunk on my dining room table like a briefcase (in recent weeks there'd been several car burglaries in the West End). Then he pulled out a wallet-sized photo of his muscle-bound American boyfriend.

"He must never find out I was here," Nino said. "He would kill us both."

"Oh. Thank you for sharing that," I said.

Then, tucking away the photo of his homicidal boyfriend, Nino put his arms around my neck and straddled my lap, grinding his crotch as he kissed me. He had thick, porn-star lips and dark skin that was warm to the touch. Reaching under his designer shirt, my hands found a smooth hard chest with firm, eraserhead nipples. We went to bed. After ten minutes of cocksucking, Nino was dressed and out the door without bothering to take a shower. I wanted to see him again. Nothing doing, he said. I understood.

Over the next couple of years, I ran into Nino on the street a few times. He always recognized me with a smile, which was pleasant. Then he disappeared. I thought he'd moved – made his way to Toronto, moved to the US with his jealous boyfriend, or returned to Manila. But one day I was told by one of his Filipino friends that he was living out his final weeks in a hospital bed, dying of AIDS. Among Nino's infections was CMV retinitis – a decaying of the retina which, by the mid-1990s, could be detected early and prevented from spreading. Nino had avoided doctors until it was too late. Now, I was told, he was lying in the palliative care unit with big round cotton patches covering his eyes. Could I visit him? "He won't remember you," said his friend. "And if he did, he wouldn't want to think about sex at a time like this. So just leave him alone."

∞

Leonard: Canadian-born Chinese, 27. Introduced by a friend at a piano recital in someone's garage in Point Grey. Arrived late to find Leonard and his friend Richard, both classically trained, serenading about a dozen people sitting in foldup chairs. They were playing Broadway tunes and Rachmaninoff on four baby grands that were being showcased for sale. A different way to spend a Friday night.

Donald, an opera queen acquaintance who introduced me to Leonard, was determined to play matchmaker and rather relished the role. But there was a warning attached: "Leonard's a *total* closet case. You'd never know it to see him, he's such a screamer. Really, he's fooling no one but himself. I mean, come on: a classical pianist … who plays show tunes?!" I was surprised to learn that Leonard, at twenty-seven, was still in the closet. He'd lived in Vancouver all his life and must have had access to the city's voluminous art fag network. But Leonard was the only son of an aging widower from one of the city's older Chinese families. There was still pressure to marry. He was bashful when Donald introduced us, but agreed to meet later for a date.

In retrospect, it would have been wiser to share dessert at a neutral location than invite Leonard to Vaseline Towers. By late 1990, I had come to expect getting naked on every first date. That must have been clear to Leonard, who was nervous throughout the visit. When he said he was still a virgin, it was all downhill from there. We kept our clothes on; he left after an hour. We didn't talk again until the summer, when he called to say he had just returned from Europe. He had been staying in youth hostels, he said. Places filled with horny young guys who jacked off in their beds every night.

"So, did you get any?" I asked.

"No," he replied. "That's why I'm calling. I am *so* frustrated. Plus, I was such a flake when we met last year that I just wanted to make it up to you…."

An hour later, Leonard picked me up at the apartment and drove us out to the Wreck Beach nudist colony just below the University of British Columbia. We hiked down to the gay sandbar and spread out a towel among the sunbathers. Leonard dug into his beach bag and hauled out a large tube of petroleum jelly. Then, in full view of our fellow sun worshippers, he drew closer, French kissed me, and jerked us both a shower of hot cum. We saw each other casually after that. Years later, Leonard would introduce me at parties as "the man who corrupted me." I was glad to be of service.

> Anthony: Filipino investor from LA (late 20s). Picked him up at Numbers. Should have noticed the cling-on vibes, but was too drunk to care. Staggered with him back to the apartment of a friend who'd put him up for the weekend. He lit candles, poured Grand Marnier and put on a CD of Ennio Morricone's The Mission. Bad sign. In the bedroom, vanilla sex. All gooey and lovey-dovey. Another bad sign; neither sign read.

What was I thinking? Anthony wasn't particularly attractive, and he suffered from chronic verbal diarrhea. He told me everything about his previous lovers, the California investment community, the china patterns he'd selected for his new kitchen…. After brunch the next morning, he asked if we could meet the next time he was in town. "Sure," I shrugged, thinking nothing of it. Three days later, he called to ask if he could stay the next weekend. I was too stunned to think up a good excuse to say no. "Sure," I said. Idiot.

By this point I had moved out of Vaseline Towers and was living in a co-op house where I shared the rent with three other people. Within minutes of his arrival, Anthony announced that he was cooking dinner for everyone – which, apart from being oddly intrusive for a guest, was impossible: my housemates had different schedules, and we weren't exactly the Brady Bunch. (I lived with a photographer in his early forties, an opera singer in his late thirties, and a provincial court clerk in his early twenties.) To get him out of the house, I took Anthony to a concert by the Flirtations. Bad move: I'd forgotten it was Valentine's Day, which meant the popular New York quintet would be singing mostly romantic favourites. Sure enough, the show was a mushy celebration of same-sex monogamy – one of those gay community events that come off like a Billy Graham revival meeting. "Are there any lovers out there on their first date tonight?" group member Michael Callen unfortunately blurted into his mike. Anthony clutched my arm. I cringed, smiling awkwardly at acquaintances I hadn't managed to avoid who were all eager for an introduction to this stranger I'd brought out in public on Valentine's Day. *Oh look, he's finally attached – and so out-of-the-blue!*

By the fourth day, I couldn't get any work done. Anthony wanted to take me shopping and was still trying to schedule dinner for my housemates, who by now wanted nothing to do with him. I finally had to take him aside, break it to him that he'd overstayed his welcome, and send him packing. His wounded look suggested I wasn't the first to dump him this way. A few nights later, I celebrated my relief by cracking open the $50 bottle of Grand Marnier he'd given me, sharing it in bed with a bisexual Vietnamese doorman from Numbers.

VI
Monogamy

FEAR OF INTIMACY IS ONE OF THE LEAST ATTRACTIVE qualities of the human condition. I was suffering a bad case of it not long after moving to Vancouver. Consider this entry from the sex log, a classic case of The One That Got Away:

> David. (Hong Kong, mid-20s): Best f*** yet. Met him at Aquatic Centre, drawn immediately to curvaceous, skin-tight blue Speedos. Cruised me in the change room, followed me upstairs, invited me to his apartment. First guy who could fit all of me, try any position; our bodies made for each other. Spent the night, went home in ecstasy. Arranged date at my place a few nights later; David brought videotape player, movies and overnight bag. It was all over in less than an hour....

Oh, what a catch was David: a sweet, handsome, good-natured music student (classical piano) with the body of a gymnast. And ambitious: he had just graduated from university and was planning to continue his studies at a prestigious school in London. The night we met, we fucked for hours at his apartment. Then he wanted to see me again. What more did I want?

Looking back on it now, it seems like only a few minutes elapsed between David's arrival at my apartment, the sex, the simultaneous orgasm, David's suggestion that we watch a movie in the living room, and the moment the magic disappeared forever. For just as I was lying there on the couch with this hot Chinese guy, his arms wrapped around me and our chests heaving in unison, I suddenly felt paralyzed by an inexplicable panic – a bizarre attack of nihilism, a sense of the world collapsing around me. David must have felt the vibes, for he soon asked what was wrong – why I felt so distant. So I told him: it wasn't his fault, but for some reason I couldn't explain I had to be alone. David was stunned. Then appalled. Two minutes later he was out the door – video machine, tapes, and overnight bag in hand.

A few months later, we bumped into each other on the Stanley Park seawall. David was with a boyfriend, but civil. Two years later we met again, at the Safeway on Tenth Avenue. This time, he was single. He gave me his number, and I dropped by his basement apartment a few days later. Inviting me in, he showed me his piano and played a few bars. He was good. Then we watched some porn, sucked each other off, and fell asleep on his hide-a-bed. The next morning I told David I wanted to see him again. He smiled and shook his head.

"I don't think so," he said, seeing me to the door.

I understood. If I couldn't let in someone like David when he was there for the asking, what claim did I really have on a second chance? When we'd first met I had thought that David was moving too fast, inviting a degree of intimacy neither of us had earned yet. But with that kind of thinking, it would be many years before I was ready to "get serious" with any of my Asian lovers.

∞

My first real boyfriend appeared on the last night of the 1980s, at a New Year's Eve party held in a one-level, 1960s-era bungalow near the university. It was one of those swishy, stand-up bachelor parties that often take place on leafy boulevards populated mostly by university professors. There were lots of cliquey art fags, dinner jackets, and martini glasses. Tapes of Billie Holliday on the stereo were barely audible through the cacophony of educated laughter. The rooms were dimly lit, with ceiling-to-floor bookshelves, hardwood floors, and Persian rugs. The feeling was cozy and collegial. About an hour after midnight, guests began pairing up with their first flings of the new decade.

At first, I was convinced I would end up with the Jordanian Cassanova I'd been flirting with all night. Ahmed was an androgynous Arab dreamboat with a long, thin frame, caramel smooth skin, dark pools for eyes, and jet-black hair that seemed to shine in the dark. Just after midnight we began our mating ritual: leaning back to back and rubbing our heads together, side by side, like two genies in a bottle. At one point I excused myself to go to the toilet. When I returned, Ahmed had disappeared. Sitting down to wait for him, I dozed off in my chair. I awoke to find him standing in front of me – doing our head-rubbing routine with another guy. Just as the sting of abandonment began to register, I felt my right hand being stroked by someone sitting next to me.

Fingers were running patterns over the back of my hand, then my palm underneath. It felt like I was getting a massage and having my fortune told at the same time. But the touch of this warm hand, which had a jade ring on one of its fingers, was more intimate than that. Looking up at its owner, I found a cherubic, bespectacled Chinese face that nodded and smiled back. Introducing himself as William – an oddly English name, I thought, even for a Canadian-born Chinese – he continued stroking my hand. I was caught between my longing for Ahmed, now doing the head rubbing with yet another partner – and the surprising appeal of William, whose fingers were walking through my defences. I turned to face him again. There was a quiet confidence behind those wire rims: after a few minutes of stroking, he offered me a ride home. I smiled, squeezing his hand. Ahmed seemed surprised by our exit.

For the next day or two, I would fret about my missed opportunity with the Jordanian studmuffin. But it was the right move. Other than a few polite greetings on the street over the next six months, Ahmed vanished from my radar; William was at the centre of it. Through him, I was introduced to the world of educated, bourgeois gay life. William was a self-described "culture vulture" who worked for a local arts centre and lived and breathed classical music. He played clarinet for the philharmonic, had season's tickets to the city symphony and opera, and was a serious balletophile. He also spent time with a married couple of former alumni from his music society days, often flying away with them for holidays in New York. Life was art; art was life.

With William by my side, the Gay Nineties promised to be just that. Together we went to concerts, plays, and the ballet, often double-dating with a couple who'd met at the same New Year's Eve party. It was an endless string of laughter-and-calorie-filled nights: from January dinner parties and post-concert pastries to springtime picnics in Stanley Park. The four of us drove around from one good time to the next in a mint-condition, powder blue 1962 Parisienne. For a time, "high" culture and homo culture were one. Throughout all this, ethnicity never seemed to be an issue: William was every bit as "western" as I was. His father's family, part of Vancouver's first wave of Chinese immigrants from Canton in the mid-19th century, had been in Canada longer than my father's had. William's dad was a partner in one of the downtown's more established notary public firms. He had sent his three boys to the best schools and raised them in the English language. William was born into Canadian society – not integrated into it. So hyphenating him as "Chinese-Canadian," as some strangers did in conversation, seemed unnecessary.

On the other hand, cultural tradition did have a role in William's life. At twenty-seven, he still lived with his parents – like most Chinese bachelors before marriage. He didn't feel at liberty to spend the night anywhere but in the soft, familiar bed whose sheets his mother had changed all his life. Night after night we'd return to my apartment after dinner or a show for more talk, a glass of wine, and then sex – only for William to announce bashfully, once we'd cum, that he had to go. With a peck on the lips, he'd be dressed and out the door, leaving me naked and alone. At the time, his protestations of family respect and fear of losing his "place" (inheritance?) seemed like convenient excuses to avoid intimacy.

But William's behaviour was not unusual, and it hadn't occurred to me that other Chinese men who'd spent their entire lives in North America spoke of the same dilemma: traditional Asian values reached all corners of the diaspora, suffocating every gay Asian male in their wake. (This was before I met Jason, the Taiwanese rich boy, and Leonard, who stayed in the closet until he was twenty-seven.) By the time I met William, I was still about halfway through the ACT-UP stage of gay liberation consciousness: drunk on queer chauvinism after years in the closet, I had little sympathy for those I thought should have been more "out." William, an art fag with progressive, left-leaning politics, was ashamed of his failure to parade our relationship. But he also felt awkward with the kind of activism embraced by his younger brother, who also happened to be gay. Prescriptive liberation politics that pushed the cultural envelope and made demands of others didn't come naturally to William. The only reason he came out to his parents when he did was that his brother had forced his hand by coming out first.

But telling the folks he was gay was one thing; providing the evidence quite another. And so, my nodding acquaintance with William's mother and father remained just that. Despite my having attended one dim sum gathering and several parties at the family home – and despite William's having attended my sister's wedding as my date – he never introduced me as The Boyfriend. But then, partner invisibility was inevitable in the early stages of homo romance when a Chinese family was involved – as anyone who has seen Ang Lee's film *The Wedding Banquet* would attest. But it was this invisibility, combined with William's disappearing act after sex, that began to chip away at our romance.

Five or six months after we began seeing each other, we had our only fight. I said something hurtful about one of William's spiritual mentors – a woman I'd met only once over dinner whom I had disliked immediately. We decided not to see each other for a while, and I encouraged the idea that we'd broken up because of religion: I was on the fast track to atheism while William was into spiritualism, crystals, tantric healing, and other things I dismissed as New Age flake-o-rama. (Even though it was his "healing" hands that had drawn me to him in the first place.) But the real reason we broke up was that I wasn't willing to wait however long it took for William to move out of his parents' home and into his own apartment; I was too impatient to be introduced as Son-in-Law Number One. But we both got over it quickly. Before long we were meeting for coffee again. In the end, our transition from lovers to good friends turned out to be more enriching than the same process with most of my other exes. I felt lucky things had turned out that way.

In the years to come, William and I would never talk about the short time we spent as boyfriends. If he was ever resentful about my lack of empathy for the traditional ways that so constricted his movements in 1990, he never said so. But I doubt he would have allowed such feelings to fester. If you asked him, he'd probably say it was only a matter of time before I came up against the same realities with another East Asian guy, and that whatever cultural conflicts I experienced with him would be nothing compared to the challenges I'd face with a recent immigrant. And he'd be right.

My experience with William turned me off steady boyfriends for the next three years. Instead, I embarked on a sex life that was not unlike my approach to freelance journalism. Wandering from one lover to the next like I did in search of a hot story, I'd drop the last one without a second glance, having learned all I thought there was to know about that particular "subject." Single life suited me, and the gay Asian males of Vancouver made sure it stayed that way: by my third year in the city, about ninety percent of my lovers had been of Far East extraction. Even during a six-month sojourn in London in 1992, I found myself gravitating to Thai and Vietnamese immigrants whose life stories seemed more interesting than those of the English locals. But not even the sweetest of these romances led to anything serious. By the late spring of 1993, when I was back in Vancouver and living in a basement suite not far from the university, I was tired of being single. My antennae were up.

One of the prettiest guys I met during this period was a wiry, twenty-six-year-old Filipino with thick eyelashes named Ferdinand. One night, after flirting with him at Numbers, I brought him home. There wasn't a lot to talk about the next morning over Chinese breakfast, and we never hooked up again. A few weeks later, I met another Filipino at the university swimming pool. Alfonso, a year older than me, wasn't pretty like Ferdinand, but his megawatt smile and warm laughter were enough for me to invite him home. After sex, we exchanged phone numbers. But he seemed awkward, vaguely guilty, when he left, and we never called each other. By the time I'd moved back to the West End a few weeks later, I'd forgotten about him. Then one night I returned to the pool, and Alfonso was there. This time, we drove back to my new apartment on Barclay Street for the night.

Alfonso worked for a local architectural firm; he was a fully trained architect, but his degree had been deemed worthless outside the Philippines. He and some of his family members had been in Canada for eight years. For the last seven, he'd been living with a man who was a decade older. They were still together and shared ownership of an upscale, two-bedroom West End condo a few blocks from my apartment. So what was he doing with me? Was this just a case of Seven-Year Itch? Quite possibly. The bloom had faded with George, a closeted technical writer from California who looked a bit like the actor Kelsey Grammer.

From Alfonso's version of events, George was a cruel bastard. One morning, Alfonso had woken up bleary-eyed and walked into the hallway wearing only his briefs. Reportedly George violently shoved him back in the bedroom, closing the door and ordering him not to come out for another two hours. A client was arriving any minute for a meeting, he said: did Alfonso want the whole world to know he was gay? (As if the piss elegant china set, fey tapestries, and West End postal code weren't enough of a clue.) George was also a grumpy workaholic who, Alfonso added bitterly, wasn't responding to his caresses anymore. And so, over the next few months, Alfonso spent more nights at my apartment.

Taking me on as his mistress was one of the many contradictions in Alfonso's life. Still a devout Roman Catholic, he and his Filipino friends saw nothing odd about attending mass every Sunday morning after a night of drinking and casual sex. Seeking heavenly forgiveness for one's sins immediately after committing them is the way they do things in Manila, I guessed. The one time I joined Alfonso at Guardian Angels parish, Ferdinand was there: the first time I'd seen him since the morning after fucking him in the basement suite in Point Grey. Alfonso hadn't mentioned that he and Ferdinand were best friends; judging from Ferdinand's expression, Alfonso hadn't told him about me, either. For the rest of the mass, Ferdinand kept winking at me when Alfonso wasn't looking.

To compensate for his profound unhappiness with George, Alfonso smothered me with affection. He was generous to a fault, taking me out to expensive steak and seafood restaurants, buying me clothes I didn't ask for, sending flowers to my apartment, driving me on errands, and letting me use his office photocopier for my freelance work. He also brought me Tupperware containers filled with leftovers of tasty Chicken Adobo and other Filipino delicacies he'd prepared for George only hours earlier, after a long day's work. Did George know of my existence? Yes, said Alfonso, but he accepted it. Somehow I doubted that, but I didn't challenge him on it. Not yet.

The good times rolled for three years. During the summers we went sailing on my friend Warren's boat, cruising the Gulf Islands from Saltspring to Cortez. In Alfonso's Mazda, we took two trips to Long Beach on Vancouver Island, went camping at Gray's Harbor, Washington, and pitched a tent near the Kalcheek Suspension Bridge near Whistler. On our second Christmas, we visited all but one of my siblings on a driving tour of the Pacific Northwest and the Kootenays. After three years, my entire family had embraced Alfonso as one of the clan. Only two questions remained: when were we going to move in together, and why hadn't Alfonso – shades of William here – introduced me to *his* family? His mother lived only a short drive away in Richmond, a suburb south of Vancouver. We'd visited once, but Alfonso had described me as "a friend" and never brought me back again.

My position was clear. We'd move in together *after* Alfonso and George had financially dissolved their union by selling the condo; *after* Alfonso showed enough confidence to present me to his mother as George's replacement; *after* he stopped pressuring me to get a desk job; and *after* he stopped being so possessive. Some nights I was happy to stay in and watch a video together. But not *every* night. I needed to get out more often, find out what was happening in the city. But after three years, our so-called relationship was stuck in neutral. What's more, I couldn't attend a single arts function in the city where Asians might be present without Alfonso assuming I was out trolling for a fuck.

Of course, such assumptions have a way of becoming self-fulfilling prophecies. By our third year together, I had confessed to a few flings. This infuriated Alfonso, who had assumed I was being "faithful," even as he was returning to George's bed for days at a stretch. After my disclosure, he began to nag about my roving eye – a condition that afflicts all Rice Queens but of which, in myself, I was blissfully unaware.

"Of *course* you don't notice you're doing it," he said one night, mimicking the raised eyebrow and nodding head of my alleged cruising gestures like a Bobblehead doll on speed. "You're too busy slobbering." A few nights earlier, he noted, we had bumped into a former dancer from Beijing I'd once slept with. In expressing my pleasure at seeing him again, I'd had the audacity to (a) maintain eye contact for longer than the regulation three seconds, and (b) *not* conceal my obvious rapture at the sight of his still gym-fit torso. After that, I was more careful about eye contact when Alfonso and I went out together.

At the same time, Alfonso – bundle of contradictions that he was – did his best to accommodate my voracious carnal appetite. In our final spring together he made several heroic attempts to save our sputtering relationship, even spicing up our sex with a couple of ideas I wouldn't have expected from a Filipino Catholic obsessed with monogamy. The first involved driving out to Boys Town and picking up a hustler to take home for a threesome. This was an act of great sacrifice on Alfonso's part, since his ideal fantasy "type" couldn't have been further removed from the white, teenaged bad boys we picked up on separate occasions. Knowing that I, on the other hand, could gobble up such ephebes for breakfast, Alfonso was offering me a special treat. His reasoning? That if he consented to, paid for, and witnessed me getting it on with a rent boy – especially if I enjoyed it – then this subsidized naughtiness would presumably satisfy me enough that I'd resist any temptation that came my way when he wasn't around. Call it the Filipino Catholic Guilt Trip version of the Mercy Fuck. (As in: *That's all right, dear – you just go ahead and have your fun with the street urchin while I shut my eyes and think of Richard Gere....*)

Alfonso's other idea was to go cruising, together, in the forested ravine above Vancouver's nude sand bar at Wreck Beach. He knew I'd been doing this alone for quite some time and had grown suspicious every time I left the apartment for a bike ride (typically assuming that I'd have my tongue up some Asian boy's crack in the amount of time it takes to boil an egg.) So one evening in May, after a sun-drenched picnic at Spanish Banks, he suggested we explore the nearby trails together. This way, he might find someone more to his liking than a skinny young hustler. If he enjoyed himself, then I would understand what it's like to feel jealous – and thus have empathy for the anguish I'd caused him.

Alfonso parked the car just outside the trail, then set the rules: "We go in opposite directions, then come back here in twenty minutes."

"*Twenty minutes?!*" I said. "You've got to be kidding."

In the shadows of this dense, several-hectare forest, twenty minutes was barely enough time to find anyone, much less enjoy a "quickie." But Alfonso wouldn't budge on this point. After watching him disappear down one trail, I turned in the other direction and headed toward the setting sun. I found my prize in about ten minutes, standing under a tree at a fork in the trail: a big, strapping Chinese hunk with long hair and tattoos on his chest. By the time we'd finished necking, sucking, and jerking each other off, forty-five minutes had passed since I'd left the car. When I got back to the Mazda, Alfonso was fuming. He'd found someone, too, he said, but he'd stuck to the twenty-minute deadline.

That was the end of our "nature walks" at Wreck Beach.

Gradually, Alfonso adopted the position that we needn't wait until his formal "divorce" from George before moving in together: since George had decided to return to the us, I could simply take his place in the condo. Was George really selling his share, I asked? Not yet, said Alfonso. So I vetoed the plan. There was no way I was moving into a home still half-owned by my boyfriend's "ex." Fine, said Alfonso: but there was no way *he* was going to sever his financial ties with George as long as his current lover couldn't keep his dick in his pants. And so we reached a stalemate. The condo issue was eventually settled when George sold his portion a year later. But by that time, Alfonso had rented a U-Haul and driven all the way to California to help George resettle. It was all but over between us.

The beginning of the end came on a hot Sunday afternoon at the end of July, when I fell head over heels for a twenty-three-year-old Russian boy I met on the sands of Britannia Beach. Drawing the older of two sons away from a family picnic scene that might have taken place on the Black Sea, I found myself in a summer seduction ritual worthy of an Isherwood novel – or, at least, a Bel Ami porn video. After wading out to an old shipwreck and fondling each other underwater in its hull, Alexei and I swam around the corner, climbed a twenty-foot rock, and swallowed each other in broad daylight. It was *al fresco* perfection: we both climaxed with the Howe Sound vista stretching out before us and the sun glowing from the west, seagulls hanging on a warm breeze above our heads as the six o'clock whistle of the B.C. Rail dayliner sounded in the distance.

Alexei's beauty was like something out of a Weimar Republic photo by Herbert List. After worshipping at the sun-kissed altar of his golden youth, I lost my head. In the coming days, I tried to prolong the fantasy back in the city by pursuing the Russian boy with Alfonso's full knowledge. But after one sordid rendezvous at Alexei's house – drunk on Absolut vodka, he fucked me on his bed as trashy synth pop played in the background, then slept on the couch – it went nowhere. In the end, the fair-weather fuck had been a cry for help: I wanted out of the relationship with Alfonso, but didn't know how to get out.

Alfonso made things easier by leaving me for good in the spring of 1997. A year after that, with the condo now sold, he was preparing to move to the US. He said he was going to Phoenix, where I knew he had clients. But later I found out he had actually gone to California and was back living with George – proving, once and for all, that I'd never had a serious chance in our entire four years together. Now and then, I would gaze at a wall hanging of the Filipino machete Alfonso had given me as a gift – amazed that in all our time together, neither of us had tried to use it on the other.

It's easy to overstate the negative when recalling a relationship gone wrong. But it's important to note that my four years with Alfonso, in fact, broke several stereotypes of the Rice Queen/Potato Queen dynamic. Rather than being a skinny little ephebe, the Asian guy in this love affair was a bit on the chunky side and a year older than the white guy. Rather than being a gold-digging "money boy," the Asian guy had the financial leverage; it was the white guy who was the "plaything"/mistress. And, in the end, it was the Asian guy who finally dumped the white guy rather than the reverse. But the most important departure from the neocolonial equation was that it was our similarities – not our differences – that had really brought Alfonso and I together. As much as I dismissed the Roman Catholic Church and thought I'd left it behind, there was something about Alfonso's sense of community and ritual – even his social conscience – that I found oddly familiar and reassuring. He was an ambitious, middle-class kid from a large family, as I was. He was loyal and dedicated to a small circle of friends, as I was. He was a lover of camp Hollywood divas and sultry torch song singers, as I was. And, like me, he was a Scorpio control queen who didn't like losing. Really, he knew me as well as anyone could. Now that he was gone, I was in no hurry to let anyone else in.

VII
Butterflies

LATE ONE NIGHT AT NUMBERS, a gay bar on Davie Street, I was standing in a stairwell that led to a basement section the regulars referred to as the "Rice Pit." Most of the men here were either Asian or the white guys pursuing them. After catching the eye of Raoul, a Filipino, in the upstairs bar, I followed him to this spot where he presented me to three of his friends, also Filipinos. Raoul began chatting with them in Tagalog. Standing before this group as the racial minority, I felt as though I was no longer at Numbers but had entered some foreign territory, with its own cultural rules and customs. All three of Raoul's friends were middle-class immigrants. But in this darkened stairwell their sweet coquettish smiles, fluttering eyelashes, and come-hither teasing had magically transformed them into upcountry go-go boys working a stage in Manila. Raoul, selling their attributes, was now their bar host/pimp.

"Which one do you want?" he smiled at me.

The "Rice Pit" was one of several public venues in Vancouver that catered specifically to, or at least provided space for, East Asian gay men. There were places like it in most western industrial cities with large East Asian populations. Postmodern academics referred to such places as "homoscapes," or "transnational scene[s] of sexual spaces, commodities, communications and identity performance ... inhabited by the coded rituals of looking and cruising, the negotiations of consent, and ultimately of course, the protocols of sexual exchange."[1] During the 1990s, some of my favourite pan-Asian "homoscapes" were located in the alternative art scene. The tension of sex was always in the air at a modern dance performance by Alvin Tolentino at the Firehall Theatre, a mixed media exhibit by Nhan duc Nguyen at the grunt gallery, or a screening by various queer Asian producers at Video In.

One night, during intermission at the Video In, a crowd began to form around a slim, giraffe-like figure in the back room. Pushing through the

1. Thomas Waugh, "Fung: Home and Homoscape." *Like Mangoes in July: The Work of Richard Fung*, edited by Helen Lee and Kerri Sakamoto (Toronto: Insomniac Press, 2002).

hallway for a closer look, I was struck by how the bohemian chic of his black leather was offset by an oddly Zen-like combination of buzz-cut hairstyle and wire-rim glasses. It was a hot look, and – with the typically Rice Queenly thought progression that tends to unfold when an intriguing Asian is within stalking distance – I began to wonder what he looked like naked. After introducing ourselves, we talked for a while about the evening's programme.

Then I told him I was thinking of writing a book called *The Rice Queen Diaries*.

His face did a Mona Lisa.

"Interesting," smiled Richard Fung.

For many artists and activists familiar with his work, Richard Fung is a post-colonial guru of minor deity proportions. To queer film director John Greyson, he's "the Cesar Chavez of the Gay Asian Fruit Pickers Association" and a "verbal enabler" of uncommon gracefulness. More skeptical observers regard Fung and the artists he has inspired as multicultural careerists who have padded their resumes with politically chic representations of minority grievances. Richard Fung is *both* pioneer and poseur, but the latter doesn't disqualify the former. He deserves credit, at the very least, for identifying the "cultural schizophrenia" of Asian gay existence in the West: a state in which the gay Oriental male "related on one hand to a heterosexual family that affirmed [his] ethnic culture and, on the other hand, to a gay community that was predominantly white."[2]

Videos such as "Chinese Characters" (1986) or "Steam Clean" (1990) were clever, funny, and – at the time – refreshing. The former juxtaposes background images of gay white porn with a Chinese man disrobing and acting out his fantasies in the foreground. It's a powerful illustration of how gay Asians expressed their desire and how it was treated in gay white porn of the day. "By introducing an Asian male presence where it [had] previously been excluded," one admirer has noted, Fung was serving notice to the two opposing sides in the porn/censorship debate – sexual libertarians and anti-porn feminists – that "neither camp can account for [gay Asian men's]

---

2. Richard Fung, "Looking for My Penis: The Eroticized Asian in Gay Video Porn." *How Do I Look?: Queer Film and Video*, edited by Bad Object-Choices (Seattle: Bay Press, 1991).

experiences of sexuality."[3] This kind of representation was long overdue.

Fung is perhaps best known for his 1991 essay, "Looking for My Penis: The Eroticized Asian in Gay Video Porn." One of the most widely quoted and republished essays in Asian American studies, "Looking for My Penis" is a somewhat arch, post-modern, Revenge-of-the-Nerds jeremiad in which Fung exhorts all queer Asians to reclaim their erotic power. The problem of stereotyping, he argues, goes beyond the realm of gay porn and is symptomatic of western mass media in general:

> Asian men have been consigned to one of two categories: the egghead/wimp, or – in what may be analogous to the lotus blossom-dragon lady dichotomy – the kung fu master/ninja samurai. He is sometimes dangerous, sometimes friendly, but almost always characterized by a desexualized Zen asceticism. So whereas, as Fanon tells us, 'the Negro is eclipsed. He is turned into a penis. He is a penis,' the Asian man is defined by a striking absence down there. And if Asian men have no sexuality, how can we have homosexuality?[4]

Butterfly (noun): an insect with four often brightly coloured wings and knobbed feelers.
– *Oxford Paperback Dictionary*, 2000

Butterfly (noun, colloq): one who leads an idle, gay life; an idler, a trifler.
– *Webster's Twentieth Century Dictionary*, 1937

In the art world, "butterfly" is the operatic diva of Puccini's *Madama Butterfly*, a fragile Asian beauty who is abandoned by her western lover. Or, it's the Asian transvestite of David Henry Hwang's play *M. Butterfly*, a spy

---

3. Kyo Maclear, "From the Seminal to the Sublime: A Richard Fung Videography." *Like Mangoes in July: The Work of Richard Fung*.

4. Fung, "Looking for My Penis."

who becomes "The Perfect Woman" for his hapless western lover. In gay Asiana, a "butterfly" is someone who flutters from one lover to the next like a Lepidoptera to a flower. When a gay Asian male refers to a Rice Queen as a "butterfly," he's either teasing him about his slutty behaviour or cautioning other gay Asians about it. Of course, anyone can be this type of "butterfly" – gay Asians included.

One of my favourite lovers was Johnny, a Filipino-American from Washington, D.C. I met in a Vancouver bathhouse one night, not long after Alfonso left me. Johnny was a hard-toned, barrel-chested gym stud the likes of which I'd never fucked: guys like him were usually out of my league. He also defied my narrow lineage of desire by turning out to be much older than I'd first thought: he was forty-one, not twenty-five. Taking full advantage of his youthful appearance, Johnny had spent the last few years on a perpetual sex tour in which Vancouver was merely a whistle stop. Several times a year, he took holidays in the gay capitals of America and Europe. After trolling the bars, saunas and shrubs in search of young white meat, he would send e-mails that revealed the extent of his voraciousness.

Johnny took great delight in describing his conquests in San Francisco, L.A., New York, New Orleans, Miami, Minneapolis, Chicago, and Boston – not to mention Prague and Budapest, two nerve centres of the East European flesh trade. Despite the repetitive nature of his itinerary, he never grew tired of sharing the details of sex: cock sizes, skin types, and other stats of the men he seduced – usually straight-looking, straight-acting varsity jocks or yuppies he'd sniffed out in parks, public toilets, or nightclub dark rooms. I was happy to volunteer as the Vancouver fling on Johnny's exhaustive travel agenda. But I couldn't help wondering how his body and psyche were coping.

Physically speaking, I needn't have worried. Johnny had the perfect career for a globetrotting slut: he was a paramedical lab tech whose job was to test blood, urine, and semen samples for the very diseases he had every intention of avoiding in his own sex life. But what about his spirit? Catholic guilt was a non-issue: he was far beyond redemption, despite that sexy little crucifix around his neck. But didn't he ever get lonely? While his boyish appeal was enviable for someone in his early forties, what would he do when the Dorian Gray canvas began to shrivel up – as it one day inevitably would? And how, come to think of it, did he ever find time to work, sleep, read the paper, or … go to church?

Two years after his first visit to Vancouver, Johnny returned with a couple of Filipino-American travel companions from Orlando and Fort Lauderdale. After meeting them on Denman Street for coffee, I took the trio for a walk around nearby Stanley Park. When I told Johnny's friends about the Lees Trail cruising ground, the older one pricked up his ears. For the rest of his first trip to Vancouver, he would spend most of his time exploring the trail's nooks and crannies, finding nothing else in the city to interest him. Johnny had to tear him away from the shrubs to get him to join us for a weekend trip to Long Beach on Vancouver Island. In hindsight, we should have left him in Lees Trail.

The night before our departure, I broke my collarbone in a bicycle accident. Still woozy on painkillers, I decided that sticking to the Long Beach plan was a better idea than staying at home and moping. Cancelling would have been a big disappointment to Johnny, who had booked a cottage on the beach over the Internet and was looking forward to the trip. But once the four of us were crammed with our belongings into a rented suv, and Johnny and I were suddenly the captive audience of two chatterbox queens from Florida, I knew I'd made a mistake. From the Horseshoe Bay ferry terminal until our arrival in Tofino, Johnny's friends never shut up. I needed something stronger than Tylenol to dull the pain.

Long Beach, on Vancouver Island's west coast, is the main attraction of Pacific Rim National Park. A rich evergreen forest of huge, old-growth conifers where bald eagles circle the treetops a few dozen feet above one's head, the park is bordered on the ocean by a crescent-shaped shoreline of smooth white sand that stretches for miles. Because of its remote location – it takes nearly seven hours to get there from Vancouver – Long Beach is rarely crowded with tourists and has thus retained much of its natural beauty and rugged, unmolested biodiversity. I couldn't wait to see the reaction of my Filipino-American companions the moment they saw it for the first time.

Johnny and I, standing on the sundeck of our rented cottage, watched his two friends sprint to the beach. Gradually they slowed their pace and stopped about ten metres from the shoreline. Standing in the middle of a picture postcard view of one of Canada's most spectacular natural settings, the Florida twosome threw up their hands … in despair.

"What is *this?*" one of them wailed in the distance.

"Where are the *men?*" cried the other, a gust of wind carrying his lament through a thicket of Douglas firs.

"You said you were bringing us to a *beach!*"

I couldn't help thinking of a famous scene from a Bugs Bunny cartoon in which Daffy Duck jumps out of Bugs' rabbit hole and begins running through a sand dune toward a distant shoreline. Wearing a full-body swim-suit and carrying all the ingredients for a day at the beach, he tears off at breakneck speed in search of the water – only to slow down, deflated and defeated, as he gradually realizes that he hasn't landed on a beach at all but is stuck in the middle of a desert. Here in front of us, the two Florida bar queens were suffering similar disillusionment – despite, unlike Daffy, having actually arrived at a beach.

Weighed down by their gold trinkets and Tommy Hilfiger sweaters, reeking of Calvin Klein's "Obsession" and gazing through jade-tinted Armani sunglasses, these two ghetto clones wanted something they couldn't possibly find at Long Beach. They wanted a "scene," with white boy college jocks and gym studs galore. They wanted ice cream vendors, hot dog stands, Señor Frog's, Planet Hollywood, and gay bars lining the shore. Instead what they got was an empty sandbar, a postcard vista, and a handful of surfers in wetsuits out in the water, paying no attention to them. There wasn't a jet ski, a franchise restaurant, or a preening hunk in a Speedo to be found. And that depressed them.

Johnny and I, standing on the cottage balcony, gazed out at these two forlorn figures on the sand and shrugged. It was true that Long Beach was more of a lover's paradise than party central. But Johnny knew this already. He simply hadn't told his friends when he booked the cottage, because, he said, he had wanted to spend a romantic weekend with me.

"So why bring *them* along?" I asked.

"I wanted them to see more of your country, not just the bars and the bathhouses," he sighed. "And I felt guilty leaving them alone in Vancouver."

Guilty, he says. At times like this, I wanted to call up the Vatican and chew someone out for colonizing every corner of the planet.

Johnny's friends wanted to leave right away. Back at the cottage, there was a lengthy argument in Tagalog as he tried to calm them down. Apparently, they were trying to convince him to forfeit the two nights' rental fee, get back in the van, and return to Vancouver, pronto – despite our having just spent seven hours to reach one of the most beautiful places on earth. And all because they couldn't do the very same things they did every weekend in Florida. Up till now, I had thought that every Asian immigrant retained at least some of his culture in North America. But these two, who had lived in the US for less than a decade, challenged that quaint notion. Whatever part of their South Pacific heritage they may have shared in private was all but invisible here. I found it hard not to regard them as anything but the sum total of the name brands they wore, TV sitcoms they quoted, junk food they ate, and pop hits they listened to. Another market category for a Disney World focus group.

The best compromise Johnny could work out was an agreement to leave at dawn. And so, while Miss Fort Lauderdale stayed in the cottage to watch television, Johnny and I dragged the younger one along to town to pick up some takeaway supper. At the local deli, Miss Orlando couldn't resist cruising the tall, blond youth serving submarine sandwiches. Sliding up to the counter, he purred in his general direction: "Oh please, I want a twelve-inch!"

The young local was in good form. It wasn't every day that a creature like Miss Orlando sashayed through Tofino, and he took full advantage.

"A twelve-inch *what?!*" was his Mae West-like rejoinder.

One night in Chinatown, at the Club 23 on Cordova Street, I was enjoying another of Vancouver's pan-Asian homoscapes: "Red Lantern," a Chinese theme party for the gay Asian community and friends. "Red Lantern" offered Vancouver's queer, mostly Chinese immigrants a nostalgic taste of the old country – the Asian equivalent of those steak-and-beer barbeques the US Army held overseas. The bar on these nights was typically decked out with red silk banners and rice paper. The sound system played the latest chart toppers from Hong Kong. And cute young Asian waiters in slinky kimonos chatted you up while taking your drink order. On this night I caught a whiff of incense as I parted the red satin curtains at the front door. Within seconds of entering the bar, I felt as though I'd walked into a homoerotic episode of *This is Your Life.*

In one corner, I exchanged greetings with a Singaporean guy I'd met at the Club baths, gone home with, and seen a few more times. Then I spotted a Canadian-born Chinese (CBC) pianist I'd known for years – yes, it was Leonard. We chatted while a member of the recreational hockey team I played on waved hello on his way to the bar. Then I recognized a model from Hong Kong I'd seen naked but couldn't recall exactly where or when … then recalled it. It was that photo spread for *Oriental Guys* magazine. I hadn't slept with him yet, so I made a beeline toward him. Just as I approached, the Chinese-Canadian art dealer I'd been meaning to call up for coffee blocked my path.

While we were chatting, I caught the eye of the Indonesian shoe salesman who had parted his thighs for me at Wreck Beach a few days earlier. He was still very much on my mind – one of the hottest lovers yet – so I was glad when he approached. I introduced him to the art dealer. Then, as the three of us stood there, a Chinese go-go boy hit the stage above us and began gyrating into a shimmery sweat. Hadn't I seen that chest before? Of course I had: I'd nibbled on it one day the previous summer, at Wreck Beach.

"What's so funny?" smiled the shoe salesman.

"Oh, nothing," I blushed.

Only the inevitability with which the past, present, and future of desire can present themselves all at once.

VIII
Diasporama

IN JUNE OF 1997, I FLEW TO WINNIPEG to visit a friend from university days who had moved to Manitoba. Since he and his Mennonite wife were living on the outskirts of the city, I wasn't able to sample Winnipeg's club scene until my last night in town. One of the busier clubs was Gio's, an urban gay disco in the heart of the Great Canadian Prairie. After spending a couple of hours chatting up its regulars, I was about to leave when I caught the eye of a slender Asian boy wearing a white-and-blue striped sweater and snug-fitting white trousers. He asked if I was from Winnipeg. I said no, that I was just visiting.

"You're lying," he said. "You know everyone at this bar."

When I showed him my British Columbia driver's licence, he pronounced it a fake. Peter, whose own ID revealed him to be from Vietnam and a month short of twenty-one, invited me out for a ride with his friend, another Vietnamese guy barely over twenty, who had just picked up a white guy in his mid-forties. With the two Vietnamese leading the way, we headed out to the parking lot and stopped between a pair of new Honda sports cars – one white, the other black.

Peter and his friend began conversing in Vietnamese, then turned to their white dates. "Get in the car," Peter's friend said. "We're going on a race."

My fellow Caucasian laughed in my direction: "Why not? They're the ones who'll get busted."

But the two Asian youths were well acquainted with the streets of Winnipeg. As both cars approached warp speed on an inner city highway, there wasn't a traffic cop to be found.

"Where are all the police?" I asked, a little nervous.

"Where do you think, silly?" laughed Peter. "They're all at Tim Horton's."

Then he turned up the volume on the stereo: the Eagles' "Hotel California." A few years from this moment, at a whiskey bar in rural Thailand, I would be asked to sing this song as the only white person in attendance. I would then think of Peter because, as the world's most overplayed guitar riff plodded toward the opening verse and Don Henley's whining lead vocal, he insisted I sing along with it. And I did. I actually sang "On a dark desert highway, cool wind in my hair…" while racing through a Canadian prairie city with a Vietnamese immigrant who, after only two years in this country, was evidently earning more money than me and was already hip to local clichés about lazy police officers and Tim Horton's. Before the night was through, Peter would think nothing of ruining those immaculate white pants of his by sliding on his ass down the muddy banks of a recently flooded Assiniboine River, all in the chivalrous quest to find us a discreet location in which to exchange blowjobs.

About the same time I was tearing through the streets of Winnipeg with a naughty Vietnamese stockbroker, academics had begun to examine the emerging Gay Asian Diaspora – and scenes like my adventure with Peter – as an increasingly common symptom of the global economy. Australia's Dennis Altman, a member of the new generation of gay activists from the sixties, was one of them. A professor of social sciences at La Trobe University, Altman by the mid-1990s had spent a great deal of time flying between international gay and lesbian conferences. During this period, he had begun to notice a pattern in the English language usage of the Far East Asian men he was meeting.

Groups such as Occur in Japan, Ten Per Cent in Hong Kong, Pink Triangle in Malaysia, and the Library Foundation in the Philippines were embracing the notion of a universal "gay," "lesbian," and even "queer" identity in their rhetoric. And they were using these words, or translations of them, in their own countries. This, said Altman, was consistent with a contemporary theory of "master identity": the large-scale construction of lesbian and gay identity as a central social one, a western development that began some time after the end of the 1960s.[1] "Asians who adopt lesbian/gay identities are conscious of and in part moulded by Western examples," wrote Altman. "[In] the development of significant communities of 'Gay Asians' in the Diaspora, a self-conscious Asian gay consciousness has emerged over the past decade in the United States, Canada, Australia and Britain…."[2]

---

1. Dennis Altman, "The Question of Cultural Identity." *Modernity and its Discontents*, edited by S. Hall, D. Held and T. McCrew (London: Polity Press, 1993).

2. Altman, "The New World of 'Gay Asia.'" *Asian and Pacific Inscriptions: Identities, Ethnicities, Nationalities,* edited by Suvendrini Perera (Victoria, Australia: Meridian, 1995).

A year later, Altman had a name for this phenomenon: Global Queering. Like it or not, he argued, the overwhelming influence of the United States as a global economic, political, and cultural superpower – including the influence of its civil rights movement and other forces for social change – had reached all corners of the planet with significant or visible queer populations. "There is a clear connection between the expansion of consumer society and the growth of overt lesbian/gay worlds," Altman wrote. "The expansion of the free market has also opened up possibilities for a rapid spread of the idea that (homo)sexuality is the basis for a social, political and commercial identity."[3]

Consequently, as "Global Queering" found its way into the Gay Asian Diaspora, more Asian guys seemed to be dating white guys. These relationships, noted Altman, were complicated by two contradictory trends in the gay Asian consciousness: on one hand, the gay Asian male's need to assert his universal gay identity – which highlighted his similarity with westerners – and on the other his proud embrace of a newly-asserted "Asian-ness" – which could potentially undermine his "assumed solidarity" with gay white men. The tension between these two opposing motivations was something I encountered with almost every East Asian immigrant I met in the West. This wasn't a tension I found especially troublesome. In fact, I rather enjoyed it.

In the spring of 1992, I decided to drop everything I was doing and live in England for a few months. I had never been to the old country, the birthplace of my grandfather, and was eager to see London for the first time. After arriving in England and spending a few weeks house-sitting for a cousin in Cambridge, I returned to the city and stayed with friends in North London. For six months I lived out of a suitcase in Chalk Farm, Islington, Highgate, Hackney, and East Finchley. When I wasn't lounging in Hampstead Heath, scribbling notes in Camden Town, or job-hunting in Oxford Street, I managed to get a few articles published. But money was tight, and I never earned enough to afford my own apartment. This made dating rather difficult.

One night, as I was waiting for the tube at Earl's Court station, a tiny

3. *Ibid.*

Asian boy smiled as he walked past me on the platform. He was barely five feet tall and had the cherubic face of a pre-teen. But something about the twinkle in his eye suggested an older person. And the black clothes and expensive jewelry he wore – along with the scent of cologne – gave the distinct impression of an evening spent nightclubbing. When the train arrived, he turned around and winked as he entered the car. Following him in, I took the seat facing him and leaned forward to ask his name; he bounded from his seat to join me. His name was Thai Van Tran. He was twenty, from Vietnam. He had come to England as a boat person with his mother. I told him my name. Then he took my hand in his much smaller ones.

"If you would like to see me some time," he said, "here's my phone number."

The next day I took the tube to Hammersmith, where Thai lived alone in a tiny studio flat. His lodgings were simple: a bed, a dressing table, and a wall divider made of rice paper and balsam wood. The place was brightly decorated with the colours of Vietnam: jade stones, red and gold silk kimonos, rice paper wall hangings, and black and gold masks. But the décor was oddly offset by the accoutrements of Rome: crucifixes, votive candles, and miniature portraits of Jesus and the Virgin Mary. Thai was a devout Roman Catholic – a true believer in the colonial faith, like so many *Viet Kieu*, or diasporic Vietnamese, I'd met. Later – after we had lathered each other up in the shared bathroom down the hall, returned to his room, and had sex under candlelight – I asked him how he reconciled his queerness with the dogma of a homophobic Church. "My faith and my gay life are two separate parts of me," he said, without irony. At first, such earnestness baffled me: I couldn't understand how Thai could pull off such a contradiction without feeling like a hypocrite. But perhaps I had less reason for faith, having spent the 1960s and '70s in relative contentment growing up in a middle-class North American suburb. Thai's childhood, by contrast, had been a living hell.

He was born in Bien Hoa, on the outskirts of Saigon, in December 1971. Bien Hoa was a major US air force base and chemical weapons depot during the war. In the late 1960s, American pilots – in an attempt to weed out the Viet Cong from their jungle hideouts – sprayed the city's surrounding area with 7,500 gallons of Agent Orange, a chemical defoliant contaminated with TCDD, the most dangerous form of dioxin (a fact that convinced me, though I could never prove it, that this was one reason for Thai's diminutive stature). When Thai was three, his father was killed during one of the last battles before the fall of Saigon. In 1980, when he was eight, his stepfather was killed during hostilities with Cambodia. Then, shortly after midnight on May 8, 1981, Thai and his mother boarded a small fishing vessel with sixty other people and fled Vietnam in the middle of a hurricane. The boat nearly capsized.

Drifting in the South China Sea for two weeks, they were finally intercepted by a Norwegian cargo vessel bound for Japan. Thai and his mum spent the next two years in a forested compound near Kyoto before being offered a transfer to the United States or Great Britain. Since Thai's sister had already been admitted to Britain, the choice was obvious. When I bumped into him at Earl's Court, Thai had been living in England for nine years. Ever since his arrival, he had made it his mission to do good for others – his way of thanking his adoptive country for the gift of new life. Thai's volunteer commitments included the Red Cross (which would eventually put him on its payroll), work with the disabled and the homeless, and drag performances for AIDS charities. A lover of pageantry, he felt equally at home in his role as an altar boy for Easter mass in London as sitting on the lap of Boy George at the "Europride" gay festival in Amsterdam.

Later, after I'd left England, the Catholic archbishop of London would invite Thai on a special visit to the Vatican, where the diminutive Vietnamese refugee would share a brief private audience with Pope John Paul II. In a photo taken at that meeting, His Holiness appears to be examining the red AIDS ribbon on Thai's lapel. I would take perverse delight in juxtaposing this image with one of a semi-clad Thai, posing as cover boy for a sexy Asian guys calendar. This kind of paradox appealed to my subversive sense of irony. What made less sense to me was Thai's enthusiasm for *Miss Saigon*. The musical's *Madama Butterfly*-inspired storyline – not to mention its superficial treatment of the war in Vietnam – was so crassly Orientalist that I couldn't fathom how a Vietnamese boat person, of all people, could embrace it. Thai had attended several performances of *Miss Saigon*, been invited backstage to meet the cast, and even performed in drag as its lead character.

In North America, East Asian immigrants held protests in every city where *Miss Saigon* was staged; there was even a politically correct bedtime story lampooning it. (In Kirby Hsu's "The Fairy Tale of Ms. Saigon," the love triangle is between an American soldier and two Vietnamese men. In the final scene, soldier boy Chris shoots himself when Kim – "Ms. Saigon" – rejects his love and runs off with Trung, who has dumped Chris for beating him all the time.) Thai didn't share my objections to *Miss Saigon*. As a refugee, he thought the quest for freedom was the musical's most important message. Racism was a non-issue, he said, because discrimination is a fact of life for *all* immigrants. A little name-calling now and then wasn't going to sour him on Great Britain, which had delivered him from a grim existence back in Vietnam.

After spending some time with Thai, I could see that the joy he derived from his gay life and the humanitarian causes he supported was consistent with his faith. In the time we spent together, he made London feel like a small town. He seemed to know everyone, and it wasn't unusual to bump into him anywhere in the city north of the Thames. One Saturday afternoon, we met by accident in a crowded Oxford Street. Thai, after running up to embrace me, invited me to a nearby pub where he ordered hot tea for himself and a beer for me. Then he sat on my lap, drawing cold stares from the mostly non-gay clientele. Thai also introduced me to a peculiar social circle which, I soon discovered, exists in most urban centres with large populations of Far East Asians: the Long Yang Club, an association that promotes fellowship among, and organizes leisure activities for, gay Asian men "and their friends."

Cynical observers dismiss LYC as a thinly veiled dating service for Potato Queens and the Rice Queens who love them. But its activities include fundraising for various causes and – true to the spirit of multiculturalism – the Club is very welcoming of white men … particularly thin, reasonably attractive white men under the age of thirty. One night, Thai brought me to a restaurant and introduced me to Sonny, the club's twenty-four-year-old Singaporean president. Thai had to work the next morning, he said, so he couldn't stay long at the bar next door where an LYC social was being held. But if I hung around with Sonny, he added with a wink, I'd have a place to spend the night. Sonny confirmed this with a nod and a smile.

When we arrived at the club, the only other customers were half a dozen gray-haired white men sitting at the bar. But gradually the place filled up, and soon there were about fifteen Asians for every white man. When a beefy, Caucasian exotic dancer took to the stage and began stripping, the place went nuts. The Asian majority whooped and hollered at the white, muscle-bound studboy; I joined my fellow Caucasians on the periphery, staring into our drinks. Later, with Thai gone home and the crowd getting drunk, Sonny took me back to his Canary Wharf condo. After sniffing some poppers, he straddled me naked as I lay on my back in his bed.

On another night at Sonny's condo, the LYC threw a party. Being one of the few white men in attendance meant accepting the fact that (a) long stretches of conversation would occur in languages other than English (some of them, no doubt, focusing on the few white men in attendance), and (b) the feeling I'd have of being regarded as a juicy piece of prime rib was not unlike that experienced by many an Asian man caught in the crosshairs of Rice Queen lust. Toward the end of the party, I was sitting alone on the living room floor, staring out at Canary Wharf, when a young Chinese queen fluttered into the room. After popping a tape into the VCR he turned off the lights, sat down beside me, and put his hand on my thigh as the porn video began. It turned out he was trying to win a bet with friends, who were watching from the doorway, that he could seduce me in a few minutes (Rice Queens never turn down sex with an Asian, right?). It didn't work. But at least now I knew what some Asian guys must have felt like whenever I came on like gangbusters. Turnabout is fair play.

As much as I appreciated Thai's generosity in "sharing" me with his LYC friends, he was the only club member I was interested in dating who was still single. But several factors prevented this from happening. Apart from Thai's being too busy with charity commitments – I took to calling him The Little Ambassador at one point – I was in no position to commit to another person, much less another country. I adored Thai Van Tran, but I was plagued by self-doubt: afraid of the age difference between us, afraid of not measuring up to Thai's goodness, and afraid that my marginal existence as a freelance writer would be no match for any of his potential suitors down the road. After six months in England, I was on a plane back to Vancouver. For years I would second guess the decision, wondering what might have happened had I taken that leap of faith – had I stuck it out in London, scraped my way into a career, and embraced a twenty-year-old, devout Catholic *Viet Kieu* as my boyfriend. At least I kept one promise I made to Thai Van Tran before leaving England: we would meet again one day – but in his native country.

Late one night in the summer of 1999, I was cruising the aisles of the twenty-four-hour Supervalu on Davie Street when I spotted him in the dairy section: an Asian grunge boy, about twenty-two, with long unbrushed hair and a green army jacket, carrying a backpack. His big brown eyes seemed to gaze into my soul when his cart brushed mine.

"Excuse me," he said, "can you tell me where to find the two percent?"

"It's over there," I said, pointing the way.

Later, spotting him at the checkout counter, I joined him in the queue. He paid for his groceries, then waited by the exit while I paid for mine. Watching me, he pulled out a card from his breast pocket. *Ah yes, here it comes,* I thought. *First he'll give me his number. Then he'll offer to take me home. Within ten minutes we'll be back in his high-rise apartment, lying naked on his couch. Gee, it's great being white.*

Quickly grabbing my bags, I tried to conceal my excitement as I approached him at the doorway. Then he handed me the card. There was no name or phone number on it – just a colourful design featuring a heart-shaped ring of beads, a setting sun, and a lotus flower. *Huh?*

I turned the card over to find a Buddha image, the mantra *Om Ma Ni Pad Me Hum* ("Hail the Jewel and the Lotus Flower"), and an earnest instruction to repeat this phrase "100 Million Time" (sic).

"Do you pray?" the young man asked.

"Yeah," I sighed, "all the time."

I thanked him for the card and moved on. I knew that *Om Ma Ni Pad Me Hum* was Tibetan. But that was not the country that came to mind when I gazed at the lotus flower image. For what would not be the last time, my thoughts turned to Thailand.

I, Sex Tourist

Then it seemed to me that in these countries in the East the most impressive, the most awe-inspiring monument of all antiquity is neither temple, nor citadel, nor great wall, but man.

– W. Somerset Maugham, *The Gentleman in the Parlour*

To the appeal that an attractive person might possess in our own country is added, in an exotic land, an attraction deriving from their location.

– Alain de Botton, "On the Exotic," *The Art of Travel*

IX
City of Angels

Bangkok
February 3, 2000

IT WAS JUST AFTER MIDNIGHT, AN HOUR after I arrived in the Far East, when my taxi pulled up to the Malaysia Hotel on *soi*[1] Ngnam Duphli and I was greeted by three middle-aged Thai bellhops wearing red jackets and blue polyester slacks. As I entered the hotel doorway, I recognized a western man in his early forties who was on his way out. I didn't know him by name, but the last time I'd seen this man, the previous summer at Wreck Beach, he and I had formed the Caucasian half of an *al fresco* foursome.

"You're going to love it here," he smiled, before taking my taxi.

Inside the hotel, the lobby and coffee bar were filled with interracial, intergenerational male couples. The Thais were all in their late teens or early twenties, their neatly cropped hair all spiked with gel, their tight-fitting nightclub pants and tank tops showing off their firm little buns and flat stomachs. Their white companions, all gray-haired and over the age of fifty, wore loose-fitting, floral cotton shirts that concealed their flab. The Thais chattered away on their cell phones while their sugar daddies ordered food or stepped away to check their e-mail on computer terminals in the lobby. The last time I'd seen a human assortment like this was in a West Hollywood cocktail lounge: there, fresh young men from the Midwest wearing varsity jock attire pretended to be budding actors; their older companions wearing Armani suits pretended to be studio bosses. Here at the Malaysia Hotel, there was an air of civility and respect for the illusion. The staff carried out their duties with quiet professionalism, insisting only that Thai visitors leave their ID cards at the front desk before going upstairs to entertain hotel guests.

The hotel was located in a tiny pocket of the gay tourist ghetto that blended into a local Thai neighbourhood known as Sathorn. Apart from the Just One garden bistro on the corner that connected Ngnam Duphli with Sathorn *soi* 1, and the Babylon sauna another minute's walk away, there wasn't much to it. And yet the Malaysia-to-Babylon axis was the centre of Thailand

1. The Thai word for "street."

for countless foreign gay tourists who passed through Bangkok. For a small number of them, it *was* Thailand; for me, it was base camp.

∞

The path I was about to embark on was very well trod. Westerners had been setting foot in the country formerly known as Siam since 1537, when the German traveller Mandeslohe visited Ayutthaya, the former capital, and pronounced it "The Venice of the East" – a title later conferred on Bangkok until the city's *khlongs*, or canals, were gradually replaced by superhighways, concrete, and office towers. In the five centuries since, an endless procession of western explorers, traders, diplomats, charlatans, and sex tourists had arrived in the Kingdom to stake some claim, or define it, for themselves.

In 1858, the French Protestant adventurer Henri Mouhot, acting under the auspices of the Geographical and Zoological Societies of London, began a journey through the Kingdom "in the cause of science." Mouhot spent most of the last four years of his life exploring the interior of Siam, Cambodia, and Laos. Motivated mainly by an interest in ornithology, entomology, and other areas of natural history, he felt more at home in the Thai countryside than in the capital. "At Bangkok, I felt stifled and oppressed. That town does not awaken my sympathies," he wrote in his journal. "The sight of so great a number of human beings annoys me." The Siamese people, he concluded, were "an indolent race" whose entire society was in "a state of prostration." A nation of slaves.

And yet, paradoxically, he also believed that Siam lived up to its name, which meant "kingdom of the free." After witnessing a royal barge procession on the Chao Phraya river, Mouhot was impressed by the sense of civic pride among the Bangkok multitudes that day:

> I was surprised to see the gaiety and light-heartedness
> of the people, in spite of the yoke which weighs on
> them and the exorbitant taxes they have to pay; but the
> softness of the climate, the native gentleness of the race,
> and the long duration of their servitude from generation
> to generation, have made them oblivious of the bitterness
> and hardships inseparable from despotism.[2]

2. Henri Mouhot, *Travels in Siam, Cambodia, Laos and Annam* (Bangkok: White Lotus Press, 2000)

That was Bangkok in 1858. Some would say the description applies today – although the source of "despotism" has shifted from the monarchy to the military to the telecom capitalists.

In 1923, another westerner stopped in Bangkok. Accompanied by his long-term partner, Gerald Haxton, and an entourage of servants, William Somerset Maugham passed through the city half way through an ambitious journey from Rangoon to Haiphong he would later immortalize in his travel journal, *The Gentleman in the Parlour*. Like Mouhot, Maugham was not fond of Southeast Asian cities. And like Mouhot, Maugham was an unreconstructed Orientalist who expressed his disdain with a cranky, racist arrogance that wouldn't win him much sympathy today.

It was impossible to think about these cities, wrote Maugham, "without a certain malaise. They are all alike, with their straight streets, their arcades, their tramways, their dust, their blinding sun, their teeming Chinese, their dense traffic, their ceaseless din...." Furthermore:

> They have no history and no traditions. Painters have not painted them. No poets, transfiguring dead bricks and mortar with their divine nostalgia, have given them a tremulous melancholy not their own.... They are hard and glittering and as unreal as a backcloth in a musical comedy. They give you nothing.[3]

On the other hand, Maugham wrote in his next breath – and this seems a rather significant "but":

> When you leave them it is with a feeling that you have missed something and you cannot help thinking that they have some secret that they have kept from you. And though you have been a trifle bored you look back upon them wistfully; you are certain that they have after all something to give you which, had you stayed longer or under other conditions, you would have been capable of receiving.[4]

3. William Somerset Maugham, *The Gentleman in the Parlour* (Bangkok: White Orchid Press, 1995).
4. *Ibid.*

The second part of Maugham's statement appears to discredit the first: cities like Bangkok *were* elusive to the visitor, revealing only what the visitor was ready to have revealed. That final sentence, sixty-seven years after Maugham wrote it, captured the essence of my first visit to Bangkok.

∞

Before getting on the plane in Vancouver, I had relied on the usual sources to prepare for the trip: Internet searches, phrase books, travel guides, and novels about Thailand. But using an online dating service to arrange for local "guides" (thinking I would need such assistance in a foreign land) was a bad idea. Establishing contacts with half a dozen strangers before I left, then setting up meetings with each, removed the element of serendipity I enjoyed most about travel. It also clogged my agenda with the kind of lonely hearts who depend on cyberspace to make friends. By the time I first reached Babylon, I was cursing myself for not having improvised from the start.

Less than forty-eight hours removed from the sub-zero chill of a west coast Canadian winter, I was still adapting to the humidity that had engulfed me the moment I'd stepped through those sliding glass doors at Don Muang airport. After a busy day of *tuk-tuk*[5] rides, markets, and the Grand Palace, I was ready for my first pilgrimage to a place described in travel literature as one of the best – if not the best – gay saunas in the world. So I walked up Sathorn *soi* 1 until I reached a five-storey, postmodern stucco building covered with vines. Babylon was a refuge from the concrete, gridlock, pollution, and high-decibel chaos of Bangkok – an oasis of tropical flora, teakwood steam baths scented with eucalyptus, and gently flowing rock fountains.

Passing through the giant front doors on my first visit, I was assaulted by a blast of air conditioning and a Vivaldi string concerto on the house music system. After paying at the front counter, I passed through a turnstile and continued through the lounge area with its black marble floors and leather furniture. On each landing, a glass door revealed various temptations inside: a workout gym, cruising hallways, a restaurant and bar (where a professional musician played jazz favourites on a baby grand piano), a massage room and, at the top of the stairs, a rooftop garden bar overlooking the lush, tropical

---

5. An open-air, three-wheeled taxi that is popular with tourists but has seen less use in recent years because of its heavy exhaust fumes and deafening motor.

greenery of Sathorn *soi* 1. On the patio, towel-clad couples enjoyed drinks, cigarettes, and casual banter. In the covered section, waiters picked up drink orders at a bar facing the patio. Between the bar and another section of tables, an exit led to another stairwell. Then there was a steam room, dry sauna, open-air shower, and a third stairwell at the opposite end of the patio, beside the barbeque facilities. I spent nearly an hour wandering through this labyrinth.

It was at about nine o'clock, when the ratio of young men in towels had reached about ten Thais for every foreigner, that I passed through the restaurant on my way back upstairs and heard a raspy, baritone voice call out from behind me: "Hello, handsome *farang*!"[6] Turning around to see which foreigner was being addressed, I noticed that the only other two people in the restaurant, both young Thai guys, were seated together. One of them was a plain-looking teenager with long, spiky hair that stood up like porcupine quills. But his friend, who called out a second time ("Come here – sit down with us!"), was something else altogether.

He had the kind of international beauty that's ethnically hard to place – rather like that of the American actress Halle Berry – and native to no people in particular. On this young man of about twenty, it was the sculpted, symmetrical beauty and delicate features of a Buddha, or a princeling: he had a long, narrow face with pencil-thin eyebrows and rose petal lips that seemed carved to perfection. Tall, slim, and dressed in black, he had a blinding smile and long, dark lashes that highlighted his big brown eyes. I had barely been in Bangkok for a day, and already I had found The Most Beautiful Boy in the World.

He said his name was Toy, and that he was from Bangkok, but I didn't get much more information than that. "Tell me everything about *you*," he smiled, taking my hand and stroking it as he gazed into my eyes. Toy asked a lot of questions, but only two – how long I was visiting and what hotel I was staying at – seemed to really interest him. Perhaps because I so rarely came into contact with such young beauties in Vancouver, I was too busy ogling to take note of certain details – the overnight bag he was carrying, the kind of questions he was asking – that would later become such red flags when I was

6. Translates literally as "guava fruit," and is the word Thai people use to identify white western foreigners, not foreigners in general.

chatting up a gorgeous Thai guy. Instead, when Toy asked if he could spend the night with me, my ego inflated to the bursting point.

Outside Babylon, he hailed a taxi with his friend.

"It's only a five-minute walk to the Malaysia," I said. "Why bother?"

"Oh, we're going to DJ Station. Do you want to come dancing?"

Not yet over the jetlag, I begged off. "But you're still going to stay, aren't you?"

"Of course," smiled the Buddha-prince, handing me his overnight bag.

Toy didn't show up until four in the morning. Even then he seemed eager for sex, which excited me out of my slumber enough for me to slather his young body with my tongue before fucking him. Disappointingly, Toy was self-absorbed – concerned mostly with his own pleasure. But this was before I realized that the best "performance" on my part would have been stuffing his underwear with a thousand-baht note the next morning. Instead, I bought him breakfast and took him on a *tuk-tuk* ride to Wat Pho.[7]

The oldest temple in Bangkok, Wat Pho is also one of the Kingdom's most spectacular. Its Reclining Buddha, at forty-six metres long and fifteen metres high, is the largest in Thailand. When Toy and I entered the Great Hall to see it, we joined a procession of Thai locals who were dropping little medallions into bronze pots that formed a continuous column around the giant gleaming Buddha. Murmuring a mantra at each pot before moving on to the next, Toy dropped his own medallions into the pots, contributing to an almost hypnotic, repetitive metallic sound that echoed through the Great Hall.

Later, we took a stroll through the fresh market and had lunch in a noodle shop on the banks of the Chao Phraya. Then we returned to the Malaysia Hotel. That morning, I'd explained to Toy that I had booked an afternoon meeting with Tau, one of my e-mail contacts. Toy, taken aback that I was seeing someone else, assumed that sex would be involved. "It's not like that," I said, embarrassed by the insinuation, but also aware that my explanation probably wasn't very convincing: "I arranged for him to be a guide before I even met you." When we got back to the hotel in the

---

7. *A wat*, Somerset Maugham noted in *The Gentleman in the Parlour*, "is a collection of buildings used as a Buddhist monastery" that is "surrounded by a wall, often crenellated so as to make a charming pattern, like the walled enclosure of a city."

afternoon, there was an awkward scene in the pool area where I wasn't able to avoid introducing Toy to Tau, who was waiting when we arrived. Tau didn't know what to make of Toy and seemed confused by his presence. Toy, still assuming I was dumping him for another sex partner, suggested we all go to Babylon together. Gently, I told Toy that I'd call him the next day. When I did, I got no answer. A month later, when I was back in town after a trip to the South, he would finally reply to an e-mail I'd sent weeks earlier, then fail to show up for our arranged meeting.

If you chose two people at random from a crowd of Thais, they couldn't have been more opposite than Toy and Tau. Toy was working-class and worldly-wise. He had parlayed his good looks, charm, style, and language skills into a constantly filled dance card. By contrast, twenty-seven-year-old Tau was a bespectacled, middle-class academic with plain features, a science geek wardrobe, and almost no English. As I stood between them in the Malaysia Hotel pool area, I felt mildly irritated by the social mess I'd created. I wished I hadn't bothered keeping the appointment with Tau, an e-mail contact I'd never met. But it was too late to back out, and so, tearing myself away from the ravishing Toy, I went out for dinner with Tau.

Of all the men I met on that first visit to Bangkok, Tau was the only one who had nothing to do with the tourist economy. Unlike Toy, he had never been to the Malaysia Hotel, Babylon, or any bar popular with foreigners. He had only posted a personal ad on a gay website because he wanted to improve his language skills ("My English is *pool*," he had written) while carefully cultivating a friendship with a *farang*. The latter required a long period of time before the subject of sex could be broached – and then only in the context of monogamy and commitment. Tau lacked the spontaneous will toward excitement that ruled the younger Toy. Rather than going dancing or drinking, he was happy to take a dinner cruise on the Chao Phraya, a stroll through Chattuchak weekend market, or a quick visit to MBK, one of Bangkok's giant shopping malls. Before I left the city Tau lent me his camera, developed a roll of film, and paid for the prints, and then, on the day of my departure, showed up at the train station to hand me a loaf of bread for the journey. Later, on my final return to Bangkok, he would take me to a royal mansion and a Thai boxing exhibition.

Tau provided my earliest clue that not all Thai guys were money boys or regarded foreigners as walking ATMs. He enjoyed the challenge of conversing in English, and made no demands of me beyond what I was prepared to give. I wouldn't have minded seeing more of him, but he was difficult to reach by phone and preferred limiting our meetings to short visits. Despite his many acts of kindness, at no point was I invited to see him in his own environment. Partly due to closetry, and partly to a middle-class cultural stigma that precludes involvement with westerners, he shyly deflected my requests to visit him on campus or at home. When we lost contact after my return as a resident, I would wonder what he could possibly have gained from our brief acquaintance.

By Day Five, I was spending too much money. It was time to downgrade hotels. The obvious choice for new digs was Khao San Road, the famous backpacker strip in Banglamphu that had recently been the subject of a withering critique in *The New Yorker*. The august weekly had reduced Bangkok's low-end tourist ghetto to a sad-sack holding pen for the West's forgotten human roadkill. Apart from holidaying students who used it as stopover during their whirlwind tours of Southeast Asia, Khao San had an overabundance of hucksters trading in fake jewelry, overpriced watches, and bogus passports or journalist ID cards. And too many burnt-out hippies seemed to have landed here decades earlier but lost their way home and, well, blended into the scenery.

I could appreciate the *New Yorker* writer's wide-eyed amazement at Khao San's postmodern jungle mix of contradictions. On one hand, the street life was a throwback to Haight-Ashbury. Rastafarian vegan children of mixed parentage sat for their henna tattoos or dreadlock hair-braiding; sixties music blared from guesthouse restaurants and bootleg CDs sold by the truckload; dope dealers plied their trade in coffee bars; clothing boutiques were filled with tie-dye or ethnic hilltribe peasant clothing; and bearded young men wandered earnestly about in their Che Guevera T-shirts. On the other hand, the hippie-dippie vibe was diluted by a manic devotion to commerce. Streetside vendors competed with 7-Eleven stores for business. And the guesthouses created a 24/7 cacophony of media noise, constantly outblasting each other with music videos, premiership football matches or B-grade Hollywood action movies.

All the same, Khao San had its charms. There were a couple of fine second-hand bookstores, some half-decent Indian restaurants, and plenty of cheap but quality clothing stalls. It was possible to get a good package deal to Cambodia or Laos. And a few guesthouses, while hardly three-star fare, offered clean rooms and friendly service for less than 500 baht a night. For my last two nights in the city, I checked into the Siam Oriental.

The night before switching hotels, I thought I should spend at least a few hours in the gay bars of Silom and Patpong, the world-famous Disneyland of sex tourism. At this early stage of first exposure to Bangkok, fascination ruled my every move. Thailand's capital was oozing with sensuality from every pore – from the garbage-cluttered, neon-lit *sois* to the glitzy skytrain ads promoting heartthrob singers. Like many a white western male getting his first taste of the city, my daily decisions in that first week were determined as much by a burning desire and sense of bedazzlement as any enlightened interest in discovering a foreign culture at its source. There was a freshness to the Thai come-on, an irresistible charm in the local male's eagerness to please, that was exhilarating to a newly arrived *farang* with a predilection for Asian men.

The fact that I was hardly lacking for amorous attention back home didn't matter in the least. In Bangkok, the constant fussing by so many beautiful young men was hard to resist – even when motivated by the expectation of cash. At this stage, the discovery of entire neighbourhoods organized around the sex trade was too exciting in its novelty, too alluring in its promise, and too interesting as cultural anthropology to allow for much teeth-gnashing about the politics of economy. That would come later, as boredom, guilt, and saturation set in. Of course, I was already aware of a stance that condemned sexual activity of any kind by Westerners vacationing in Thailand. But if I were to arrive at my own conclusions, I thought, I would have to get a first-hand look at what all the fuss was about.

Just after five o'clock in the afternoon, well before the action usually begins, I was passing through *soi* Thantawan when I was startled by a collective shriek. A quartet of young Thai waiters, all dressed in low-cut shorts and tank tops, were standing on a verandah beneath a sign that read "Tomahawk" – complete with phallic cruise missile logo. They were surrounding the bar's only customer, a middle-aged European who was quietly drinking his beer. The foursome shrieked again as I approached, instantly abandoning the European and transferring their affections onto me. All four were under twenty, skinny, and pretty, and each took turns sitting on my lap. After my third beer, when I went to the toilet, nineteen-year-old "Film" escorted me to the urinal, held my cock as I did my business, and wiped it dry with a tissue.

When I returned to my table and breathed in the warm, sweet scent of "Film" and his three friends, I briefly considered a late afternoon orgy with these four heat-seeking Tomahawks. However, having decided to downgrade hotels because of my budget, I opted instead for a quiet beer at the Balcony pub in Silom *soi* 4. Balcony is the Thai male version of the American Hooters franchise: rather than big-breasted young waitresses, Balcony features smooth young Thai guys in Hawaiian T-shirts and snug-fitting shorts that show off their asses and crotches. ("Baskets," come to think of it, would be an appropriate name for the place.) But unlike Hooters' buxom servers, Balcony waiters were more than just friendly: after their shift – or, for a 200 baht "off" fee to the bar during it – you could whisk them away for the night and pay the going rate for their company.

By ten o'clock, it was time to go to Screwboy, a famous go-go bar in the middle of the Patpong night market. I had to stop at this bar: its acrobatic fuck shows were legendary. A friend back home recalled one night at Screwboy when a pair of naked young Thai guys had taken their act into the audience, the masculine "top" carrying his stereotypically feminine "bottom" – still planted on his member – to my friend's table. With one hand clutching his partner's ass cheek, the boy being fucked leaned over backward until he made upside down eye contact with my friend. Then he threw out his other hand, palm upward, and winked: "Tip?" He got one.

But I never did get to see the show. Within moments of taking a seat in front of the stage, I was hit on by a beefy, twenty-year-old farm boy from the North. Sliding in beside me and squeezing my thigh and arm, he offered to take me upstairs. He was wearing nothing but white thong underwear with a red plastic heart pin bearing his number "10." He was very butch, with long thick hair, creamy smooth skin, hard muscles, and a pleasant scent. Suddenly the bar manager appeared out of nowhere and whispered in my ear, "This boy is the very best – he will do *everything* for you. Only 300 baht." *Three hundred baht?* That was less than ten bucks US. It seemed both an insult to the boy and a very, very unlikely fee for the privilege. Smelling a scam, I paid for my drink and bolted, leaving Screwboy without seeing the fuck show. As I left the club, I turned around to steal another glance at the stage. A dozen smooth young Thai guys were shuffling about in their bare feet, wearing nothing but their smiles and their white thong underwear.

To get out of the *soi*, I had to run the gamut of Patpong's sidewalk stalls and neon-lit girlie bars, past all the touts (hard-sell promoters) who'd walk up and ask, "Mister, you want sexy girl show?" (or, in my favourite display of staccato ESL patois, "Sexy-boy-fuck-show-big-stiff-cock-shooting-cum-this-way-please-sir"). Then it was on to my last stop of the evening, DJ Station disco, where I hoped to find Toy. DJ Station, in Silom *soi 2*, was Bangkok's most popular gay nightclub. When I got there, the dance floor was packed. But being a white man under forty and new to the city had its advantages: as soon as I walked in, the crowd parted and a receiving line of cuties turned to look. A forest of soft Thai hands reached out, a few grabbing my ass. Toy's were not among them.

When I reached the top of the stairs, I made eye contact with a shy little fellow dressed in black. Standing alone, he was about a foot shorter than me and had a tiny, retroussé nose, a bashful grin, and neatly cropped, gelled black hair that was upturned in the front, giving him an impish cowlick. His name was Wit, and he was from the Northeast. When I asked what he did for a living, he said he didn't have a job – which meant he was "freelancing." No matter: I was so smitten by the soft, dulcet tone of his voice that I told him where I was staying.

Like Toy, Wit had probably been to the Malaysia with dozens of western men before me. But back at the hotel, that was the last thing on my mind as we began stripping off each other's clothes. After losing Toy, getting the arm's-length treatment from Tau, and spending four days in a strange place on my own, a full evening in Silom-Patpong had turned my brain into mush. There was simply too much stimulus; I had to have release. What I couldn't have anticipated, when Wit and I woke up the next morning and fucked again, was that a simple exchange of e-mail addresses would lead to a long, awkward romance that would ultimately take its toll on my wallet and psyche. But that was still many weeks, many more kilometres, and far too many boys into the future. For now, Wit and I said our goodbyes and *choc dee*: "good luck."

∞

My first stop in Bangkok had lasted nearly a week. Like Somerset Maugham, I felt I had only scratched the surface when I left; that whatever the city had to reveal was lying dormant, waiting for my return. The days had been marked by a constant tension between a thirst for knowledge and a hunger of the body. And all too often, the body won out. Apart from the ravishing Toy and persuasive Wit, there had also been Jack, a young businessman I'd met on a second visit to Babylon, and Beer, a student I'd picked up at a bus stop on my last day in town and brought back to my Khao San bed.

The friendliness of the Thais and the imperatives of the tourist economy are a potent mixture when sexual attraction rears its head. For a western traveller unaccustomed to such lack of inhibition toward bodily pleasures, the possibility of meeting someone new every day becomes an endless source of temptation that is hard to resist. In the real world, there's no such thing as "heaven." But on this trip, one angel after another kept fluttering his wings in my direction. These glittery illusions, which began with Toy, would turn out to be the spark that transformed a three-month journey into something more significant.

X
On the Beach

"Did you know anyone there?"

It's late December 2004. I'm sitting in front of a TV set with a friend, witnessing the aftermath of the Boxing Day tsunami that wiped out the island of Koh Phi Phi in Southern Thailand. Yes, I tell him, I did know someone there. But only for a heartbeat: my one visit to the tropical beach paradise in early 2000 hadn't lasted more than twenty-four hours. Five years later, scattered moments from an overnight excursion, and the time I spent on the island with a handsome Thai companion, remain fixed in my mind as I contemplate the giant, rolling waves that have just enveloped it. In a few short minutes, the tsunami has left a mind-boggling trail of death and destruction, obliterating one of the world's most heavenly places. As television coverage reveals the enormity of the disaster – which has engulfed neighbouring Patong Beach in Phuket, where I have also been, resulting in the worst of the carnage in Thailand – it occurs to me that the cataclysm has also finished off every preconceived notion I once had of "paradise": what defines that elusive concept, how to reach for it and, of course, how to behave there once you think you've found it.

Like many urban dwellers of the First World North, I've always been attracted to the notion of the tropical beach holiday. I love spending several days in the sun, sand, and surf – wind-blown and naked, the mind approaching Zen-like bliss. In Thailand, my interest in beaches was greater than usual, thanks to a Hollywood movie filmed on Koh Phi Phi the year before my visit. *The Beach*, starring *Titanic* heartthrob Leonardo DiCaprio, just happened to be opening in the United States the same week I was travelling south to visit some of the beaches where the story took place. The film would open in Thailand a few weeks later.

The Beach was based on a 1996 novel of the same name by British author Alex Garland. Richard, the book's protagonist/narrator, is a young sensation seeker on his first trip to Thailand. A chain-smoking, post-literate video game addict, he sees everything through the prism of television. When the story begins, he's in Khao San Road mulling his options for the next destination. Eager to venture beyond the *Lonely Planet* circuit, he thinks he has struck gold when he finds a map pinned to the door of his guesthouse room – a parting gift, just before his suicide, from the deranged hippie stoner in the next room. The map points the way to a hidden oasis in Ong Thang Marine National Park, in the southern Gulf of Thailand. Together with a young French couple, Richard sets out to find this tropical paradise. The rest of *The Beach* becomes a sort of *Lord of the Flies*-meets-Jonestown/*Apocalypse Now* nightmare in which Richard and his friends find the beach, become part of its cult-like utopian community, and are nearly consumed by the self-destructive narcissism of the enterprise.

Apart from his youth, his chain-smoking, and his video game addiction (or any resemblance to DiCaprio), I wasn't all that different from Richard. I was a white western male on my first visit to Thailand. I was seeking sensation in an exotic locale, and I was prepared to wallow in the physical once I found it. I had no agenda while I was down in the South, really, other than to follow some of Richard's footsteps in *The Beach*. The tourist in me wanted to see whether the places Garland wrote about bore any resemblance to the fiction; the traveller wanted to see if I could find my own version of paradise along the way.

The only person I knew who'd ever been to Koh Samui, Thailand's third largest island, had gone there in 1980. Back then, Samui was a lush, green oasis with not a single luxury hotel or chain restaurant. Fishing was the main industry in an ocean-based economy, the forest was sacred, and everyone smiled at *farang*, who were about as common a sight on the island as a solar eclipse. At least, that's how it seemed in the grainy slide photos my friend Harry presented one night over dinner, just before I got on the plane to Thailand. But the place I found after getting off the ferry at Nathon pier, the morning after leaving Bangkok on the overnight train, bore no resemblance to Harry's Samui.

Nearly every beachfront had been developed; the local economy was dominated by tourism. Samui had become another Puerto Vallarta, with Chaweng, its main beach, just another bar strip cluttered with McDonald's, 7-Eleven, and Starbucks outlets, overflowing dumpsters, and piss-stained sidewalks. I absorbed all this while choking on exhaust fumes from the back of a taxi pickup truck that took me along the main road that snakes around the Samui perimeter. I couldn't believe it. The island was forty-eight square kilometres large. Wasn't there more to its coastline than this? Sure enough, there was. After renting a motorbike, I finally found my piece of Shangri-la on a hidden stretch of road that ran through Bangruk, one of the least developed beaches on the island's northern coast.

The Como resort had seaside bungalows facing Big Buddha Bay, just west of the ferry to Koh Pha-Ngnan. My shaded hut was the last in a row of private, stand-alone A-frames that sat less than ten metres from the shore. From the front door I could see the gleaming, gold statue of Big Buddha in the distance. To the right were several hundred metres of sparse jungle. On the beach itself, there were no vendors, only the occasional sunbather. Early in the morning and again at dusk, a Thai fisherman would slowly wade into the water up to his waist and cast a line from a recycled plastic Javex container. There wasn't a sound but the gentle breeze and soothing hiss of waves lapping the shore. I laughed at my good fortune as I unpacked my bags on the first day. On the bathroom mirror, a faded sticker proclaimed: "Life is a Miracle."

If you're a city person, there's a funny thing about solitary beach holidays. Once you've got everything you want – the scenery, the atmosphere, and a good place to read – it isn't long before you're hankering for that city energy once again. Boredom and loneliness are inevitable, especially if you know there's a happening scene not too far away. After three days of reading and writing, I was eager for some company. So I fired up the motorbike and took off on a narrow, paved road that zigzagged through several kilometres of jungle toward Chaweng. It wouldn't take long for the city complications to arise.

By February 13, I had booked a date for the next night with Nut, a twenty-eight-year-old Thai guy from Pattaya who was running a small beach bar on Chaweng. As much as I liked Nut, the date was not my idea. Nut's *farang* boyfriend from London, thirty-eight-year-old Mark, was on Samui at the same time; I wasn't interested in playing mistress. But Nut insisted on visiting my bungalow and couldn't wait until Mark went home the following week. So there it was: a dirty date on Valentine's Day. When I saw Nut at Christie's pub the night before our scheduled rendezvous, he was just leaving for the Green Mango disco and wanted me to join him there. I begged off, telling him I wanted to stay at Christie's and watch Koh Samui's best drag show. As a result of that decision, I never did hook up with Nut the next night.

A few minutes after he left Christie's, I was sitting at the bar when a glittering troupe of Thai ladyboys, or *kathoeys*,[1] hit the stage. Forming a chorus line of pistol-packing Bond girls, they lip-synched a flawless rendition of "The Man With the Golden Gun." Cubby Broccoli himself would have appreciated their dazzling re-enactment of the opening credits sequence for his 1974 movie, which was filmed in Phang-Nga province long before most of these *kathoeys* were born. The performance was appropriately ironic, given the context of sex tourism that defined nightlife in Chaweng.

The bar captain that night was a twenty-two-year-old northerner named Chai. Dressed all in black, he was five-foot-six, with the broad jawline and high cheekbones typical of his native Chiang Rai. From the moment I saw his face, all thoughts of committing Valentine's Day adultery with Nut vanished. Chai's sparkling beauty, and his upcountry earnestness when we chatted, stood out from the crowd of jaded queens and con artists which – if a brief survey of the beach and main drag that day were any indication – seemed to infest the Chaweng scene. So when I invited him out for a drink at the end of his shift, I was thrilled when he accepted.

After leaving Christie's, we walked down a dusty *soi* off the main street and passed by an outdoor restaurant where a group of ladyboys recognized Chai. They bolted from their chairs, whooping and hollering. Chai smiled: he had brought me here to show off his prize *farang* catch, just as Beer, a young student, had done at a shopping mall on my last day in Bangkok. One *kathoey* ran up with a glass of ginger ale and ice, imploring me to take a sip. I politely obliged. So did Chai. The *kathoey* and her friends all seemed to regard us as a couple, even though I'd only met Chai a few minutes earlier. Sitting behind me on the motorbike as we rode back to the bungalow, Chai wrapped his arms tightly around my chest. "Slow-ly!" he murmured in a thick northern accent, his lips brushing my neck, when my driving made him nervous. Until Wit, I'd never been fucked by someone shorter than me. But after that night's romp with Chai, I wondered why not. The next morning, we rode to a quiet

---

1. Thai transvestites and transsexuals.

beach north of Chaweng for lunch. Then, dropping off Chai at his home, I asked him out for dinner that night. He wasn't working, so he was pleased that I asked – although Valentine's Day was culturally irrelevant to him.

When I arrived to pick him up, I was shocked by the squalor of his apartment. Chai and his friend Pukha had been living there for several months, the place looked as though the last tenants had just moved out and that Chai and Pukha were living among the leftovers. Dust, filth, and piles of abandoned boxes were everywhere. Chai, dapper and handsome in a clean white shirt and pants, was an island of beauty amidst all the trash. I could tell by the way he sat cross-legged on the floor, oblivious to the clutter as he carefully combed his hair, that he probably grew up in Chiang Rai this way. But I put those thoughts aside as I took him and his friends out for supper at the Swordfish, followed by drinks and a Thai cabaret show at the Pink Lady. When the two of us returned alone to the bungalow, I sang in the shower while Chai got ready for bed. But by the time I slipped under the covers with him, something had shifted in the air. When I slid my naked body beside Chai's, he turned away. When I asked what was wrong, he wouldn't speak. What had I done?

"I leave you now," said Chai. "I go home."

"What? You can't go home now, it's two a.m."

It was dark outside. Chaweng was a long ride away, and I was too tired to get back on the motorbike. More to the point, I was disturbed by Chai's sudden mood swing.

"Come on, Chai," I pleaded. "Just go to sleep. I'll take you home in the morning. We'll talk about it then."

But there was no persuading him. He got dressed and walked out the door, heading out on foot down the same unlit country road we'd just taken on the motorbike, all the way back to Chaweng.

It wasn't what I had done that was the problem; it was what I *hadn't* done. Chai worked for minimum wage at Christie's – about us $100 a month. If he wanted to eat well, tips and cash gifts from foreign flings became important. Also, the bar was supposed to receive a 200-baht "off" fee, just like in the city, when I took Chai off his shift (he hadn't really finished work when I snapped him up). I hadn't given him a single baht, either for the bar or himself, in all our time together. He hadn't asked because, I suppose, he thought I knew the drill. But when our second night ended and I still hadn't shelled out, he got fed up and left. Waking up alone late the next morning, I felt depressed.

This was my first confrontation with the rules of the tourist economy, the opening struggle in an internal dialogue about the inequality that separates most Thais from the *farang* who visit their country. The good times I enjoyed with so many gorgeous Thai boys only happened because an entire infrastructure had been created to ensure that they would. Such infrastructures tend to exist in poor countries where there aren't enough better opportunities for young people to get an education or otherwise forge lives and careers within their own communities, independent of foreign currency. But at this stage of my journey, I was living in a bubble of neocolonial narcissism that didn't allow for much analysis. Here's what typically goes on inside such a bubble:

(A) Back home, Travelling White Boy (TWB) doesn't consider himself a "consumer" of sex because he can get it whenever he wants and, therefore, doesn't pay for it (this conveniently ignoring the fact that, back home, his Asian objects of desire are likely his status equals, if not superiors);

(B) Because he sees himself as objectively desirable, TWB assumes there should be no difference in how he cruises, romances, or otherwise ends up having sex with guys in Thailand;

(C) TWB believes that paying for sex in any form amounts to prostitution, a financial exchange that – despite his laudably liberal attitudes toward older friends who indulge – he categorizes in strictly western, Judeo-Christian terms whose assumptions are grounded in moral judgment;

(D) TWB is in deep denial. Because of all of the above, he truly believes that all the hot, young Thai guys he meets are interested in him only because of his wonderful personality, great looks, and stellar performance in bed (rather than, say, the fact that his whiteness, education, and possession of a plane ticket are likely indicators of relative wealth).

The fact that I was unable to connect the dots between "A" and "D" guaranteed that I would make a lot of mistakes with Chai. Instead of recognizing our basic inequality and seeing things from his point of view, I took it personally that Chai had walked out on me. Instead of seeing that my failure to shell out might have seemed insulting to a Thai person in Chai's position, I felt that his departure had cheapened our time together. Instead of seeing his filthy apartment as a clue that I should have been more generous, I assumed that taking him and his friends out for dinner was enough. Reality had fucked with the fantasy, and now I felt sordid. How did I deal with it? By going out and doing something that would ultimately feel even worse: riding the motorbike to Chaweng and showing up at Nut's bar to redeem his earlier offer of a fling.

Mark, Nut's hairdresser boyfriend from London, wasn't at the bar when I arrived and sat down.

"Hey, where you been?" Nut asked, joining me.

He didn't seem offended that I had broken our Valentine's date, so I told him – careful not to reveal precisely which bar boy it was I'd taken home from Christie's, lest I fall afoul of the Samui gossip mill.

Nut shrugged: "I've got a lunch break. Let's go to your bungalow."

Minutes later, we were on the motorbike, driving back to the Como for some afternoon delight. After fucking me mechanically with a sand-speckled condom, Nut asked for some money so he could buy cigarettes. I gave him some, then drove him back to Chaweng. I felt like shit. With Chai nowhere to be found and my encounter with Nut amounting to nothing but a fix for his nicotine addiction, Samui wasn't looking very much like paradise. The next day, I locked up the bungalow and took the ferry to Koh Pha-Ngnan where I rented another motorbike, checked into a bungalow on the northwest coast, and attended the Full Moon Party in Hat Rin. That night I met a group of Thai revellers from Bangkok – one of whom, noticing my boner, led me into the jungle for a closer look. Back on the beach, we exchanged phone numbers (we would reconnect a month later in Bangkok, at a bar called Sperm). The next morning, I felt refreshed enough to return to Samui.

By late afternoon I was sitting at the Sharkfin, scribbling a few notes during happy hour, when I felt a tap on my shoulder. It was Chai. I was stunned to see him. He had the pick of the whole beach that day. If he was really looking for *farang*, why come back to me – the tightwad who'd given him nothing? Offering him a seat, I apologized for my behaviour, handed him a beer, and gave him 400 baht for his troubles. It was mere pennies, of course, but it was all I had for the moment. Chai accepted it, and my apology, with a smile and a *wai*.[2] When I told him I had been stupid and thoughtless,

---

2. A folded-hand greeting Thais use as a gesture of respect.

it seemed to bridge some of the gap between us. Rather than talking about it, Chai was ready to move on.

"So, you make plans? What you do?" he asked.

"Well, I want to visit Ong Thang tomorrow," I said.

"You like me to come?"

"Yes, Chai," I said, taking his hand. "I would like that *very* much."

Apart from craving Chai's company, I was eager for us to part on a happier note. As we were leaving the bar, he asked if he could spend the night at the bungalow so we could head directly for the pier in the morning. This time, Chai kissed me as he fucked me, then slept like a baby in my arms. By noon the next day, we were swimming through coral reef caves and hiking up the towering limestone crags of Ong Thang Marine National Park, where *The Beach* was set. Chai waited halfway up as I climbed one of the 500-metre rocks. Later, in a thicket of trees at its base, monkeys darted about in front of my camera. The next morning, I was off on another bus.

Ten days and about two thousand kilometres later, I would run into Chai on a street in Hua Hin. He was on his way north to visit family and was stopping to see some friends in Prachuap Khiri Khan. Could he join me at my guesthouse? Sorry, I said; I had to meet someone in a few minutes. With a sad look in his eye, he kissed me tenderly on the cheek before turning around and walking away forever. Still spinning from a serial sex marathon that hadn't stopped since Bangkok, I was starting to feel like a US marine who's become desensitized to all the collateral damage in his wake. I couldn't imagine how these young Thai men must have felt, to be constantly swept off their feet by foreigners – only to be discarded like the household trash when it was time for the next destination. Now I actually felt something for Chai, but it was too late to do anything about it: my travel itinerary had pre-empted romance. "Goodbye, stranger," an old song goes, "it's been nice. Hope you find your paradise...."

As with Samui, I only knew one person back home who'd ever been to Phuket. And, like Samui, Phuket had evidently become an over-polluted tourist ghetto since that person was last there. But instead of moving on to Krabi, Koh Lanta, or other points south, when I arrived in Phuket City I decided to tough it out in Patong Beach, a sailing and diving resort heavily promoted in the gay press. Shortly after sunset on my first night in town, I was out for a walk when the shrill din of cicadas began to drown out conversation in the beachside bistros. Passing through a *soi* at the end of a soccer field, I noticed a swank little eatery called Bicycle Bar. Outside the entrance, a group of young male hosts wearing identical navy-blue T-shirts stood posing for passers-by. The bicycle logos on their chests clashed with the establishment's wicker chairs, white linen tablecloths, and garden fountain gnomes.

It had only been a day since my last embrace with Chai, so I wasn't in the mood for the stud-mechanic porn fantasy. I just wanted a drink. But when I entered the patio area, I was immediately swarmed by Bicycle boys – the beefiest of whom, Korn, kept making kissy-face gestures at me. I almost walked out until a tall, skinny waiter with a mild case of acne pushed his way through the crowd. An odd-looking character, with a disproportionately large head, nose, and ears, he had a poise and self-confidence that set him apart from his fellow hosts. Introducing himself as "Soup," he sat me down at a patio table, ordered another waiter to get me a beer, and then joined me at the table.

Sitting next to me, Soup gently brushed his cheek against my ear as he leaned in to look at my guidebook. His skin was smooth, warm, and moist.

"Soup," I said, "really, I'm just here to have a drink. I don't want to – "

"Sssshhhhhh," he said, putting a finger to my lips. "Don't worry – I come to your hotel room after I finish work. I no charge you, because I am gay. Not like the others. They are all straight."

I turned to look at the handsome Korn, who was still doing his kissy-face routine. Then I turned back to Soup, who was stroking my palm.

"Okay," I shrugged. "See you at eleven."

Soup spent the night. He was a good lover, and fun to be with. I wanted to see him again, but he told me he'd be busy running errands for the rest of the week. His mother in Phetchaburi was bankrupt, he explained. He needed to make some more money. "So don't feel bad," he said, "if you see me in boy bar with older guy, okay?"

Patong was pretty much all downhill from there. I only saw Soup once more that week – at Uncle Charlie's Boys cabaret, with a Swiss man in his late fifties. After a brief chat there, I wouldn't see him again until we met in Hua Hin, on my way back to Bangkok. In the meantime, I would suffer a series of misadventures that began to sour me on the whole idea of beach holidays.

First there was Manoon, a twenty-five-year-old hustler who accosted me in the street one afternoon after I'd turned him down on the beach. Despite my several attempts to politely get rid of him, Manoon used humour to sweet-talk his way into a drink and then a taxi ride to my guesthouse. When he followed me in and began, uninvited, to strip off his clothes in my room, I knew the only way to get out of this would be to let him fuck me and then shortchange him. It worked: he left in a huff when I gave him only 250 baht. Then there was Mon, a go-go dancer I picked up at Uncle Charlie's Boys a few minutes after Soup left with the Swiss guy. Mon, twenty, stood out from the others with his pixie-like face and smile. The moment our eyes locked, it was game over.

Mon bounded up to my table, sat on my lap and – wrapping his body around mine – French-kissed me. He poured on the charm, made sweet conversation, and wouldn't take his hands off me until I'd paid his bar captain the 250-baht "off" fee and agreed to pay him 1,000 baht for whatever happened next. No sooner had we left the bar than the fantasy dissolved: Mon turned off the smile, pulled out the cigarette, and behaved like a cold, wet dishrag for the rest of the night – even fucking me with perfunctory strokes that made no secret of his crashing boredom. After taking him to a bank machine to pay him, I sent him on his way and returned to the guesthouse feeling utterly pathetic. Getting ripped off by a sex trade worker is hardly news. What amazed me was how jaded this one had been, putting on a display of consummate acting skill to attract a customer – only to abandon the principle of customer satisfaction the moment he secured the sale. The fact that the song playing during Mon's onstage performance had been that cheesy, sixties lounge hit, "Can't Take My Eyes off of You," only rubbed salt into the wound.

After Mon, I wouldn't visit another bar in Phuket and briefly lost my appetite for sex altogether. Apart from a Thai boxing exhibition followed by a snake charmer, I avoided contact with people and buried myself in books. The second-hand shops in Patong were a literary desert – chock full of Danielle Steeles, John Grishams, and New Age self-help titles. But one boutique had a copy of Jose Saramago's *Blindness*, a bleakly Orwellian novel about human rights, exploitation, and totalitarianism. The story revolves around a city whose residents, one by one, lose their vision. Government authorities then terrorize them with a litany of abuses: quarantine in squalid and cramped conditions, food and sleep deprivation, hoodlum justice, gang rape and summary execution, et cetera. It said something about my state of mind at this point that I preferred the soul-wrenching company of this harrowing novel to any human companionship available in Patong.

∞

Two days before heading back north toward Bangkok, I was walking along the main drag at Patong when I noticed a sandwich board advertisement outside a travel agency: *Overnight Excursions to Koh Phi Phi.* "Go snorkeling, kayaking and cave exploring…. Swim the emerald waters…. Confer with the multicoloured fish…. See the islands where *The Beach* was filmed…." Well, that last bit was an odd marketing ploy: the year before my visit, Koh Phi Phi had been the scene of an international controversy when a group of residents accused Twentieth Century Fox of destroying the local ecosystem to film *The Beach*. The film's star, Leonardo DiCaprio, adopted their cause when it became apparent that soil erosion, tree cutting, and coral reef destruction were garnering the film a lot of bad press back home. The studio ended up replanting some trees and paying for cosmetic improvements. But the activists launched several lawsuits anyway and boycotted the film's release in Thailand.

The controversy was enough in itself to pique my curiosity about Koh Phi Phi. I wanted to know what was so great about this island; why it had been chosen to represent Garland's *The Beach*. But whom could I take on such a trip? Soup was nowhere to be found – probably on his way to Hua Hin already. Returning to the guesthouse a few minutes later, I was passing by an ATM when I spotted a young Thai athlete I'd met during a rainstorm a few days earlier. He and a friend had been caught in the downpour, like me, when we passed each other going opposite ways. He'd been wearing a skimpy tank top that clung to his muscular chest, highlighting his nipples and the curves of his torso. He'd said his name was Ut and that he worked at a clothing store. But he had an appointment, so he had to run.

Only after he'd gone had I realized that Ut may have wanted my room number but was too shy to ask for it in front of his friend. I hadn't seen him since and cursed myself for letting him get away: he had a job, a pleasant manner, and a hot, studly body to boot. If we had clicked, he could have spared me the dreadful memories of Mon and Manoon. Now, here he was

– just after I'd been wondering who to take along to Koh Phi Phi. When I invited him on the trip, he said yes and came back with me to the guesthouse. Minutes later, I emerged from the bathroom to find him lying naked in bed, his hands behind his head, his armpits facing me. From then on, Ut's body and the natural beauty of Koh Phi Phi would combine to fill a void, compensating for all the bad karma of the past few days in Patong.

The next morning, we took a taxi to Phuket City and boarded a group excursion boat to Koh Phi Phi. After exploring some limestone caves together on the first of the two islands, Ut stayed on the boat while I slipped off the side with a snorkel and mask to catch my first real glimpse of tropical marine life. Koh Phi Don, where we spent the night, featured a cove almost identical to the one on Koh Phi Le where *The Beach* was filmed. The view from the shore was a postcard vista of clean white sand leading to a placid bay of crystal-clear, aquamarine perfection. Out in the distance, towering crags of limestone jutted out from the water. Stepping into a kayak the next morning, we paddled into the postcard and left behind the still waters of the bay.

Throughout all this, my emotions swung between euphoria and melancholia. Still recovering from the Mon disaster, my heart was aching for Chai and I was haunted by memories of the boys I'd met in Bangkok. Back in the cabin, Ut helped me forget by fucking me three times. At the restaurant, I rewarded his prowess in bed with all the expensive seafood he could eat. But something was bothering him. I could see he was sad, like me, and that nothing I said, did, or spent would shake him out of it. What was the problem? Ut said he liked me well enough but had only come to Koh Phi Phi because he was bored and had nothing better to do. What's more, he was living in Phuket because he didn't want to stay in Bangkok with his father, who hated homosexuals. In the South, the only men he ever dated were tourists like me, who trolled their way through holiday romances that ultimately led to nothing. Such excursions were always about *us*, not him. Did we ever stop to think how many times *he* had done this, and with how many foreigners? Too many to count, Ut sighed.

Five years later, the restaurant where we had that conversation is now history, along with the entire section of buildings that surrounded it. So is the hotel cabin where we fucked, the beachfront business where we rented the kayak, the dock where we arrived, and, no doubt, some of the local Thais who served us with a smile. When I think of Koh Phi Phi now, I prefer to dwell on the beautiful memories: the clean white sand; the aquamarine waters we paddled through; the stillness of the secluded beach where I skinnydipped while Ut (declining my overtures for sex in the water) chased away a family of monkeys trying to steal our belongings from the kayak; and, finally, the taste of Ut's hairless body when I licked the salt water off his skin back in the cabin.

I don't know where Ut is today. I don't know if he ever left Phuket or if he was still living there when the tsunami hit. For all I know, he could have been among the thousands of Thais who were swept away that morning. It's hard to fathom the last moments of all those unlucky people, just before the waves hit: their realization of nature's monumental force, their awareness of impending death, their final thoughts as the water carried them away to oblivion. When I do allow such things to enter my mind, I can no longer view my own quest for paradise with nostalgia of any kind. It was a quest, after all, that ultimately revealed more about the seeker than about the destination.

XI
Thais that Bond

HUA HIN, ONCE A SMALL FISHING VILLAGE in the northwestern Gulf of Thailand, is now a popular beach resort favoured by Thai families, golf enthusiasts, and the elderly. His Majesty the King has a holiday residence there, and every now and then the federal government holds cabinet meetings at one of its five-star hotels. Hua Hin is also popular for its sand and surf, but I'd had quite enough of beaches by the time I arrived there in early March of 2000. After a month in Thailand, I was eager to experience some local, traditional culture. My wish would be granted sooner than expected, thanks to Soup – the Bicycle Bar waiter I'd met on my first night in Patong, the fling who'd abandoned me so he could earn some extra cash from older, richer sex tourists.

I woke up with a start at four o'clock in the morning when my train screeched to a halt on the outskirts of town. Grabbing my bags and getting off, I hailed a *tuk-tuk* and drove around until I found the only guesthouse open at that hour. After checking in, I slept until noon. After lunch, I dug out Soup's number from my bag and called him from a pay phone. I thought the plan was to spend a day or two together in town. But when Soup finally arrived at the guesthouse that night, his mother and a chauffeur were waiting outside.

"Come on," he said. "Pack your bags, let's go."

"What's the big hurry?" I said. "I've paid for another night. Why don't we –"

"No. You're coming with us. Just pack up and check out. Mama's waiting outside in the van with her chauffeur, and she's in a hurry."

It turned out that Soup had told his family about my visit and had made plans for my arrival. But first we had to drive to Chumphon because "Mama" had errands to do. It was only after I'd gotten into the sport utility vehicle and was introduced to Soup's mother, a no-nonsense businesswoman in her early fifties, that I recalled that Chumphon was a five-hour drive south toward Surat Thani – the same direction from which I had arrived that morning. I politely mentioned this to Mama, and she got the chauffeur to drop us off at a bus stop. She then continued south with her driver while Soup and I boarded a bus headed for Thayang, the family's hometown in Phetchaburi province. On the way there, Soup called home on his cell phone to arrange for motorbikes to pick us up at a stop outside the town centre. Our bus got there ten minutes before the motorbikes did – enough time for an elderly, drunken local to stagger up with a smile, shake my hand, and then (after realizing my connection to Soup) make lewd copulation gestures while hissing at my host.

∞

> The family remains a central pivot of most Thai homo-
> sexual men's lives, and for the majority, the main prob-
> lem is not how to establish an independent lifestyle, but
> how to fit their homosexuality in, around and between
> the restrictions and demands of a home life dominated
> by heterosexual expectations.[1]

As progressive as western people like to think of ourselves, most non-western people who visit the United States, Canada, England, or France would not expect an invitation to the home of a typical family in one of those countries as the result of a casual sexual acquaintance with one of its members. But in the upcountry homesteads of rural Thailand, this kind of thing happens all the time. By accepting Soup's invitation to spend a few days at the house in Phetchaburi province, I was continuing a grand tradition that had begun not with sex tourism, but with the old explorers of the imperialist project. Foreigners were always welcome in Thai homes because they were seen as exotic, rich, and glamourous. But such invitations were also an honour for the visitor, for they showed that at some level the foreigner was trusted to fit in with the locals and make the most of his privileged exposure to Thai culture. Turning down such an invitation – which I wouldn't have done, given how starved I was for this kind of experience – was seen as highly disrespectful.

During the ten-minute motorbike ride back to the house, I didn't realize that the longhaired *kathoey* Soup was riding with was his brother, nor that the younger male I was riding with was his brother's boyfriend. I would figure that out later, once we'd finished riding through clouds of dust to arrive in

---

1. Peter A. Jackson, *Dear Uncle Go: Male Homosexuality in Thailand* (Bangkok: Bua Luang, 1995).

a residential sub-district full of Portuguese townhouses. The four-storey home in which Soup's family lived was one of these buildings, with a huge garage-door entrance that exposed the entire ground floor. Converted from a warehouse some years earlier, it was badly in need of upkeep. But the clutter was as much a symptom of the family's peculiar makeup as of its uncertain financial status.

Apart from an older sister who worked as a full-time nurse and didn't come home often, I got to know Soup's family quite well. His brother Lek, a post-operative transsexual and genuine *kathoey*, exhibited all the cross-gender behaviour and speech patterns of the classic Thai "ladyboy." Two years younger than Soup, Lek was tall (about six-foot-two) and big-boned. But she was all woman, with flowing long hair, large breasts, and the kind of round, feminine face with which nature had endowed so many gender dysphoric Thai men. When Soup introduced us at the house, Lek squealed "Oouuu-eeeee!!," a common *kathoey* expression of delight, before shaking my hand like a debutante. Lek and her seventeen-year-old boyfriend Lop, who also lived in the family home, made an odd pair. Lop was much smaller than Lek and claimed to be attracted only to *kathoeys*. While I was with them, Lek played dominatrix – nearly strangling her boyfriend in headlocks, clutching his balls, or smacking him hard whenever he misbehaved. But this was true love. Traditional gender roles meant nothing to Lek and Lop; S&M was simply their preferred mode of communication.

A few minutes after arriving at the house, Soup conducted a brief inspection of the pantry. Seeing that the mango supply had run out, he sent me back on the motorbike with Lek to get some more. Passing through the centre of town, we were greeted with catcalls and whistles from the sidewalk noodle stalls and beer bars. Lek turned to look at me, and we both laughed: as the only *farang* in town, on the back of Lek's motorbike, I was being mistaken for the new boyfriend. Just outside the town centre, Lek parked the bike in front of a small orchard. Then she held a flashlight while I climbed a tree to pick a sackful of bulging, fat green mangoes. I wasn't quite finished when Lek turned off the light and told me to get out of the tree: a dog was barking and a security guard was on the way. We were trespassing.

The next family member I met was an older brother Soup hadn't mentioned. Chon made his entrance on the following afternoon, my first full day in Thayang. I was reading a novel in a shady spot on the third-floor balcony when the familiar chords of western pop music began filtering through a bathroom window. Then I heard a shower being turned on, followed by some badly out-of-tune warbling. Five minutes later, a stocky young man in his mid-twenties stepped outside wearing nothing but a smile and a skimpy, pink bath towel. He stood about five-foot-eight and had a Clark Gable moustache, high cheekbones, and thick, sassy bangs of wet black hair that hung suggestively over his eyes. Shaking my hand, he introduced himself and pulled up a chair. Chon's English was poor, but I gathered he was a former soldier and Thai boxing champion, now a pub manager in Phetchaburi city; that he'd once fucked thirty-one women in thirty-nine days; and that, five years ago, he'd been in a motorbike accident that left him in a coma for four months, robbed him of memory, and – I couldn't help noting while ogling his otherwise perfect torso – left a patchwork of scars on his belly.

For all his machismo, Chon clearly had a soft side. "You like music?" he asked. "Come, I play for you." He motioned me to follow him inside, which I did, blinded by the sun, not knowing where he was leading me. Passing through the upstairs hallway, we entered his bedroom. While I sat on the bed, he went to the stereo and began digging through his collection of cds. First, he played some romantic pop ballads from Thailand; then he asked me to sing along to a schmaltzy, karaoke version of "Imagine" – which I did while gazing up at him from the bed. It felt weird, indulging this rather intimate request only moments after Chon had labelled himself a *puu-chai tem-tua*, or "complete man." Finally he offered that yes, he *had* had sex in the all-male military barracks once or twice and oh, by the way, I was really handsome just like all western guys, and gee, I sure had a nice voice. Gulp.

"Uh … Chon – we go outside now?" Rather than succumb to the advances of my host's "straight" brother on the first day of my visit, I thought it might be wiser to slip away from Chon's heat and remind him of his offer to make us some Thai salsa.

Back outside, Chon smiled as he peeled one of the green mangoes I'd picked the night before. He sliced it into thin wedges, his knuckles whitening on the knife handle for added effect and, using a mortar and pestle, pounded together a sharp and spicy sauce made of fresh chili, onion, sugar, and lime juice. Finally he dipped a mango wedge into the mixture, pulled it out, and stuck it in my mouth. By the end of our snack Chon was inviting me to visit his pub, which, he couldn't help noting, had an upstairs bedroom where we could spend the night if he got too drunk to drive. I thanked him for his kindness but told him I'd have to think about it; I didn't know what Soup might be planning for us.

Mama returned from Chumphon on the third day bearing a vanload of food and gifts. From all the excitement surrounding her entrance, it was clear that she was the centre of the household; all the attention Soup had lavished on his guest was instantly transferred to her the moment she arrived. Mama was a typical Thai matriarch: she worked hard, knew everyone in town, and did everything possible to improve the lives of her children. Most of all, she was a survivor. Despite having lost ten million baht during the stock market crash of '97 and being dumped by a philandering husband, she had bounced back. From what I could see, her connection to her children was straightforward, unconditional, and emotionally uncluttered. I liked her for that.

But a stare from Mama in the middle of a group conversation could be intimidating. Somehow she had convinced herself that I understood the Thai language simply because I had *wai*'ed her in greeting, said *sawatdee khrap*, and pronounced her food *arroy*. She would speak to me at length in Thai, punctuating everything with *Cao jai mai?* and nodding her head in satisfaction, as if I'd had the slightest inkling of what she was talking about. Mama grew quite attached to me over the week. Maybe she liked the way I gathered the neighbourhood children for photos. Or maybe it was the fact I had paid an old woman from across the street twice the going rate for a massage.

> Most lower-class young men who work as barboys do not tell their families, who in turn do not ask too much. However, gays of this class do have a place in their families, and I have never heard of a case where a working-class Thai gay man has been ostracised by his family or friends.[2]

At this point, I had no idea what a "typical" Thai family was. Soup, his

2. Eric Allyn, "Trees in the Same Forest: Thailand's Culture and Gay Subculture." *The Men of Thailand: Revisited* (Bangkok: Bua Luang, 1991).

siblings, and their mother were merely a random sampling from the limited range of Thai society I'd been exposed to as a tourist. But as a Thai family, it seemed that this one had dealt with the challenges of modern development and shifting social values with real aplomb. While recovering from an economic crisis that had affected all of Southeast Asia, Soup's family had stuck together in ways that, to me, seemed heroic. This family had not only lost its fortune; it had also lost face by losing its patriarch to adultery. And yet despite its difficulties it had incorporated the socially disapproved sexual identities of two of its sons – one a gay bar boy who had assumed some of the father's leadership role, the other a transgender *kathoey* who was allowed to shack up in the family home with her teenaged masochist boyfriend. Ironically, the socially approved sexual identity of the eldest son had proved the most problematic: Chon was "straight" and had a girlfriend, but the few times I met her I sensed a weariness typical of all women who get stuck with a philanderer.

Before Mama's return from the South, things were pretty relaxed around the house. *Ahan chao*, or breakfast, was no different from lunch or dinner: we ate spicy dishes of trout, prawns, and pork with stir-fried vegetables and rice while sitting cross-legged on the cement floor of the garage. Chon ate with his fingers; the rest of us used a fork and spoon. In the early afternoon, Chon would go upstairs for a nap while the rest of us drove out to a beach or went swimming in a local *khlong*. When we returned, I'd spend the late afternoon reading on the rooftop sundeck while Soup visited friends he hadn't seen in months. Then we'd get together for dinner in the garage, following which Soup would go across the street to play cards, Lek and Lop would repair to their bedroom to watch TV or have sex, and Chon would get on his motorbike and drive to his pub to work. I'd stay in and read. Later, just before midnight, we'd all meet again to go out and *kin khao*, or "eat rice," at an open-air restaurant in downtown Thayang. The country version of *som tam*, or papaya salad, turned out to be much spicier than what they served in the resort towns. The first time I tried it, I bit into a chili and nearly hyperventilated from the result. Soup, Lek, and Lop all had a good laugh at my expense.

Once Mama returned from Chumphon, Soup instantly converted from Patong Beach money boy to provincial *kunla-gay*: the "decent," "respectable" homo who's responsible to his family above all else. Soup told me his mother didn't know the nature of his job at Bicycle Bar and I was not to breathe a word because he would lose face. I suspected that she already knew, but perhaps had chosen, with typically Thai discretion, to say nothing. Whatever the case, I would find it impossible to make any plans with Soup because, in his mind, Mama's agenda trumped all else. Even when she appeared to have no pressing need for her son to attend to, Soup left open the possibility that she would. We weren't going anywhere as long as Mama was around.

Our visit hadn't been all that intimate to begin with. Other than a single day Soup reserved for a motorbike ride to Phetchaburi City, where we toured a royal palace and visited several temples, we hardly spent any time alone. Playing host to a *farang* tourist who spoke only a few phrases of Thai had turned out to be more than Soup bargained for. By the third day, we had stopped fucking; by the fourth, I could tell that my presence was wearing on him. Part of the reason may have been my unwillingness to part with money every time he asked for it. The 1,500 baht I gave him on the first day wasn't all that much, given what I was saving in hotel bills. What concerned me was that he was using it to play poker with the neighbourhood police officer, who lived across the street. After I handed him the money, Soup knelt on the bedroom floor clutching his Buddhist prayer beads and an amulet. Then he closed his eyes, folded his hands in a *wai*, and bowed three times.

"I'm praying for good luck, so I can win at poker," he said.

"Does Buddha answer that kind of prayer?" I asked.

"Of course," Soup frowned, annoyed by the question.

When he got home at midnight, he'd lost nearly all the money I'd given him.

The next day, as we sat upstairs in his bedroom after lunch, Soup asked if I would buy a life insurance policy from Mama. "No thanks," I said, "I already have one." I was troubled by the request, given that I had just finished "lending" him 1,500 baht for the card game he'd lost – and that was *after* he revealed that he had once sought counseling for a gambling addiction. But Soup didn't seem to notice my discomfort and kept asking for more money. I turned him down after the third cash infusion.

Eventually, my curiosity about these mysterious poker games got the better of me. Eager to see a game in progress, I walked across the street to the policeman's yard in the guise of calling Soup home for dinner. I found him with the others, sitting at a table behind a large blanket that hung from a tree to conceal the policeman's illegal activity (which, of course, the entire neighbourhood knew all about). When I approached, a dozen pairs of eyes turned to look up at me. Soup translated the police officer's greeting: "Are you going to play?" I scanned the expectant faces staring at my wallet pocket.

"I think I'll just watch," I said.

The policeman muttered something and pointed the way out.

"You no play, you no stay," Soup explained with a shrug.

Toward the end of the week, I finally accepted Chon's invitation to visit his pub. Soup didn't want to join me, preferring to spend yet another night across the street losing yet another card game to the neighbourhood cop. When I told Chon I would visit his establishment – I delivered the news over Soup's cell phone, which Chon was calling on from the pub – he was so happy that he rode all the way back to Thayang, about thirty minutes away, to pick me up and bring me back. When he arrived, his girlfriend was sitting behind him on the motorbike, and she was not in a good mood. She had been crying; it was obvious they had been arguing. At first I thought she was angry at being dumped at the house while Chon whisked me off to the pub. But later, Soup explained that she was upset because Chon wanted me to spend the night with him in the pub's upstairs bedroom – where there was only one bed. Soup, for his part, was amused by his brother's shameless promiscuity.

The ride to Upcountry Pub was long and nerve-wracking. Chon was a maniac, driving at top speed in the middle of the night on a smooth, unlit stretch of dry asphalt that was dusted with sand. He wouldn't stop talking the entire way and kept turning around to make eye contact while he spoke. It was difficult to relax, knowing that the quilt of scars on his stomach was the result of a near-fatal motorbike accident. After narrowly avoiding a wipeout at one bend in the road, I couldn't stop thinking of a scene from Annie Hall in which Alvie and Annie are in a car driven by Annie's suicidal brother, played by career psychopath Christopher Walken. The brother chooses this captive moment to share his fantasy of driving into the oncoming headlights.

It was while he had me in this grip of terror that Chon suddenly made it clear he had money problems. When he asked, for the third time before we got to the pub, how much cash I was carrying, I began to wonder if he'd suffered some mild brain damage from his accident. The trip on his motorbike, which should have taken only half an hour, ended up lasting two hours. During the journey, I paid to fill up his gas tank, bought some stir-fried duck to bring to a woman Chon kept referring to as his "sister" (though I'd already met his only female sibling, and the gorgeous young woman we were visiting had a baby of uncertain paternity), and treated him to some noodle soup before promising, again, to spend at least 200 baht at his pub.

But Chon was in more than just financial turmoil. He also needed a shoulder to cry on about his place in the family. Lately he hadn't been getting along with Mama; his brothers hardly spoke to him anymore. Although he reserved a certain amount of respect for his two queer siblings – who, after all, seemed to be making their way through life with a greater deal of success – he found it incomprehensible that Mama would lavish them with so much affection when he was the "real man" of the family. I wasn't sure if I'd missed something in Chon's emotive combination of broken English, hand gestures, and facial expressions, but all was confirmed later by Soup's version of events.

Chon was what Thais might refer to as a *jik-go*, an androgynous tough guy who, as Manit Manitcharoen's Thai Dictionary puts it, "dresses ostentatiously, puts on airs and does not work." *Jik-go* was mainly a product of Thai urban youth culture of the 1950s and '60s, but country boy Chon fit the classic profile: he slept around a lot (and wouldn't turn down homo sex if it gave him some advantage), drank too much, told lies, and didn't repay debts. Soup and Lek were far from perfect, but at least they pitched in with the family chores, contributed to the household budget (apart from his Bicycle Bar wages and "tips," the little money I lent Soup that he didn't lose playing poker he gave to Mama), and included their mother in every aspect of their lives. Mama's acceptance of Soup and Lek's openly queer sexual orientation – including Lop's live-in arrangement and my own presence as a freeloading *farang* – was commendable in a traditional Asian culture which, while not outwardly homophobic, saw homosexuality as an unfortunate aberration to be pitied.

When we finally got to the pub just after midnight, there were only three customers sitting at a table in a corner next to the door. The pub was not much larger than a two-bedroom apartment in Vancouver, but one corner of it was devoted to live, amplified music. The band hadn't arrived yet, and Chon left me alone to talk with his staff. When he joined me a few minutes later, I handed him the 200 baht I'd promised to spend. He then fetched two more large bottles of beer than I'd paid for, insisting that I go ahead and drink them. Later, as the canned music seemed to improve with each bottle, he grabbed me by the hand and pulled me onto the dance floor. A few minutes later, we were holding hands and spinning each other around the floor while the Eagles' "Lyin' Eyes" played on the sound system. I had trouble not bursting into laughter as I sang "You can't hiiiiiiiiide ... your lyin' eyes ..." while gazing straight into Chon's big, brown, duplicitous orbs.

By the time the house band arrived for its first set, there were about a dozen regulars in the bar. After starting off a bit rusty with some western tunes – they sounded like a shithouse college outfit playing their first gig – they finally hit their stride with a traditional Thai rocker that got everyone up on the dance floor. Getting me even more in the mood was the band's twenty-two-year-old lead guitarist – a tall, lanky, caramel-skinned country boy who looked more Hispanic than Asian. At one point I was forced to submit to the command performance for any visiting *farang*: joining the band to sing "Hotel California." As my country boy and another guitarist dueled their way through the song's famous, extended coda, I was suddenly transported back to Winnipeg and the drag race with a young Vietnamese stockbroker who had asked me to sing the same song. The moment was surreal. How had I ended up here, at some anonymous hole-in-the-wall in the Thai countryside, being hustled by my host's brother while getting a serious hard-on for a young rock guitarist I'd never see again? Soup didn't seem to care what I did while I was with his family, as long as it didn't cause him any trouble. I wanted to discuss this when I got home just after midnight (mercifully, Mama's arrival in the van spared me another ride on Chon's motorbike), but Soup was still out playing cards and wouldn't slip under the covers beside me until four hours later. By the time he awoke after lunch, I was on my way out the door with Mama, accompanying her on a string of errands that would take us around the province.

After driving to the insurance office where I met Mama's staff, we headed back on the road and into the country, stopping by a rice field for a chat with some farmers. Then it was on to a salt packing factory where Mama had more clients. She was like a campaigning politician, this woman – she seemed to know everyone in the province. By the end of the visits, though, she sensed my weariness at all the driving around and smiling at strangers amused by the *farang* in their midst. So our final stop was just for fun: a pop concert held in a public square in Phetchaburi city. Mama dragged me to the front of the stage where, in front of a thousand local Thais, she encouraged me to buy a rose for the young male singer. I wouldn't realize until a month or so later that the teen heartthrob being showered with garlands was Goong, then near the top of the charts as one of the most popular *Luuk Thung* (traditional Thai folk music) performers in the country. I wasn't the only man who handed Goong a rose that night, but I was too stunned to lean forward and kiss him on the cheek like everyone else appeared to do.

The crowd roared as I handed him the flower.

"*Khop khun mak krap,*" he smiled warmly as I gave it to him, bowing and folding his hands in a *wai.*

The next night I was on the road back to Bangkok, lying in the back of a pickup truck with Soup, Lek, and Lop while Mama sat in the front with her chauffeur. Along the way, we stopped at a music festival where we were invited backstage to meet the performers and take photos of them in traditional garb.

My week of full immersion in Thai country family life was exactly the kind of situation I'd been seeking: deep in the Thai heartland, off the tourist track, and totally unpredictable. Months later, I sent Mama copies of the photos I had taken in Phetchaburi, plus a thank-you card. I sent Chon some Canadian coins for his collection, and I sent Soup my best wishes. Much later, when I had moved to Bangkok, Soup would invite me back to the family home. But I'd never take him up on it, and he'd never take up my offer to meet in the city.

XII
Economies of Love

THE DAY AFTER I LEFT BANGKOK FOR THE first time, an invitation arrived in my Hotmail "In" box. Wit, the young freelancer I'd met at DJ Station and slept with at the Malaysia Hotel, was offering a place to stay the next time I was in town. In my reply, sent from an Internet shop on Koh Samui, I thanked him for the invitation and promised to let him know when I'd be back. A month later, just before my return, we exchanged e-mails. Then I called his cell phone from Phetchaburi to arrange our rendezvous at his Sukhumvit Road apartment. I took it for granted that we'd be sleeping together, and given my experience with hosted housing in Thailand up to then, I was looking forward to the same hospitality from Wit. It didn't occur to me that staying in a bachelor suite with a bar boy in Bangkok might have an entirely different set of consequences than staying in a provincial townhouse with a bar boy's family.

It was six o'clock on a Sunday morning when I rang the buzzer at Wit's apartment building on Sukhumvit *soi* 52. He wasn't home, but that was hardly surprising: our appointment was for ten o'clock the night before, and I had been forced to keep postponing it while my ride into Bangkok from Phetchaburi kept getting delayed. After my last apologetic phone call at about midnight, Wit must have given up, gone out to a bar, and spent the night with someone else. Not knowing where else to go now that I was at his apartment, I decided to wait for him by lying down on a bench in the parking lot. Before passing out, I noticed someone staring at me from the building's office window and picking up a phone; the next thing I remember is being nudged awake and thinking I was under arrest. But the Thai man staring down at me was in his early twenties and had big red lips, Carmen Miranda eyes, and peroxide in his hair. He said his name was "Bee," and that he was taking me to his apartment. "Don't worry," he said. "I best friend Wit."

Bee shoved me into a taxi, got in himself, and then directed the driver to a twelve-storey complex off Sukhumvit *soi* 81, a few blocks away. Inside a small bachelor suite on the seventh floor were three other young Thai guys, all of them snoring. Bee shoved one of them off the bed to join another on the floor, then slid under the sheets beside the third and invited me to join them. A few hours later, he woke me. "Ssssshh," he said, putting a finger to my lips. Then he led me to the toilet, closed the door, and locked it. Slipping off his undies, he then pulled mine off as well, turned on the shower and slid his tongue in my mouth. After we finished cumming and toweling each other off, he led me back to bed and wrapped his naked body around mine. His roommates continued snoring. "Don't tell Wit," he smiled.

When Wit arrived in the middle of the afternoon, he didn't seem bothered that I had missed our appointment the night before and then slept with his best friend. Moments after greeting me, he joined Bee and the others for a game of poker. When the game was over, we hauled my bags to his apartment on *soi* 52 and fucked for half an hour before rejoining the others for dinner. The next morning, Wit showed me his bank book to prove how broke he was. I gave him 1,000 baht. We still had six days to go together, and I knew I'd be shelling out again before leaving for Chiang Mai the following Sunday.

What Wit hadn't said when he invited me to stay with him had become rather obvious the moment I woke up in Bee's arms: Wit and Bee were part of a small but tight-knit group of Sukhumvit freelancers, and Bee's bachelor suite was Money Boy Central. Both of these young men, and most of their friends, had moved from the Northeast and met in Bangkok. None had gone to university, and a few hadn't finished high school. Most made ends meet by cruising the bars, where the occasional fling with a *farang* could supplement the income of a low-wage day job. In Bee's building, eight or nine freelancers lived on the same floor. In the week I spent with these young men, a sort of Stockholm Syndrome of the flesh trade set in: constant exposure to the money boy existence led me to identify with their world as if it were like any other.

Before staying with Wit, I had set a total weekly spending limit of $350 Canadian for a three-month journey through Thailand and southern Vietnam. But during our single week together, I spent $600. By most global standards of casual involvement with a sex trade worker, Wit was a bargain at $250 for an entire week. But I was lost in an ethical and philosophical haze; still at a stage of enchantment with Thailand that allowed me to believe I wasn't really participating in an "economy" as such because my Thai lovers seemed to be having as good a time as I was. Hadn't I told them that I was staying in cheap guesthouses and didn't use plastic? If they knew I was telling the truth and they still wanted to be with me, then money must not have been an issue, right?

Well, wrong. The reality that had confronted me first in Samui and Phuket, and then in Phetchaburi with Soup, was finally becoming clear on my second visit to Bangkok. It was this: just because the protocols of exchange as I understood them in the West did not apply in Thailand did not necessarily mean I was *not* engaging in prostitution by hanging out with bar boys. By this point I knew enough about the culture to understand that Thai people do not tend to engage foreigners in open discussions about money or sex. But my thinking was still clouded by the big myth of "global queering": the assumption that the kind of socializing one does in the West – including all the visual symbols and pick-up lines of "cruising" – can be transported to another culture.

Back home, I saw myself as young and presentable enough to meet the kind of lovers I wanted, no strings attached. But here, the kind of guys I found hot were quite often farm boys from Isaan or the Golden Triangle – this made them, automatically, much poorer than my objects of desire back home. The fact that the Thai upper- and middle-classes were a significant minority, combined with my attraction to younger, "out" guys, amounted to a high probability that my Thai lovers would be involved, to some degree, with trade. There was nothing wrong with this; the problem was that my hypocritical views about prostitution were tainting *any* transaction of cash involving a Thai male. Instead of being generous to my hosts, I had approached every encounter hypersensitive to any perception that I might be "enabling" Third World prostitution. This despite the fact that I'd hired a hustler in Vancouver on at least three occasions. This despite the fact that I saw nothing contradictory or obscene in the fact that I was trying to experience everything in Thailand, including all the "fun," on a backpacker's budget. Who the hell was I kidding?

An ideology of deviance disempowers sex workers. It would be more useful to realise the central role played by the bar workers in a complex pleasure economy, and that a diverse workforce extending from the ice vendors and waiters to pimps and accountants depends on this economy to make a living.[1]

Sex work for some men can provide a long-term, sometimes permanent, escape from life as an unskilled farm labourer.[2]

By staying with Wit for a week, I would learn much more about the realities of the sex trade. One common *modus operandi* among Thai money boys, especially those from Isaan, was the "sob story": an elaborate tale of woe – a parent desperately requiring chemotherapy treatment, a house wiped out by a flood – designed to get the tear ducts, and the cash, flowing. Sometimes the sob story was bullshit, but quite often it was true. Wit never resorted to this tactic with me, but then he didn't have to: one day I took him out for lunch and, with journalistic intent, paid him 700 baht to tell his life story. Here's the result....

Wit was twenty-three. His parents broke up when he was only a month old, and neither wanted to raise him. He said he didn't know why. Instead, he ended up bouncing back and forth between relatives until he was a teenager. By the time he decided to move to Bangkok at age fifteen, he had completed one year of schooling, two years as farm labourer outside his home town of Udon Thani, and one year at a temple as a novice monk. For his first three years in Bangkok, he worked at a clothing factory where he earned 1,500 baht per month (then about us $30). Then he worked for Paitoon Footwear, a shoe manufacturer that churned out mountains of Nike, Reebok, and Adidas runners. Wit earned just over poverty-level wages, up to 6,000 baht a month. But even that was barely enough to cover rent and utilities at the dingiest studio flat in Bangkok, and still have enough left to eat anything more interesting than street vendor noodle soup every day.

His boss at Paitoon wanted him to be a junior supervisor, but ordering people around did not come naturally to Wit. He tried it for a month and then quit when a job at a furniture company came up: given the choice of

1. Graeme Storer, "Rehearsing Gender and Sexuality in Modern Thailand: Masculinity and Male-Male Sex Behaviours." *Lady Boys, Tom Boys, Rent Boys: Male and Female Homosexualities in Contemporary Thailand*, edited by Peter A. Jackson and Gerard Sullivan (New York: Harrington Park Press, 1999).

2. Malcom McCamish, "The Friends Thou Hast: Support Systems for Male Commercial Sex Workers in Pattaya, Thailand." *Lady Boys, Tom Boys, Rent Boys: Male and Female Homosexualities in Contemporary Thailand*, edited by Peter A. Jackson and Gerard Sullivan (New York: Harrington Park Press, 1999).

becoming a management stooge in a textile multinational or earning nine to ten thousand baht a month, Wit went for the money. But the new job was no better: some days he worked a sixteen-hour shift. After seven months, he was fired for complaining about the hours. He spent the next year working for The Mall department store chain, but conditions were no better there.

Wit turned twenty-one with no education or prospects. So he was intrigued when a friend told him about a gay bar in Saphan Kwai where he could earn a lot of money from "tips." His new place of employment was not a disco, as he'd been told; it was a low-end karaoke bar where, once in a while, a *farang* might "off" him and pay him 1,000 baht for sex. It was at this bar, The Eagle, that Wit first learned about Bangkok's biggest red light district. "I saw someone working there from Twilight bar," he recalled. "He say to me, 'If you want to change to Patpong, you can work at The Boys Bangkok go-go bar, opposite Twilight.'"

And so, with about as much trepidation as saying "yes" to a new hairstyle, Wit joined the ranks of a million or so other Thais who were part of the country's biggest growth industry. On his first night at Boys Bangkok, Wit was offed by a Japanese man. He said he was lucky, since the Japanese were the most generous sex tourists in Thailand; in many go-go bars, it wasn't unusual for groups of Tokyo businessmen to approach a dancer and stuff 500-baht notes into his crotch. ("The Japanese are big tippers, three to five thousand baht," one bar owner in Pattaya has said, "and they generally only want to be fucked."[3])

Wit said the Japanese customer "took" him twice. But soon afterward, business at Boys Bangkok suffered a dry spell. "I think I work there two and a half months, I have three *farang*, three Japanese – six customers in two months…." I didn't ask how much these clients paid him, but I knew the going rate for non-backpacker tourists was 1,000 baht for a "short time" and 1,500 or more for a sleepover. Even allowing for the generous Japanese, six customers in two months wouldn't necessarily earn him a lot more than he was getting at the furniture company, maybe even less.

However, Wit continued, "My friend tell me I can work another place. So I go to work at Superlek bar." I'd seen the ads for Superlek. The boys there were smaller and younger-looking, like Wit. All the dancers stripped,

3. *Ibid.*

and some took part in fuck shows. Wit spent three months there, dancing onstage and sometimes in the shower. I didn't ask if he did the fuck shows; apart from respecting the shy Thai personality (it's okay to do it, but not talk about it), I felt like we were too involved now. *I didn't want to know.* What he would say was that one of his customers from the UK had paid for a nine-month English course and helped him finish high school. Wit liked him very much. But the man, a forty-two-year-old expat living in Malaysia, dumped him for a boy from Hat Yai. Wit left Superlek shortly afterward. Once in a while, if a go-go bar was short-staffed, he would do an occasional gig while looking for other work.

When I asked how he felt about working in the sex trade, Wit looked down at the food on his plate. "After I finish working at department store, I try to work at another place – not a go-go bar, but a company or some factory," he said. "But I don't get a job, so, okay, I can try working at go-go bar. I know everybody don't like the boy bar, but I don't know what I can do. I try everywhere and I ask everywhere for the work. But I cannot wait for the job. If I wait, then I no money. Because, for a long time, my sister help me."

His sister was an unemployed single mother.

Lately, when he went out at night, Wit would join Bee onstage at Twilight, where they danced in their underwear. Other times he'd dance at Screwboy, the strip club I'd visited the same night we first met at DJ Station. Until then, I'd been eager to examine the life of a go-go boy up close. Now, the thought of seeing Wit shake his ass, jerk off, or get fucked onstage in front of drooling *farang*, then get "offed" by one of them, made me ill. So did the thought of having to ask for his keys after the show so I could return to the apartment by myself and wait for him to finish with his trick.

"I don't think I want to see you at Screwboy," I said.

"I understand," he said, managing a tiny smile. "I no want you to come."

After hearing Wit's story, I thought I'd learned all there was to know about the money boy life. But that was before a St. Patrick's Day bus ride with Wit, Bee, and four of their friends to Pattaya, a seaside resort and sin city in Chonburi province, a couple of hours east of Bangkok. Bee was excited because he was reuniting with his Dutch boyfriend Peter, who owned a beachside condo in nearby Jomtien. Bee would be staying at the condo while the rest of us camped out in sleazy South Pattaya guesthouses.

Asking where the red light district is in Pattaya is rather like asking where the "art district" is in Paris or the "fashion district" in Milan. Almost every corner of downtown Pattaya has some connection to the sex trade. Boyztown, an L-shaped strip of bars and nightclubs, contains the largest concentration of commercial gay venues in the world. On our one night in Pattaya, Wit and I waded through its ocean of bar boys and sat in a pub at the end of the *soi* called Coco Bananas. Similar to Balcony in Silom *soi* 4, the pub was a good vantage point from which to survey the passing crowd. At one point, a silver Mercedes stopped in front of us, outside the entrance to Boyz Boyz Boyz disco. A door opened, and a white-haired octogenarian got out and shuffled slowly to the front door with a cane. *Rage, rage indeed*, I thought, *against the dying of the light.*

Later, we joined Bee and his friends at Boyz Boyz Boyz, where muscular Thai men in briefs were pouring candle wax on each other and performing simulated fuck shows. None of this interested Bee, who was only waiting for his Dutch benefactor to show up. When the front door opened and a tall European in black leather walked in, Bee jumped from his seat. Peter, a fifty-seven-year-old nightclub owner from a Dutch provincial town, had silver hair that was trimmed to a youthful buzz cut. The leather and postmodern half-rims gave him the look of a Bond villain. After introducing himself, he invited Wit and me to brunch the next morning. I accepted immediately. After five days of money-boy English, I was starved for intelligent conversation.

"Brunch" turned out to be a minimalist affair. Bee met us at the door dressed only in briefs, then Peter directed us to the dining room so we could help ourselves to coffee, toast, and a tray of Dutch cheese and strawberry jam, which turned out to be the extent of the meal. Then he introduced us to Son, who turned out to be his *other* boyfriend for the weekend. Son was a skinny, sweet-smiling nineteen-year-old who was wearing nothing but a slinky pair of high-cut satin shorts. Peter, slapping his ass, sent him off to the kitchen to join Bee on cleanup duty. *So*, I thought, *this is what Bee means by "boyfriend."* I hadn't known there was anyone else, and I wondered how he felt about sharing Peter.

Before the trip to Pattaya, Bee had told me how important Peter was in his life. Peter the Patron was going to pay for his tuition and travel fees to study at a prestigious fashion design school in Paris. For this, Bee appeared willing to play the submissive, smiling houseboy/sex toy for his Dutch lover. But here, in Peter's Jomtien condo, I could tell that Bee wasn't all that keen about the arrangement. He averted his eyes when Peter grabbed the younger Son and pulled him onto his lap for a grope.

"Don't you get jealous?" I asked. Bee tilted his head and flashed a vacant, "Amazing Thailand" smile. It wasn't his turn to speak.

"I don't allow them to get jealous," Peter said abruptly. "If they get moody or jealous, I tell them they have to go home. So they always behave."

Right, I thought: *Lord of the manor. These boys exist only for his pleasure.* I bit my tongue as our host stood up from his chair and took me by the arm, directing me to his patio garden overlooking Jomtien Beach. On our way out the door, Peter turned and pointed a bony finger at my companion.

"Wit," he said, "why don't you clean the coffee table? There's a good boy – Bee will give you a cloth." Snapping to attention at the sound of his name, Wit nodded and silently complied. I was still adjusting to the shock of realizing that Wit had likely been one of Peter's boys – their exchange of glances seemed a giveaway – when Peter once again directed me to the sundeck.

"Come," he said, "let us talk like men."

Peter wasn't being pretentious. This was who he really was: a wealthy Dutch ephebophile for whom the colonial era had never quite ended. After converting three bar businesses into one successful nightclub – who knows what else he was up to on the side? – he had enough money to fly to Thailand three or four times a year, buy a beachside condo with modern furniture and a state-of-the-art stereo system, and keep several boys (and even their families) happy for months, if not years. The trade-off was that the boys had to behave like concubines while on his turf. Bee was on his best behaviour in Pattaya. Back in Bangkok, he was leader of the pack. But here, under Peter's watchful eye, he could switch to "servile" in a heartbeat. Later, out on the beach, Peter and I sat in tanning chairs while Bee, Wit, and Son frolicked in the surf. At one point, Peter clapped his hands twice; Bee, like a slave, led the others back to his chair.

I was disturbed by my ambivalence about Peter. On one hand, I was appalled by his treatment of the Thai boys as his personal chattel; on the other, he did have a certain charisma I found impressive. The boys fawned over him, competing to impress him. Imagining a life of nightly threesomes with the likes of Son and Bee, I was reminded of a line from *M. Butterfly*. "While we men may all want to kick Pinkerton," says Gallimard, describing a colleague who keeps a harem of young Asian women, "very few of us would pass up the opportunity to *be* Pinkerton." Was this what I had to look forward to in my late fifties? Would I, too, given the same wealth, surround myself with submissive Asian boy toys who could attend to my every need? Peter's quintessential Rice Queendom – all that was missing, it seemed, was the smoking jacket – was like a mirror reflecting my own desires. But it wasn't right. I didn't like what I saw in the reflection.

The place I was visiting after Pattaya, and the things I'd end up doing there, would not dispel such fears. If I thought my Thai adventure up to now had been an endless campaign of hedonism, Chiang Mai was the Fuckfest coda. Taking the night train to the old Lanna kingdom was supposed to be a relief for my body and psyche, which by now were battered from too much sex and emotional stress. I needed a break, and Chiang Mai's rolling hills, lush green forests, and cool climate seemed the right solution. My plans were modest: apart from doing some research on the hill tribes, I would visit a few temples, go to Chiang Rai, do a motorbike tour of the Golden Triangle, hang out in coffee bars, and swim at the Mae Rim waterfalls. In the end, I would do all these things – but not without a thorough working over by the local gay scene.

The House of Male was a men's sauna located in a teakwood mansion whose gables were festooned with ornate wooden carvings typical of the North. Surrounded by bamboo and rubber trees, it was situated just outside the old city, not far from Chiang Mai University, behind a large shopping mall. On the ground floor was a fenced-in swimming pool and patio, a restaurant and bar, workout gym, showers, and locker room. Upstairs was an outdoor seating space with a private meditation room designed in traditional Lanna style. Behind a row of beaded curtains was an open-air TV room with large throw cushions that led to a cruising maze. An adjoining teakwood chamber contained private rooms with vinyl mattresses on the floor. On my first afternoon in town, it seemed a good place to relax after a long train ride.

Within minutes of arriving, I was heading upstairs with a beefy gym stud who cruised me in the shower room. Returning to the pool area afterwards, I got a disapproving look from the next local man I met.

"Chiang Mai," he warned me, "is like noodle soup: you mix the ingredients in a bowl, and they don't take long to blend. Sooner or later, everyone knows everyone else. And everyone knows everyone else's business."

It seemed that Phan, a twenty-eight-year-old Thai chef from a wealthy family, knew a lot about *my* business. He turned out to be the local contact that Ronald, a Vancouver acquaintance, had recommended before my trip. Ronald, who'd known Phan for years, had forgotten to give me his number; now here he was, on my first day in town, meeting me by accident. True to his "noodle soup" metaphor, Phan already knew my occupation, travel plans, financial status – even intimate physical details Ronald must have gotten from Jason, my Taiwanese fling of a decade earlier. Later, Phan investigated those details for himself in an upstairs cabin – despite having chided me for being such a slut.

Phan had a way with metaphors. One night at Bubble disco, where I joined him for drinks with another Canadian, my attention was diverted by the arrival of a group of handsome young Thai men.

"Ah yes," smiled Phan. "It's the Air Crew."

"'Air Crew'?" I asked.

"Yes. These boys compete to see who can get the most foreigners in bed, and from the most countries," he said. "Their sex lives depend on airplanes. So we call them the Air Crew. We like to say they 'fly' England, they 'fly' Germany, they 'fly' Australia … who knows? Tonight maybe they'll 'fly' Canada." Given Phan's interest in François, the twenty-eight-year-old businessman from New Brunswick he'd been chatting up, I knew his last comment was directed at me.

My dalliance with two members of the "Air Crew" marked the turning point in my northern adventure – the moment I lost my head. The sexier and more masculine of the two, Deuan, and his cuter but fey housemate, Saen, were like an erotic tag team: their complementary attributes made it hard to choose between them. Deuan got to me first, inviting me home after a snog on the dance floor. But just before he took me back to their townhouse, his roommate exacted a promise for us to meet at my hotel the following day. At their townhouse, Deuan and I took turns fucking each other.

The next day, I was late returning from a trip to Mae Rim with Phan, François, and another friend, and I missed my appointment with Saen, who hadn't given me his phone number. So I went looking for him at the Night Bazaar. Chiang Mai's largest market was an assault on the senses with its spicy food aromas, cigarette smoke, incense, and exhaust fumes, its cacophony of bargain-hunters, merchants, and *tuk-tuk* motors, and its open-air food court with its live music. The gay bars were hidden behind beaded bamboo curtains in the middle of the Bazaar, in an alleyway lit by pink neon. Like most other gay bars in Chiang Mai, the Night Bazaar pub row was a gathering place for money boys.

Saen wasn't there, so I decided to return to my hotel. But as I was leaving the alleyway a handsome, dark-skinned young man in a white cardigan sweater grabbed me by the arm. Wisut seemed adorable, but I didn't feel like making any more new friends. I told him I was tired, but he didn't seem to hear me. "If you pay for the motorbike rental and our food," he said, "I happy to stay with you tonight. Then I take you to orchid farm and waterfall." Wisut spent the next two nights in my arms. By the time I dropped him off at his home on the second day, exhaustion was beginning to set in.

Back at the House of Male that afternoon, I was approached by twenty-year-old Mon from Chiang Rai, one of the sauna's most popular masseurs. I'd had a crush on Mon since the first day, and he'd acknowledged it by flirting with me ever since. Phan's "noodle soup" analogy had already come true: Mon knew about my flings with Wisut, Deuan, and Saen. But that only seemed to encourage him: at one point he conspired with two other House of Male masseurs to give me a "special welcome" in a quiet corner of the upstairs terrace. From then on, the noodle soup began to boil over as I bounced between Deuan and Saen's townhouse and the House of Male.

First it was a night in Deuan's arms during a rainstorm, then a quickie with Saen, followed by private sex with Mon at the House of Male, after which a student named Paisal took me back to his apartment to have his way with me. Finally, at the House of Male on my last night in town, I met a twenty-six-year-old freelancer named Chai who had a gymnast's body and twice brought me to orgasm in an upstairs cabin. Later, as we frolicked in the swimming pool and I contemplated moving to Chiang Mai to become Chai's personal sex slave, Saen showed up on the patio. He was followed by Paisal, the graphics student, who was then followed by Deuan. Their glares burned a hole through me. Chai disappeared, as did Paisal. That left Saen and Deuan. When I began to approach Deuan, his roommate thought I was making a final choice. Saen swore and flapped his arms about, mocking my "butterfly" behaviour.

Six months later, when I returned to Bangkok as a resident, I would pay for my greed in the north when I spotted Deuan one night with an older *farang* in Silom *soi* 4. When I approached him to say hello, Deuan would only hiss and glare, like a cat on the defensive, before blanking me for the rest of the night. This reaction told me, among other things, that I had been more cynical than Deuan about our time together; that if I had given our acquaintance any more than I had, he might have reciprocated. Instead, I had likely misled him into thinking that I cared more about him than I actually did, and so my failure to keep in touch after leaving Chiang Mai must have hurt – even if, as one of the "Air Crew," he had learned to expect exactly such treatment from *farang*.

Sometimes, when I'm asked what I did on my first visit to Thailand, I blush at the thought of all that prolific humping. On the other hand, I'm relieved that I came out of it with body and mind intact. During a subsequent visit to Chiang Mai, I arranged to meet an American acquaintance at Adam's Apple, the city's most popular gay go-go bar. After one of the shows, we were sitting outside in the garden pub when a young *farang* walked up to us. An American in his early twenties, he was very distraught. He had flown in from Seattle to reunite with a go-go boy he'd met at this bar the previous year, on his first trip to Thailand. The two had kept in touch by e-mail, and the man had told his young lover that he was coming back to see him. But the Thai boy's trail had run cold as soon as the American arrived: he wasn't at Adam's Apple, his apartment, or anywhere else in Chiang Mai. Apart from being worried, the American was growing impatient with his lover's workmates, who weren't being very forthcoming.

I felt sad for him. Truly besotted, he appeared to believe that he was the only *farang* in this boy's life. Contemplating his angst later that night, I couldn't help thinking of a young sex worker from the countryside who had taken part in a study on bar boys in the north, an entrepreneur of the sex trade whose story had been recorded as cultural anthropology:

> By the age of 19, Thirayut had 23 farang men sending him money, mostly on a monthly basis. He had to write almost 50 letters a month to keep the contacts going, and he had to manage his time very well in order not to let two of his sponsors meet each other in Thailand. For example, if one of his sponsors was to arrive on say the 3rd of July, and another on the 5th of July, then he would say to the July 5th man that he had to study until the 10th, after which the July 3rd man would have left. None of the 23 overseas men knew that other people were also sending money to Thirayut. At one point, there was 400,000 baht in his bank account, which he used to build a new concrete house for his parents....[4]

Before my journey through Thailand, I used to see the Asian men I was attracted to as part of my universe – not the other way around. If I liked them, and the feeling was mutual, they came into my orbit – not the reverse. I was the Great White Subject; they were the Immutable Asian Objects. Seeing them as participants in my erotic narrative, I could not possibly account for my own behaviour while I was with them. But after ten weeks in an Asian country, my false dichotomy had been turned on its head. No matter how much sex I was having, nor with how many partners, it was impossible to conduct these relations on any terms other than those of my hosts. In Thailand, I was entering their orbit – not the reverse. Things were often not as they seemed, and I could not control events. And thus I realized that I was no longer the subject of this erotic narrative but, all too often, the Flawed White Object.

---

4. Jan W. De Lind van Wijngaarden, "Between Money, Morality and Masculinity: Bar-Based Male Sex Work in Chiang Mai." *Lady Boys, Tom Boys, Rent Boys: Male and Female Homosexualities in Contemporary Thailand.*

Good Evening, Vietnam

Vietnam is still, more than most places, new to the world. It does
not know what to make of us, nor we of it. Its pleasures feel
unrehearsed, and surprise is still a growth industry.

– Pico Iyer (1991)

XIII
Snapshot: Saigon

It was a hot, humid Saturday night in Ho Chi Minh City – the end of my first day in Vietnam. I was sitting in an open-air sidewalk café in District One, marvelling at the gridlock of motorbikes in front of me, when a group of intoxicated young Vietnamese men arrived at the table next to mine. There were five of them, all in their early twenties, their faces crimson from too much whiskey. They were at that stage of drunkenness when some young men get friendly and others want to fight. Thankfully this group, an odd assortment of jocks and science geeks, belonged to the first category. When one caught me staring, the others turned to look. The one sitting closest, a bookish but handsome fellow with wire-rim glasses, leaned over and breathed his whiskey into my face.

"Why did you come to Vietnam?" he asked. "Why are you here?"

It was a good question. What *was* I doing here? When I landed at Tan Son Nhat Airport that afternoon, I had no credit card or traveller's cheques, and only five American dollars in my pocket: half of what I owed the cab driver bringing me into town and half the going rate for a single night in a two-star hotel. It was my good fortune that the only bank machine in Saigon actually worked.

My hotel, located half an hour's walk from the café, was one of those French colonial walkups with the inner courtyard and winding, wrought-iron staircase that leads to the roof. The hallway-facing window of my fourth-floor room was secured on the outside by an iron grid, my privacy guaranteed from the inside by a gaudy pair of satin drapes. After taking my first shower in Vietnam that afternoon, Thailand already seemed a distant memory – even though just a few hours had passed since my last shower on Khao San Road.

The streets surrounding my hotel were dusty and dry, the air thick with kerosene fumes and motorcycle exhaust. Among the clusters of family shophouses and sidewalk bistros, every other doorway seemed to contain a shirtless young male leaning in its frame, vacantly stroking his belly. Earlier in the evening, a smile from one of these strangers had drawn me to his family's restaurant, where I paid us $1.50 for a heaping plate of fried rice with chicken leg, and a large bottle of Tiger beer. After the meal, I wandered through District One, trying to ignore the humidity that had slowly enveloped me and seemed more oppressive than Bangkok's. My shirt was stuck to my skin, but I didn't stop walking until I found this café. Now, as I waited for my second beer, these pickled youths wanted to know why I'd chosen their country to visit.

∞

> An acid nightmare of modern warfare spilled its devastating horrors across a once tranquil, outstandingly beautiful land. We should have come to learn, to liberate ourselves, rather than obstruct their liberation.[1]

The first time I heard the word "Vietnam" was at the end of January in 1968. I was four years old and depending on my father, who himself was depending on Walter Cronkite, for perspective. As a young boy, I had a vague awareness that terrible things were happening in some faraway jungle. But the grim realities of the war in Southeast Asia were beyond even adult comprehension. In 1979, when I was sixteen, I got hooked on the war narrative of Vietnam when I saw those helicopter rotors fade into the ceiling fan above Captain Willard's bed – the drunken hallucination scene that sets up one of the more memorable opening lines in late-seventies cinema: *Saigon ... shit. I'm still only in Saigon.*

Apocalypse Now was the first Hollywood film to pitch the Vietnam War as surrealist nightmare, with American soldiers being driven insane by a war they no longer knew why they were fighting. The absence of the Vietnamese people themselves as fully realized characters in the film only fueled my curiosity. Who *were* these people? I wouldn't find out much more from the us film industry, which saw Vietnam chiefly as a backdrop for navel-gazing American psychodrama. "Vietnam is no longer a nation or a people," one writer said of the Hollywood syndrome, "but a nexus of signs and sounds that describe, simultaneously, American guilt and American prowess. The 'real' Vietnam, elusive and incapable of

---

1. Tim Page, *Derailed in Uncle Ho's Victory Garden* (London: Scribner, 1999).

realization as it may be, is never even given a chance."[2]

By the early 1990s, when I had grown up and was living in Vancouver, I'd met several Vietnamese men whose families had immigrated to the West. Nhan, an artist whose work graced the walls of my West End apartment, was a smiling trickster who taught me not to take the world, or myself, too seriously. (In a bizarre coincidence, I wouldn't learn until recently that, at the age of nine, he'd been an extra in two scenes of *Apocalypse Now* shot in the Philippines.) Van, a bisexual doorman at Numbers, captured my heart for several months. Peter, the naughty young stockbroker who took me on that joy ride through the streets of Winnipeg, was one of the more thrilling quickies. And Thai Van Tran, my big infatuation in London, still sent Christmas cards eight years after we met. But all these relationships had taken place in the West. With the exception of the feasts Nhan's mother used to lay out for his friends, none involved much exposure to Vietnamese culture. All I knew about the Vietnamese was that they had beaten back several Chinese invasions over the past 1,500 years, fought off the French colonialists, and confounded the US military industrial complex. I also knew that they held book learning in such high esteem that a centuries-old temple devoted to literature was one of Hanoi's main tourist attractions. Brilliant military strategists *and* intellectuals? Clearly, a people worthy of respect.

Now, with the twenty-fifth anniversary of the fall of Saigon approaching, my interest in this country was greater than ever. I wanted to know what kind of life the families of my Vietnamese lovers had left behind – or, at least, what they'd be missing now. I wanted to know how a country could survive so many invasions, and then a quarter century of Communist rule, and still retain a strong sense of itself. And I wanted to discover how my own sense of the Left and romantic visions of class struggle might be challenged by direct exposure to a Communist state. But I didn't know how to say all this to my first acquaintances in Vietnam.

"Vietnam has been talked about a great deal in the western media, but not often accurately," I told my drunken young friends. "Your country has preserved its tradition despite constant attacks from the outside. I find that fascinating. Oh, and I came here to celebrate Liberation Day on April 30."

2. Justin Wintle, *Romancing Vietnam* (New York: Pantheon Books, 1991)

My new comrades nodded approvingly at the last comment, and we raised our glasses in a toast to the New Vietnam. There was a brief exchange of numbers and addresses, and the handsome one – who introduced himself as Le Van Si – wanted to stay and talk with me alone. But he was too drunk, his friends were pestering him to leave, and I was tired, so we said our goodbyes. As I began the return walk to my hotel, the streetlights blacked out – a periodic budget remedy by the local authorities, I was later told. Wandering back in the darkness, I couldn't help thinking about curfews and late night visits by the secret police. When I arrived at the hotel, I had to bang on the gate several times before Som, my host, let me in. Som, who had fallen asleep on the lobby couch while watching television in his pyjamas, was bleary-eyed, but smiled when he greeted me at the door. He was used to foreigners staying out late.

Twenty-five years after the end of what locals called "the American war," the Communist Party's grip on the people of Vietnam was loosening. The process had begun fourteen years earlier with the introduction of *doi moi*, or "openness," the Vietnamese equivalent of Mikhail Gorbachev's *glasnost* and *perestroika*. *Doi moi*, which was supposed to usher in a new era of freedoms for the people, did not gain the expected momentum following the collapse of the Soviet Union. But by the late 1990s, when a brief surge in the economy was followed by a recession, Hanoi was seeking a closer relationship to the West.

Saigon was now Vietnam's centre of trade and business – the city which, under Ho Chi Minh's name, would jumpstart the economy. But it was also a city frozen in time: the "Paris of the Orient" that had never quite cut its ties with the old Gallic occupiers. After a few hours here, one could see why the French might pine for the good old days, much like Cuban exiles in Miami gushed about Havana during the Batista era (the difference being that the French were now welcome in Saigon). With its freshly-painted City Hall and Eiffel's famous Post Office, to the corner patisseries where one could still sit under an awning and read *Le Monde* while sipping French espresso or chomping on baguettes stuffed with camembert, Ho Chin Minh City 2000 could have been Saigon circa 1952, the colonial backdrop for Graham Greene's *The Quiet American*.

One happy coincidence of my visit to Saigon was a reunion with Thai Van Tran, the *Viet Kieu* refugee I'd met in London in 1992. The two of us had kept in contact since I'd left, and it turned out we were both visiting the land of his birth at the same time. Before flying to Southeast Asia, I had imagined the two of us standing outside Reunification Palace on Liberation Day, among the masses, waving our little red flags as a procession of Socialist Republic army tanks rolled by. "Long live independent Vietnam!" I would shout with Thai Van Tran. "Down with imperialists and colonial exploiters!"

The reality was far less romantic. For one thing, this was not my first reunion with Thai: we'd met in Amsterdam two years earlier. Nor was this Thai's first return to Vietnam: he'd been back twice since 1994. Furthermore, he was not arriving alone but with David, his English boyfriend of four years. Finally, Thai did not share my sentimental view of the milestone. For him, April 30 was merely a dark day in history that had made his flight to the West inevitable. As long as his relatives and most Vietnamese remained shackled by poverty and other effects of Communist rule, the very notion of "Liberation Day" – to say nothing of celebrating it with throngs of co-opted tourists and pre-selected cadres in a staged rally – would seem hollow and fraudulent.

Our reunion was supposed to begin in front of the Virgin Mary statue at Notre Dame cathedral – an ironic wink at all those arguments we'd had in London about Thai being the devout Asian Catholic and I the lapsed western one. But Thai and David had overslept after a busy day of touring, so I ended up knocking on their door at the Grand, the four-star hotel where they were staying, on Dong Khoi Street. This famous café strip, whose English translation is "spontaneous general uprising," was known as Rue Catinat during the French occupation and Tu Do ("Freedom") during the South Vietnamese regime. The street's current ideological name was ironic, given all the high-end business startups due to large infusions of foreign cash.

The end result of my long-awaited encounter with Thai Van Tran in Vietnam was to demystify, once and for all, his "otherness" as an Asian refugee to the West. In London, I was all too aware of the things that made him different:

from the superficialities of accent and clothing to the odd combination of Roman Catholicism and flamboyant queerness. But in Saigon, Thai was suddenly far less exotic. He and his partner David, a tall and lanky university librarian of about my age, were – apart from an extreme difference in height – as conventional a gay couple as any I'd met. On the streets of Saigon, where I watched him in action among the locals, haggling for prices like any tourist, I realized just how western Thai Van Tran had become.

Everywhere we went, Thai attracted a lot of attention – and not just because of the two western men walking with him. His eagerness to learn about his own country, and his infectious enthusiasm, turned a lot of heads. Near City Hall, he would stop to speak with young children and street people, peppering them with questions about their lives. Vendors at Ben Thanh market would turn to look as Thai, speaking loudly in English, enthused about some traditional love poem printed on scented stationery. Then there was his wardrobe. One night, Thai left the hotel wearing a high-cut pair of bright, pink shorts and flip-flops for shoes – a most unseemly outfit for an adult Vietnamese male. Children laughed and pointed; their parents glared in disapproval. Thai was oblivious. By flaunting his sexuality in Saigon, he was demonstrating a sense of entitlement – an emotional openness and confidence in his own individual worth that was completely at odds with the collectivist mores of the Socialist Republic. This was a western way of behaving that Thai would never have adopted had he and his mother not fled Vietnam in 1981.

Thai and David were on a package tour that occupied most of their days, so I had plenty of time to explore Saigon on my own. My first guide was Duc, a forty-five-year-old high school teacher moonlighting as a night watchman at my hotel. Duc drove me around on the 1950 Vespa he'd bought when he was fifteen. Thanks to regular upkeep, the little white scooter still ran like a charm, confirming a local maxim that the Vietnamese can repair just about anything. (But then, there's no such thing as "planned obsolescence" in a country where decades of war and economic embargoes make replacement parts hard to find.)

Our first stop was the War Remnants Museum. It used to be called the Museum of American War Crimes, but mid-nineties diplomacy had forced

Hanoi to soften its ideological stance. Still, despite the thaw in Vietnamese-us relations, there was no attempt to soft-pedal American brutality during the war. One display featured photos of mutilated bodies, us soldiers laughing as they held up severed heads like trophies, and children being shot as they tried to flee. To any American who thought the Mai Lai massacre was an aberration, this display provided chilling evidence to the contrary. Outside the museum, as Duc and I sat down to have lunch, we were approached by a young vendor who had a deformed right eye and stumps for arms. (Was it a landmine? Agent Orange? Both?) Carrying a large satchel of books, postcards, and photographs, he wouldn't leave us alone until I bought something. So I picked out a book: Bao Ninh's *The Sorrow of War*, a famous novel about a young North Vietnamese man who's haunted by nightmares when he has to collect the corpses of fallen comrades after the end of the us war. One of the few modern classics approved by the regime, its translated edition was, after *The Quiet American*, Vietnam's biggest selling title in English.

On another afternoon, I dropped by the Metropolitan Hotel on Dong Khoi Street to attend a photo exhibit called "Saigon in Black and White." The photos, by life-long Saigon resident Doan Duc Minh, were still being mounted and some of the captions placed as I entered the hotel lobby to meet the artist. While assistants continued with the installation, Mr Doan took a break to answer a few questions. An advertising specialist, he had worked professionally for twenty years and had an impressive resumé. His client list included most of the major local and foreign corporations in Vietnam. He was also the official photographer for the 1997 visit of George and Barbara Bush.

With "Saigon in Black and White," Mr Doan had set out to capture the human realities of Ho Chi Minh City, warts and all. On the positive side, the future hopes of the people were expressed in a delivery room portrait of the city's first baby of the year ("The baby of the New Millennium in Saigon"). The people's resilience could be seen in "Able War Veteran," which showed an amputee named Mr Quoc thriving as a fish farmer. And Saigon's burgeoning population of millionaires was expressed in "Businessman," which showed Le Trung Hieu, general manager of the Gimiko clock company – an exhibition sponsor – in front of his mansion. But just above that one was "Canal Housing in District 8," a gritty view of slum life in Saigon. "Waiting for Relatives at Tan Son Nhat Airport" showed a crowd of Saigon residents standing behind a roped-off barrier, their faces a canvas of collective weariness and anxiety.

When I asked about the effect of politics on his work, Mr Doan said he enjoyed far more freedom of expression now than a decade ago. Back then, he assured me, he could not have presented photos such as the portrait of a bed-ridden AIDS patient at Binh Trieu Hospital. But as an artist today, he was still subject to government censorship. For example, he had to get official clearance for all the photos displayed – even the wording of the captions. Mr Doan bristled at my suggestion that offering dissenting political views through art might still be a no-no in today's Saigon.

"That's not true," he frowned, before an assistant called him away. "Look around you. Everything you see on the street is politics – the way people live. You can't get away from it, you can't hide it."

I knew what he meant. Most of my time in the city had been spent in District One, but even here I could see the stark contrast between the poverties of Bangkok and Saigon. In the former, panhandlers sat quietly on the ground and *wai*'d passers-by for putting a five-baht coin in their cup. Vendors called out sometimes but always remained at their stalls; taxi drivers tooted their horns once before moving on. But here in District One, beggars and vendors alike swarmed every westerner they saw. Cyclo and motorbike drivers often followed tourists for more than a block before giving up. Every day I was approached by orphaned children, one-eyed amputees, destitute seniors, and street hawkers selling Zippo lighters, newspapers, and portfolios of watercolour folk art – sometimes whole groups of them, while I would be eating in a restaurant. Desperation is political.

Unlike Mr Doan, I was taking photographs in colour with an old, East German Praktica. One morning, as I wandered on foot through the city, I turned my lens on some of the propaganda posters that cluttered the sidewalks of Saigon all month (commemorating the quarter-century anniversary of reunification). Each of these giant, freshly painted billboards bore the classic motifs of socialist realism: the glory of the workers and their visionary leader on a flawless revolutionary path. Wandering from one billboard to the next in a fruitless attempt to find some variation in theme, it occurred to me that my feelings about April 30 had begun to evolve in the days leading up to it. Before this trip, the twenty-fifth anniversary of the fall of Saigon had seemed important only for the *endings* it represented: the final bullets fired, the closing chapter of a long war, the last gasp of foreign occupation. But now I was more interested in the *beginnings* it represented. Specifically, what life was like *after* reunification.

Vietnam's new leaders were not – unlike the Khmer Rouge of Cambodia – demented, genocidal despots hell-bent on erasing history and murdering millions. But while their stewardship of the country was restrained by comparison, the Communists could hardly be described as moderate. Some degree of authoritarianism was inevitable after a long war, especially given the ravaged condition of Vietnam in 1975. But the glory of reunification had been tarnished by show trials, summary executions, "re-education" camps, slave labour, repossession of private property, "snitch" culture, employment by party loyalty, and media censorship. The worst excesses came in the first few years after the war ended. But even now there were glimpses of the old Maoist reflex. One example occurred while I was still in the country, when a forty-three-year-old *Viet Kieu* and Canadian citizen was executed by firing squad in Hanoi.

Ngyuen Thi Hiep and her seventy-four-year-old mother had been languishing on death row since 1996, when they were convicted of smuggling twelve pounds (US $5 million worth) of heroin into the country. Despite compelling evidence that they'd been duped by a notorious smuggling ring – like others before them, they were paid to carry paintings for a supposed import/export firm – and despite an appeal by the Canadian government, Vietnamese authorities carried out Nguyen's execution and didn't release her mother from jail until months later. But I would hear nothing of the case – nor of the diplomatic outrage it caused – until my return to Vancouver. Only then would I learn that Canada had recalled its ambassador, suspended all government contact, postponed annual meetings on development aid, withdrawn assistance for Vietnam's WTO bid, and boycotted all state-sponsored celebrations of April 30 – an event I'd come to witness and, unaware of a boycott, eventually would.

Meanwhile, Thai Van Tran and his partner David had left Saigon. Continuing their tour in Dalat, they would gradually head north and spend April 30 in Hanoi before returning to London a few days later. Now on my own, I was eager to experience more meaningful contact with local Vietnamese people. So far, all I'd had were glimpses. First, there was Le Van Si, the young man I'd met on my first night in Saigon. He and his drunken friends were university students who all spoke Russian and wondered why I didn't. Then there was the khaki-clad soldier who guided me through the Cu Chi tunnels: a slender young cadre born long after reunification, he parroted every pronouncement of the Viet Cong as if he'd actually been part of the war – his historical authenticity allowing for a more satisfactory tourist experience. But gradually, the longer I stayed in Vietnam, these glimpses became suffused with desire....

Snapshot: Cai Be. On a ferry ride during an overnight trip through the Mekong Delta, I was gazing toward the riverbank, wondering what it must have been like to pass through these waters in 1968 (and how on earth the Americans expected to win this war) when I spotted a shirtless peasant boy reclining on the verandah of his bamboo house. The casual elegance of his pose was striking: the way he stared at our boat through long bangs of jet-black hair, the gracefulness of his outstretched right leg and how he kept his left leg propped up at the knee, his left hand hanging off it, like he was sitting for a portrait painter. Later, in a small island village, another half-naked youth cast a spell on me: a young rice pounder, doing his work in the back room of a corrugated tin shack that served as a rice cake factory. Dressed only in fisherman's trousers, his long hair tied back in a ponytail, this perfect specimen of Vietnamese masculinity stood beside a piping hot urn and, clutching a large wooden mallet with both hands, pounded the grain into soft, puffy rice. As he performed this ritual, tiny beads of sweat trickled down his smooth hard chest and onto his washboard stomach. Long after the other tourists had moved on to the next room, I continued snapping photos of his immaculate beauty, prompting the slightest trace of a smile from him.

Later, on a ferry across the Upper Delta, I was sitting on a bench inside the car deck when I was suddenly joined by a smooth, dark-skinned local boy with big brown eyes, thick red lips, and neatly trimmed brown hair that was dusted with blond streaks. His age was hard to place – he could have been anywhere from fifteen to his early twenties – and he looked as though he belonged somewhere else, somewhere more urban. When I caught him looking at my Praktica, he pointed at it and then at himself. So I focused on his face and snapped two close-ups. His eyes melted into the lens – he didn't smile at the camera so much as gaze into it, searchingly.

When I put down the camera he rose from the bench, still staring, and walked past me to climb a ladder to the roof. I looked around to see if anyone was watching, then followed him up the ladder. Up on the roof, I couldn't find him. A few minutes later I spotted him on the bow, stepping out of the captain's cabin. When he saw me watching him he pulled out a pack of cigarettes from his jeans, took out a stick, lit it, and puffed. I captured him in my viewfinder doing this, beneath the blood-red flag of Vietnam that flew above the captain's cabin. When the ferry reached the dock, I watched him in the crowd of foot passengers leading the way off the boat. In the village, as our van sped away from the terminal, he turned into a dark alley and vanished.

IXV
Kieu & Cai

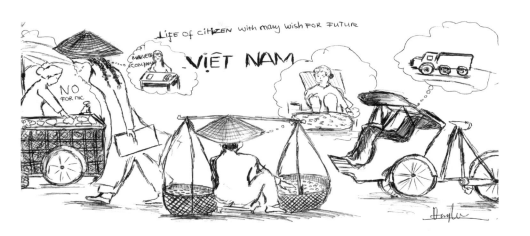

DEEP IN THE HEART OF SAIGON'S DISTRICT ONE, amid the clutter of tourist cafés and budget guesthouses, was one of those backpacker ghettoes like Khao San Road that seemed to be cropping up all over Southeast Asia. De Tanh Street offered some of the cheapest rooms in Ho Chi Minh City, which is why I decided to switch hotels and move there a few days into my visit. At the five-storey guesthouse I chose, the only vacancy was the penthouse unit. It came with an outdoor water closet in the middle of a rooftop garden that offered a panoramic view of District One. With Internet access, laundry, and restaurant facilities under one roof, it was a steal at three bucks a night.

The manager was an outgoing, twenty-eight-year-old Saigon native named Kieu. From the moment I checked in, Kieu went out of his way to make me feel welcome. Within hours of my arrival, he had taken me on his motorbike to a camera repair shop near city hall, a public swimming pool in Cholon on the south side of town, and a sidewalk café near the municipal zoo. This was well beyond the call of duty, but Kieu insisted there were no strings attached; that he was simply showing gratitude for my decision to move to his guesthouse.

Later that night, as I was sitting in the restaurant writing postcards, Kieu joined me at my table and plunked a bottle of snake wine down between us. All the other customers had filtered out into the night; the staff had gone either home or upstairs to sleep. After toasting each other's health, we proceeded to pour the rancid brew down our throats. I continued writing; Kieu pulled out a sketchpad and began drawing.

Several glasses later, he presented me with an elaborate cartoon of Saigon street scenes revealing the private thoughts of Vietnamese "with many wish for future." An *ao dai*-clad woman at a food stall, wishing she could run her own company. A vendor carrying baskets of betel nuts across her shoulders, wishing she could take a holiday on the beach. And – poetic touch – a cyclo wishing it were a truck. The cartoon was accompanied by a lengthy personal greeting in Kieu's broken English: a declaration of pride in his country, best wishes for a good vacation, and an affectionate thank you for choosing his guesthouse. When I looked up at Kieu, he was gazing into my eyes.

Kieu was not at all attractive. His features were homely, his skin pockmarked, and his body odour intense. But now, with the restaurant empty and both of us drunk, he was making overtures. I was about to thank him for the drawing and turn in for the night when he handed me a second drawing: a cartoon profile of a sad Vietnamese peasant girl. As I pondered what to do next, he took my hand and began sharing his life story. To satisfy his parents, he said, he had promised to get married when he turned forty. But until then, it was the company of men he craved most.

"What are you trying to say?" I asked. "That you want to come to my room?"

"Yes."

∞

> It's a cliché to call them children – but there's one thing which is childish. They love you in return for kindness, security, the presents you give them – they hate you for a blow or an injustice. They don't know what it's like – just walking into a room and loving a stranger.
> – Graham Greene, *The Quiet American*

Within moments of closing my door behind him, Kieu abandoned all pretense of professional decorum and came on like a lovesick hound dog. Before I could offer him a seat he was planting his tongue in my mouth, pulling me onto the bed, and begging me to fuck him – undaunted that two of his maids were sleeping on the hallway floor outside my room, only inches away from where we'd be doing it. Just before cumming, he whispered the three words that one stranger should never say to another: "I love you." When it was over, he wiped himself off, kissed me, and opened the door. "See you tomorrow," he said, gently tiptoeing over the two sleeping housemaids and making his way downstairs. I fell asleep wondering what I'd gotten myself into.

Early the next morning, Kieu barged into my room without knocking, to see how I'd slept. This was the first of four such intrusions he would make that day – a violation of boundaries indicating that ours was no longer a business relationship. When Kieu reminded me of his promise the day before to take me back to the camera shop, I insisted on going alone. But he wouldn't hear of it. When the appointed hour arrived, he burst into my room again and told me to get ready. After picking up the repaired Praktica,

I assumed that we'd come back to the guesthouse. But Kieu had other plans. Instead, he took me on an hour-long joyride that ended about ten kilometres outside District One. Only when I begged him a third time did he finally agree to return to the guesthouse.

There, on the sidewalk outside the patio, he revealed a new plan.

"I put motorbike away and then come up and lie beside you?" he asked, oblivious to the baffled looks from his staff (who must have been wondering why he had suddenly abandoned his responsibilities – and them – to serve as my personal tour guide).

"Um, I'd prefer to be alone," I said.

Upstairs, I packed a bag with swim trunks and bolted the door. Then I raced back downstairs, hailing a cyclo before Kieu could notice my departure.

"Take me to the swimming pool," I said, "behind Reunification Palace."

During the American war, the District One swimming pool was a favourite workout venue for US marines; now it was one of Saigon's most popular gay cruising grounds. When I arrived, the men's locker room was filled with Vietnamese students and yuppies, along with a few shifty-eyed white men. The patio was like a backdrop for a Bruce Weber shoot or a *Physique Pictorial* spread from the sixties. Divided by a towering white column of Greco-Roman pillars, the deck was filled on one side with muscle boys flexing their massive pecs in a makeshift gym and, on the other, youthful ectomorphs preening about the patio in bulging Speedos. A few metres from the gym, a railing separated the patio from a tropical garden and manicured lawns below. This corner of the deck offered a quiet respite from all the eye candy – or a good place to get acquainted with a new friend.

In the locker room, I caught the eye of a young local talking with an older foreigner. Dressed in a navy blue tank top and black nylon shorts cut just below his ass, he had a long, trim body with a smooth chest and firm, round buns. He also had a sweet, impish face with eyes that sparkled as I passed behind the man he was chatting with. When I came back a few moments later, he was alone.

His name was Le Van Cai. He was twenty-one, a student of English and history. He said he was getting ready to leave when I arrived, but would be happy to stay and accompany me as I swam.

"I'd like that," I said, relishing the thought of Le Van Cai in a bikini.

After a few lengths we got out of the pool and headed to the corner above the garden. Leaning against the railing, Cai turned to face me, his smooth brown skin shimmering in the late afternoon sun, still slippery from the swim.

"Foreign friend always come and go – it's boring for me," he said, repeating a theme I'd heard all too often in Thailand: "I hope I know you long time."

After getting dressed, we crossed the street for an early supper of broiled steak and tomatoes served on large wooden trays. Cai had an evening English class to attend, but wanted to meet again afterwards. So I told him to call me at the guesthouse when he was done.

Kieu was outside chatting with customers when I returned to the guest-house.

"Where have you been?" he asked with a frozen smile. He seemed irritated by my absence – as if he expected to be informed of all my plans. By this point I was feeling suffocated by him; I needed to put some distance between us.

"I went to the District One swimming pool," I said, "and met a nice boy there. I'll be seeing him later tonight."

Kieu laughed as I brushed past him and went upstairs to take a nap. I was being cruel, but I didn't know how else to deal with the situation. Surely Kieu, a professional in the hospitality industry, would understand.

But no: an hour later, he barged in again. He was flustered, out of breath.

"Telephone!" he shouted.

"Who is it?" I asked, standing up. Of course, it could only be Cai.

"He says he will be late," Kieu frowned. "You have friend?"

"Yes, I told you already. Weren't you listening?"

With that he stepped forward and punched me in the right shoulder. Then he retreated, hesitated, and lunged at me again, punching me in the chest hard enough to hurt. When I looked up at him, his face was creased with a pained grimace. He stormed out of the room and down the staircase in a huff. I followed. Halfway down, he stopped and turned around.

"If you go with that boy tonight," he said, pointing a finger, "I don't want to see you again. I will not talk to you." Then he continued down the stairs.

Was he serious? Yes: after one drunken roll in the hay, my guesthouse manager was in love with me, the effects of a bottle of snake wine earning him exclusive rights to my cock for the rest of my stay in Vietnam. The question of whether such a relationship with a foreign tourist was feasible did not seem to have occurred to Kieu. But then, it hadn't occurred to *me* that inviting a lonely closet case to my bed might, in a country like Vietnam, be playing with fire.

When I picked up the phone in the bar, Cai's cheerful voice was on the other end. He apologized for being late and promised to arrive in half an hour; I told him not to hurry. Then, after hanging up, I approached Kieu and tried to smooth things over. No luck. While speaking with Cai on the phone, I had spotted Kieu glaring at me from the outside patio as he was clearing tables. Now he was putting on a brave face – smiling for customers, maintaining his composure – but he had made up his mind. "You go find new hotel," he snapped, avoiding eye contact. "I don't want to see you anymore."

I was in no position to argue. Once I'd lost the good will of my host, there was no point staying. I had visions of Kieu in the kitchen the next morning, spitting into my breakfast coffee. Or worse.

But I couldn't move out just yet. A few minutes later, Cai showed up wearing a snug-fitting white shirt and pants, his short black hair gelled and neatly combed to one side; *very* come hither. For young gay men in Saigon, there were few better places to go for sex than the hotel rooms of the foreigners they met. I didn't know how to tell Cai, without spilling the beans about Kieu, that an upstairs rendezvous would not be a good idea. So I took him to a bar on the Saigon River, and tried to postpone our first sexual encounter. Cai squeezed my hand under the table, saying he wanted to "see" my room. I called for the bill.

Back at the guesthouse, Kieu was nowhere to be seen. But a six-year-old boy who lived on the second floor was waiting in the rooftop garden when we arrived. The moment Cai entered the water closet, he ran downstairs. Minutes later, Cai was sitting on my bed and I was about to bolt the door when I felt a strong push from the other side: it was Kieu, using all his strength to force it open. I stepped aside. Kieu's face was a mask of rage as he fell into the room.

"You have to go now," he said, pointing the way out. "We not allow this here."

Technically speaking, he was right – and had all the leverage of Vietnamese culture and law to back him up. Tourist guesthouses did *not* allow local visitors, and man-to-man sex was officially regarded as a "cultural infraction." So: would Kieu take the Stalinist route and snitch on us, knowing that a single phone call would be enough to get my new friend – and maybe even me – into a world of trouble? Looking into his frantic eyes, I doubted it. It had, after all, been less than twenty-four hours since Kieu had said he loved me as I was fucking his ass on the floor on the very spot where he now stood.

"Come on," I told Cai. "Let's pack my things. It's time to find another hotel."

The disaster with Kieu should have been my first clue that the rules governing sex and friendship in Thailand didn't necessarily apply everywhere in Southeast Asia – especially in a country that had been, until recently, a closed society. In Thailand, the influence of Buddhism and more than a century of mass tourism could smooth over even the roughest edges of contact with foreigners. But in Vietnam, where desperation was never far from the surface, nothing could be taken for granted. The strangest part was that, the longer I stayed in Southeast Asia, the greater the excitement I derived from the oddly unpredictable sense of danger in the air, the more willing I was to take risks, lose control, surrender to circumstance. There were many chances to do that in Vietnam.

A few months after my trip to the South, I flew to Hanoi to witness the appearance of Bill Clinton, the first US president to land in Vietnam since the end of the war. As I wandered through the city on the night Clinton arrived, a seventeen-year-old hustler invited me to join him and an older man on the back of their motorbike. Although it was pitch black outside, with no way of anyone tracking my whereabouts, I accepted the offer. After quietly considering the worst that could happen, I was helpless as the worst *did* happen: the teenager drove us down an even darker street before stopping at a dilapidated building, where he led me upstairs to a room with an automatic door lock. There we sat alone and crooned to each other accompanied by a karaoke machine while a "waiter" brought us drinks. Then, after aggressively unzipping me and delivering a blowjob I didn't want, the youth got the "waiter" to hand me a bill for a hundred US dollars. I bolted from my chair, pushed past the waiter, fled the building, and did not stop running until I found my guest-house in the Old Quarter. Meanwhile, a few blocks away, Bill Clinton was setting up shop in his $1,500-a-night room at the Daewoo Hotel, preparing for meetings in which he and Tran Duc Luong would share congratulatory platitudes about the wonders of globalization.

The ten days I spent with Le Van Cai in Ho Chi Minh City offered no such dangers. Instead, I got to know him personally. Like many of his countrymen born after reunification, Cai was someone whose fortunes were determined by events long preceding his birth. The first twist of fate came in 1955 in the Mekong Delta village of Thap Muoi, a few hours' drive west of Saigon. Thap Muoi was a nerve centre for Viet Minh nationalists, Communists, and other anti-French revolutionaries fighting to end colonial rule. (Later, Americans would know it as the Plain of Reeds – a crucial base for the Viet Cong.) After the French defeat in the North at Dien Bien Phu in May of 1954, the separation of North and South Vietnam was supposed to last only two years before elections were held and reunification proceedings began. But the ink was barely dry on the Geneva agreement when Ngo Dinh Diem returned from nearly four years of exile to become the new, CIA-approved leader of South Vietnam.

Diem was a right-wing Catholic mystic who lived, it was said, "in a mental cocoon spun out of a nostalgic reverie for Vietnam's imperial past."[1] A petty sadist with Vatican-like pretensions of moral authority, Diem rejected the Geneva agreement and declared himself absolute ruler of the new Republic of South Vietnam. Soon his regime began strafing Mekong Delta villages with bombs and machine gun fire to hunt down rebels. After one of these bomb attacks killed Cai's maternal grandmother, his grandfather, who was a Communist, decided to flee to the North with his son and three daughters. But the eldest daughter – Cai's mother, Hoan Thu – didn't want to go. At age ten, she was allowed to stay with an aunt in Saigon while the rest of the family fled to Hanoi. It wasn't long afterward that Diem signed a decree preventing

1. Neil Sheehan, *A Bright Shining Lie* (New York: Random House, 1988).

anyone who had moved North from ever returning to the South. Hoan Thu wouldn't see her father and siblings again for twenty years.

In 1967, at age twenty-two, she fell in love with and married a low-ranking soldier from the Army of the Republic of Vietnam (ARVN) named Van Vuong. The war with the Americans was in full swing when the couple had their first son in 1968 and first daughter in 1970. Another boy was born in 1973, another girl a year later. Just before the fall of Saigon in 1975, Vuong considered smuggling his wife and children out of the country to avoid capture by the Viet Cong. But he changed his mind when he learned how many were losing their lives in the attempt. Vuong's brother Thuc, an employee of the psychology department, was captured a few days after Saigon fell on April 30. Convicted of sending radio transmissions urging northerners to abandon Communism, he was sentenced to three years in a re-education camp. Vuong was convinced he wouldn't suffer the same fate. By war's end, he hadn't risen beyond the position of bodyguard to an ARVN colonel: what possible threat could he pose to the new regime? When the secret police came knocking three months after April 30, he found out: the government, planning its first land reform projects, needed workers to build a commune in Tay Ninh. Vuong was told to move his family there.

"The government make it sound very good, but they lie," said Cai, describing the slave labour conditions. "The land was very bad. The people have to start their lives again from nothing." Vuong needed an excuse to avoid going. When he told the police his wife was pregnant with a fifth child and expecting the following spring, they gave him an exemption. In 1976, a boy named Le Van Cai was born, and Vuong and Hoan Thu were recorded as the parents. But this boy, Cai said, was not him; it was his *cousin*. The Cai that I knew would be born two years later. So what happened?

When Vuong told the secret police in the fall of 1975 that his wife was pregnant, the authorities took him at his word. Had they bothered to check up on Hoan Thu over the next six months, they would have found no signs of swelling in her tummy. In fact, it wasn't Hoan Thu who was pregnant but Vuong's sister-in-law, who lived in another province. When the woman gave birth to a baby boy in the spring of 1976, Vuong forged a copy of the birth certificate so he could register the birth in his own province, naming himself as the father and Hoan Thu the mother of a boy who was actually their nephew. When the police visited shortly afterward, the couple presented the boy as their son and showed the papers to prove it. The plan worked: the police didn't ask questions, and Vuong's family was spared a life of slavery in Tay Ninh.

Early in 1978, Vuong ran off with another woman. At first, Hoan Thu was devastated. But soon her husband was coming back for visits – including to the marriage bed. When Hoan Thu told Vuong she was pregnant, however, he denied the baby was his and accused his wife of seeing another man. On December 1, 1978, Hoan Thu gave birth to a boy. Vuong refused to visit her in the hospital, told everyone the child was not his, and threatened to throw the baby into the Saigon River. His brother, Tu Hai – father of the boy whose birth certificate had saved Vuong from the commune – visited Hoan Thu in the hospital. Vuong withdrew his threat when he heard that the baby looked just like him, but he still refused to register the birth. Hoan Thu was desperate to keep her new child. So, after forging the birth date, Vuong gave her a new copy of their nephew's birth certificate so that their new son would also be named Le Van Cai. Until the age difference between the two boys was no longer noticeable, there wasn't a day that Hoan Thu didn't worry about being caught.

Since then, said Cai, his father Vuong had been with several other women. He now lived near the rice paddies on the outskirts of Saigon, working as a farmer. Throughout Cai's childhood, Vuong had visited the family home several times, begging Hoan Thu to take him back. But his earlier threat to drown Cai had destroyed their marriage; Hoan Thu vowed to remain single for the rest of her life. Today, Vuong still visited his wife and youngest son every month, even providing financial support. But Cai didn't regard him as a father. "I don't like him," he said. "He show no duty to wife and children."

Cai's older siblings had long since left home and raised their own families. Cai lived alone with Hoan Thu, who had raised him to be a good Buddhist. Each day, mother and son went to a pagoda and prayed for a better life. Hoan Thu was fifty-five when I met her, but she looked a decade older. Before reunification, she had been a schoolteacher. But after April 30, 1975, all the best jobs went to Communists. Hoan Tu was told she would have to learn Russian if she wanted to teach in a Saigon school again. She refused. Since then, she had spent her prime years working as a housekeeper. Now and then she earned extra cash running errands for her aunt, a privileged

Communist who had moved from the North after reunification.

Hoan Thu hated the Communists. For a choice she had made at the age of ten – to stay in the South – she had suffered ever since. When I gave Cai a Viet Cong scarf I'd bought at the Cu Chi Tunnels, he said he'd have to hide it from his mother because she would probably burn it. On the day I visited their small townhouse in District Three, far from the tourist centre in a narrow lane off Levansi Street, Hoan Thu stayed in the kitchen to make lunch while Cai rolled out a large rattan mat on the living room floor so we could have a nap. Later, Hoan Thu called up the next-door neighbour and invited him over to cut my hair. He did a fine job for two bucks. Afterward, one of Cai's sisters arrived with her baby boy. I took photos. Cai took me back to my hotel on his motorbike, happy that I had met his family.

Tuesday night was gay night at Sam Son disco – unadvertised, due to the "cultural infraction" law. The techno mix was hot, and the floor was filled with well-scrubbed young men wearing designer labels. Lovers embraced openly while, off in a darkened corner, a group of men in their late fifties tried to blend in. At first I found their presence unsettling: their dour green military uniforms suggested they were long-time party members. But Cai told me not to worry, and the longer I watched them, the clearer it became that these cadres were not there to spy on us: tapping their boots, swaying out of time with the music, they were there to boogie. These were self-repressed revolutionaries who, having waited for *doi moi* to clear the cobwebs from their souls, were only now cracking open the closet door, dusting off the ideological blinders, taking cues from the next generation on how to be In the Life.

At last, April 30 had arrived. Instead of spending it with Thai Van Tran, a *Viet Kieu* who had escaped Vietnam for a better life in the West, it seemed appropriate that I would be spending it with someone born and raised after reunification. But I didn't expect to begin the day at six o'clock in the morning, when Cai nudged me awake to have sex.

"Why so early?" I yawned, as he rolled a condom onto me. I hadn't seen a schedule of events, but I couldn't imagine the parade getting under way much earlier than noon. Cai said it would all be over by nine o'clock because the government preferred to address The People while they were still fresh.

Of course, he was right. When we arrived at Reunification Palace at nine, the speeches were over and the last of the soldiers were filing out of the gates. The front lawn was empty, except for a few scattered leaflets floating on the breeze. "It's okay," said Cai, reassuring me. "The speeches are long and boring anyway." Outside the gates, a large crowd watched the final parade entries, a troupe of dragon dancers in flaming red outfits, leave the palace grounds. Then it was time to pay our respects to the Father of Independence.

Every major city in Vietnam has a Ho Chi Minh Museum. The one in the city named for him featured some of the clothes he wore during famous campaigns, along with statues, busts, photographs and – of course – quotations. But my enthusiasm for the legend was not shared by Cai, who said nothing about "Uncle Ho" during our visit to the museum and seemed anxious to leave.[2]

For supper that night, I took Cai to the Rex Hotel, whose rooftop bar had once been a favourite watering hole of the author Graham Greene. The Rex was putting on an April 30 banquet billed as "Vui Ngay Hoi Lon," or "Happy Festive Events." But the events were not quite as "festive" as advertised. While the food was fair and the live performances top-notch, most of the tables were empty. Given its legendary reputation, I had thought the Rex would be one of the city's happening places on April 30. But instead it seemed that to all but party officials and diehard historians, April 30 was just another day. When the event mercifully ended after four hours, we returned to my hotel and crashed.

The next day was May Day: the international Communist holiday and part two of a Marxist doubleheader in Vietnam. While most of his countrymen took the day off, Cai wanted to study. That was fine with me: I had spent the better part of ten days with Cai, and I needed a break. Solitude was a privilege

2. In his comprehensive biography, *Ho Chi Minh: A Life* (New York: Theia/Hyperion, 2000), William J. Duiker argues that contemporary Vietnamese youth regard Uncle Ho more as a tourist magnet than as a guiding light for modern life: "To the new generation raised in the shadow of the next millennium, Ho Chi Minh probably has no more relevance than does Abraham Lincoln to the average American."

of travel I had come to appreciate. Back home, "solitude" meant staying alone in my apartment. In Southeast Asia, it implied endless opportunities for discovery.

∞

I didn't need any more sex on this trip. Apart from overdosing in Thailand, the fallout from the snake wine incident with Kieu had proven that casual sex was an oxymoron in Vietnam. Besides which, Cai was an eager lover; being twenty-one, he typically wanted to fuck three times a day. So I was not in a cruisy frame of mind when I paid a final visit to the District One swimming pool on May Day. This time, the outside patio was awash in Communist nostalgia. Dangling two feet above the water, on rows of cable that ran from one end of the pool to the other, were dozens of tiny Soviet Union flags. The blood red banners with their golden hammers and sickles cut a dramatic contrast with the blue sky above as they flapped noisily in the breeze. On opposite sides of the pool, two lifeguards sat Sphinx-like atop their high chairs while fresh young men wandered back and forth, making eye contact with one another. Soft Vietnamese love songs filtered through the sound system.

One of the men on the patio was a skinny nineteen-year-old in a blue Speedo who had pawed at my groin in the locker room earlier. By the end of the afternoon, Blue Speedo and I had groped each other in the water, then returned to the locker room and shared a private shower in which "cultural infractions" took place. Blue Speedo sighed as my tongue ran circles around his salty brown nipples and down his torso. Here, in a moldy shower stall at a public swimming pool in a repressive socialist republic, the body of a horny nineteen-year-old tasted like ambrosia. Someone else evidently thought so, too: for the second time that week, an intimate moment I was enjoying with a young local was interrupted by another Vietnamese man trying to force open the door from the other side. Until I saw who it was, I was in a state of panic – assuming it was the police, or some other authority coming to put a stop to our pleasure. I had visions of my name appearing in the North American press at the beginning of some lengthy extradition battle. But no: it was just another horny swimmer, a Vietnamese man in his late forties, wanting to have a go at the foreigner.

∞

Back at the hotel that night, I didn't tell Cai about Blue Speedo. I was going home the next day; why spoil a perfectly sweet holiday fling? Before meeting Kieu and Cai, I had scoffed at the clichéd notion of a "fragile Vietnamese heart" as described in *The Men of Vietnam* guidebook. But now I had learned of it firsthand. The week before April 30, I had taken Cai on a hovercraft voyage down the Saigon River to Vung Tau, once a favourite retirement spot for Soviet Russians. It had been a lazy couple of days of sand, surf, and sex. On the second night, we sat on Vung Tau's wide-open sandbar at low tide, with no one else on the beach and the moon and the stars bathing us in their glow. Gazing out at the South China Sea, Cai told me how much he wished I could stay in Vietnam and be his boyfriend. Then he sang a sad Vietnamese ballad about a man and a woman who are in love but can't marry because the man is poor and the girl's family doesn't approve of him.

Five years after our casual holiday fling, Cai was still sending e-mails, wondering when I'd be back.

Going Native

It is easy to imagine the giddy sense of freedom felt by Englishmen from rainy northern towns, or Americans from god-fearing Midwestern plains, when they came to Japan, or Thailand, or Ceylon, or wherever their idea of Arcadia happened to be. Because local constraints did not apply to them, and they were far from home, everything suddenly seemed possible.

– Ian Buruma, *The Missionary and the Libertine*

XV
Instant Expat

AFTER THREE MONTHS OF TECHNICOLOUR adventure in Southeast Asia, returning to Vancouver was like waking up in a black-and-white rerun of Rod Serling's *The Twilight Zone*. The natural beauty was still there, but the landscape had a post-apocalyptic dullness about it. After the cacophony of Saigon and Bangkok, the silence in the air was disconcerting; the downtown grid, "high density" by local standards, was like a ghost town. *Where were all the people?* Then there was the climate: while I walked around the West End wearing a sweater, shivering on sunny afternoons, other young men wore tank tops. Winter had given way to spring since my departure. But now I was cold, and everyone else was hot.

I was glad to see family and friends again, but I didn't care what they had done in my absence. Instead of asking about their lives, I kept on showing photos of my journey – sometimes more than once. In the city, things that had drawn me to Vancouver more than a decade earlier now seemed lame or uninspiring. An evening out in the Davie Street bars, which I once anticipated with a sense of excitement, no longer held such promise. And Club Vancouver, once my favourite all-night bathhouse, was depressing to behold – a stinking dungeon of bad hygiene after the pristine, garden oasis of the Babylon Bangkok.

From the moment I landed, all I could think about was getting back on the plane. Still high from the journey, I was glowing in that typical first phase of a westerner's reaction to his chosen lotusland: "sensuous and sensual delight."[1] In such a phase, every moment of first contact with one's Asian Shangri-la is recalled through the rose-tinted lens of nostalgia. One afternoon, as I rode my bike around the Stanley Park seawall plugged into a Walkman, I managed to tune out the spectacular scenery of Burrard Inlet as a recent hit song from the Thai pop charts transported me back to the Kingdom.

"Yud Trong Nee Tee Ter" ("Stop Right Here") was a lush, romantic ballad sung by Supachai Grai Yoorasean, better known as "Ford." In the song, the pop star triumphantly proclaims the end of his search for love: he has finally found the perfect woman. Ford's rich, sexy baritone and convincing

---

1. Arthur Koestler, *The Lotus and the Robot* (London: Hutchinson, 1966).

delivery made him a kind of Cupid, and his song the perfect anthem, for my love affair with his country. After repeated listenings over ten weeks in Thailand, "Yud Trong Nee Tee Ter" now haunted my every moment, bringing me back to the sands of Koh Phi Phi, the motorbike ride through the Golden Triangle, the ruins of Sukhothai, the Portuguese family house in Phetchaburi, the monk ordination ceremony in Sri Satchenalai, the Sukhumvit Road noodle stalls, the neon lights of Silom *soi* 4, and the smooth, brown thighs of all those sweet young lovers. "Stop Right Here," indeed....

I had left Thailand in the middle of *Songkran*, the country's New Year water festival – one of the few occasions that *farang* take part in a civic celebration of Thai culture. The day before getting on the plane to Saigon, I had joined Wit, Bee, and some of their moneyboy friends on Khao San Road, the centre of *Songkran* activities in Bangkok. Thousands of local Thais and foreign tourists had crammed into the backpacker strip to hose each other down with giant water guns, or cake each other's faces with talcum powder. As I forced my way through the throbbing hot mass of slippery wet bodies, hands kept stroking my cheeks, painting me with Songkran mud. One beautiful Thai stranger, pushing through the crowd in the opposite direction, found my hand at waist level as he passed. Entwining his fingers in mine, he gazed lustfully into my eyes and ran his thumb down my palm before the current of bodies separated us and he disappeared into a sea of faces. *How could I leave this place?*

As it turned out, I wasn't leaving for very long. Only six weeks after getting on the plane to Vietnam, and a month after flying home to Vancouver, I was back on a plane to Bangkok, making the transition from tourist to expatriate without so much as a backward glance. Such an impulsive decision was as much a result of good timing as euphoric enchantment. Toward the end of the Chiang Mai visit, I had begun to ponder what it might be like to live in the Land of Smiles: to learn to speak Thai; to adopt some of the cultural ways; to simmer in the "noodle soup" of desire; to "go native." It was about the same time that I spotted an ad in *The Nation* newspaper calling for foreign sub editors. I applied immediately. Two weeks later, I was sitting in the deputy managing editor's office, accepting a job offer. After flying home from Vietnam, I was to take no more than a month to sort out my affairs before returning to Bangkok on my own funds. We sealed the deal with a handshake.

For the westerner who settles in his Eastern Arcadia immediately after discovering it, the most important adjustment is not culture shock; it's the rapid transition from traveller to expatriate. In Thailand, my reception as a wandering vagabond had felt like a giant, non-stop caress – as it too often was, in the literal sense. Drunk on that feeling, like a gambler who gets lucky on his first visit to Vegas, I was convinced that all the good karma I'd experienced as a tourist would keep on flowing for me as a resident. What I hadn't considered was how the shift in circumstances – forsaking the beaches and boys for buses and business attire, so soon after returning to the scene of the fantasy – would alter my perception not only of Thailand but also of all those so-called "magical" experiences I'd enjoyed. If I had never returned to the country but instead summarized my half-baked perceptions in a piece of travel journalism, the resulting story would barely have scratched the surface. It takes far more than a whirlwind trip to understand a country, its people, or even who you are while you're there. Thankfully, my sobering passage from gallivanting sex tourist to office professional took care of that.

My new job in Bangkok, at *The Nation* newspaper, required my daily presence in a twin set of office towers on the Bangna-Trat highway, about five kilometres east of where Sukhumvit Road crosses *soi* 101 – the far southeast of Bangkok. Most foreigners have no reason to find themselves anywhere near the Bangna-Trat unless they're on a bus bound for Pattaya, Koh Samet, or Cambodia. Lined with a dreary assortment of industrial plants and scrapyards, the giant Central department store, and BiTec exhibition centre, Bangna-Trat was the Sixteen-Wheeler Row of Bangkok – a smog-filled confluence of all the concrete and traffic gridlock of the capital's south end.

At thirty years of age, *The Nation* was the English-language upstart of the Thai press, the only competitor to the *Bangkok Post*. Its reputation as the more "progressive" of the two papers was established in its early years, when it took a strong human rights stance against the military dictatorship of the day. But apart from the *Post's* higher circulation figures and more conservative editorial slant, the two had much in common. The approach to newsgathering and layout was nearly identical, as were the staff structure and general quality. Like the *Post*, *The Nation* employed a large pool of Thai nationals as reporters and senior editors, a team of Thai translators to produce rough drafts of their work in English, and about twenty or thirty western sub editors to edit the copy. "Subbing" was divided by section – news and business, features, and sports.

Whatever shape it arrived in, any story under a Thai writer's byline had to read, by the next morning's edition, as if a native English speaker had written it. That's where I came in. Subbing was an easy job, once you learned the local ways of thinking. But it was a delicate process as well – especially in news and business. For even the slightest blunder of interpretation could lead to an error, thus inspiring the wrath of both writer and subject. In Thailand, the rarest of screw-ups could result in an offense against the much-loved monarchy.

The year I moved to Thailand, the Kingdom was still reeling from two major events that had unfolded within months of each other in 1997: the regional economic crisis and the signing of the People's Constitution. The baht devaluation had led to widespread bankruptcy, massive job losses, and disappearing fortunes. The Constitution, which called for electoral reform and the establishment of legal entities to deal with corruption, was seen as the final piece of the puzzle that would lead the country to democracy. Thailand was under the stewardship of a moderate liberal government led by Democrat Chuan Leekpai, a dull but honest technocrat whose return from Opposition for a second term as premier was expected to lead the country back to prosperity. After three years, Chuan's incremental approach to economic recovery hadn't won many converts, and a new political movement was gaining steam.

Thaksin Shinawatra, a former police officer, had served in the Chavalit Yonghaiyudh cabinet in the late nineties just before Chuan resumed office. Now CEO of telecom giant Shin Corporation, he had a few things in common with another billionaire aiming to lead his country at about the same time. Like Silvio Berlusconi and his Forza Italia ("Go, Italy!") party, Thaksin had formed his own, patriotic party, Thai Rak Thai ("Thais love Thais") after becoming his country's richest man. The fact that Thaksin appealed to such a large cross section of the electorate – despite the country's intelligentsia labelling him a dangerous autocrat – spoke volumes about the country I was embracing.

Thaksin won the January 2001 election in a landslide despite his mid-campaign conviction, by the recently formed National Counter Corruption Commission, on charges of deliberate concealment of assets. In most western democracies, a frontrunning candidate who suffered such a blow would be forced by public pressure, if not conscience, to withdraw. But this was Thailand. Since the Constitution Court could not issue a ruling for at least five months, Thaksin was free to fight the election as a champion of the Little People. Casting himself as the victim of bureaucratic hair-splitting by the country's barely tested anti-corruption laws, he vowed after winning the election to fulfill as much of his platform as possible before the Court delivered its verdict.

In the end, Thaksin won the public relations war by delivering on several of his populist election promises. These included a one-million-baht "village fund" for small-scale development, a thirty-baht-per-hospital-visit health scheme, and a new national asset management corporation to handle the big banks' non-performing loans. On August 3, 2001, Thaksin was acquitted of the concealment-of-assets charge in a verdict decided by a single vote. The next day, he closed his office to the media and briefly ended all individual press interviews. In the months to follow, as reports of press freedom violations began to pile up, Thaksin's tolerance of criticism evaporated – perhaps not surprising, from a leader who boasted about becoming the next Southeast Asian "strongman" after Malaysia's Mahathir Mohamad.

A few minutes after eight PM on September 11, 2001, I was sitting at my desk at *The Nation* when a group of Thai employees standing around a television set burst into a collective shriek. Over the next few days, my shock over the terrorist attacks in the United States was matched by confusion over the response by some of the Thais. A few of my colleagues had actually giggled at replays of the exploding fireballs in New York City. A day or two later, our business section ran a story about a cell phone company with a hot a new product: the phone's liquid crystal display showed a jet plane slamming into a skyscraper. (In the accompanying photo, a teenaged girl beamed for the camera while showing off her trendy new gadget.) The *Post*, meanwhile, ran a story about a Sukhumvit Road flower vendor who worried that his business would suffer because Americans – the bulk of his customers – wouldn't feel like buying flowers. In another story, a Thai restaurant owner in a closed area of Manhattan said she was relieved, because now her rent wouldn't go up. Throughout all this, more than one taxi driver in Bangkok greeted me with the words "World Trade Center … boom!," followed by giggles. And T-shirts with heroic images of Osama bin Laden were all the rage among teenaged boys.

To those *farang* who had brought to Thailand their own culturally ingrained sense of decorum, it was hard not to conclude that the Kingdom had been infected with some bizarre epidemic of callous insensitivity. But Thai people don't like discussing politics with foreigners at the best of times, so it was difficult to identify the real reason for such reactions – or canvass the "average" Thai opinion about the tragedy. Unlike in Singapore and other Asian nations, there was no official memorial gathering. Thaksin's response had wavered from an initial declaration of neutrality to qualified support for George W. Bush's so-called war on terrorism. In a non-confrontational, Buddhist society where *mai pen rai* ("never mind" or, "it doesn't matter") is the rule, disturbing events are better left alone, smoothened over with laughter, or – as with Thailand's own tragic legacy of violence – forgotten altogether.

One recent historical event was still an open wound for many in the Kingdom. Back on October 6, 1976, national insecurity was at its peak. Three of Thailand's neighbours had fallen to Communism the year before. The pro-democracy demonstrations of 1973, which had forced the resignation of military dictator Thanom Kittikachorn, had spawned an unprecedented era of free speech in Thai society. With the progressive student movement gaining influence, and Marxism as its guiding light, Thanom's return from three years of exile to live a quiet life as a monk (and his warm welcome by members of the royal family), was met with angry protests. On October 5, Bangkok newspapers published photos of Thammasat University students hanging the Crown Prince in effigy. In response, an army radio station called upon all patriots to unite against the students and "kill Communists!"

The next day, an ad-hoc coalition of hard-core, right-wing thugs, police, and the army invaded the Thammasat University campus and unleashed an orgy of violence. Students were crushed by tanks, mowed down by bullets, lynched, beaten to death, and even burned alive. In one photo taken that day, several young men were shown gathered under a tree in Sanam Luang, their faces lit up in adrenaline smiles as a policeman, clutching a wooden fold-up chair, flogged the bloodied corpse of a young student dangling from a rope. It was images like this that the current Thai government wanted people to forget, even though many Thais were still seeking answers about the deaths of relatives whose bodies had never been recovered. By the twenty-fifth anniversary of the tragedy, it appeared as though mass amnesia was winning. Polls showed that most university students knew nothing about October 6, 1976, nor of the October 14 demonstrations of three years earlier: most Thai youth had only the slightest idea of what the protests were about. For the rest of the population, who couldn't afford a university education, life was an endless cycle of scarcity in which the value of human life was itself negotiable. Why bother dwelling on events of a quarter-century ago?

Shooting deaths and contract killings resulting from business disputes, adultery, or domestic abuse happened all the time. Countless people in Isaan and the lowland central areas, whose forests had been clearcut during the 1970s campaign to root out the Communists, were annually swept away by seasonal floods. AIDS continued to infect thousands, especially in the northern province of Chiang Rai. And crystal meth produced on the Burmese side of the border had long replaced opium as the drug of choice in Thailand. Just over a year later, Thaksin would respond to this problem with a shoot-to-kill policy targeting dealers. The no-tolerance campaign by police, in which even casual users were gunned down, was condemned by the United Nations.

Instead of wringing my hands at stupid taxi drivers or teenagers wearing bin Laden T-shirts, I reminded myself of the differences between Canadian and Thai disenfranchisement. Our poor and jobless had unemployment insurance and welfare; theirs lived in garbage dumps. With proof of address, ours could vote for an MP who might receive them in the constituency office; theirs had given up on a political system tainted by cronyism, fraud, and graft – a record that put Thailand near the top of the worldwide corruption index. Taking all this into account, it was easier to fathom some of the strange Thai reactions to September 11. Most Thais I spoke with after the tragedy said they liked Americans and never wished them any harm. So why all the weirdness?

Thai Buddhists believe that all of life is a form of suffering. But after a twentieth century redefined geopolitically by US power and might, it appeared as though the Lord Buddha had exempted Uncle Sam from this rule. Americans seemed superhuman, incapable of suffering or defeat of any kind; and their sense of entitlement was boundless. Behind their smiles of welcome, Thai people had watched in quiet humility as one American tourist after another traipsed through the Kingdom and spent more money in ten minutes than the average Thai could spend in ten years. September 11 had confirmed that Americans were capable of suffering. And that realization had driven some Thai people giddy with disbelief. The rich westerners were human, after all.

When I first moved to Bangkok, I thought I would find a community of expat writers to share notes with. But the only writers' group I discovered was the "Obliterati," a small coterie of American and British men in their fifties who wrote first-person expat novels about heroic adventures with Thai women, favourably reviewed each other's work in the local press, and held occasional readings at a Sukhumvit watering hole. Their work adhered to what I liked to call the Girls, Guns, & Ganja[2] school of fiction: Intrepid Macho Western Dude becomes denizen of the Nana/Patpong girlie bar circuit, gets ripped off in a stock market scam, and wakes up in Burma, where he barely avoids castration by knife-wielding drug dealers on *ya-baa*. Or something like that. Being more loyal to a Boys, Buns, & Babylon sensibility, I didn't bother joining the Obliterati. Nor did I hang out at the Foreign Correspondents Club.

Since I was working the three-to-eleven p.m. shift, my usual after-hours watering hole was Moo's, an outdoor pub located in a dusty old *soi* behind *The Nation*. Moo's consisted of a few bamboo tables and plastic patio chairs under a corrugated tin roof, with hanging vines lit by Christmas lights. Moo, the owner –whose name in Thai means "pork" – cooked a half-decent yellow curry with bamboo shoots, and a mean *phad kaprow moo kai dow duay* (pork basil and rice with fried egg on top), and he kept two coolers filled with ice and large bottles of Heineken and Singha. But it was important not to go

2. Borrowed from the actual title of a serious work of non-fiction: *Guns, Girls, Gambling, Ganja: Thailand's Illegal Economy and Public Policy* (Chiang Mai: Silkworm Books, 1998), by Pasuk Phongpaichit, Sungsidh Piriyarangsan and Nualnoi Treerat.

to his place more than once a week. An evening at Moo's could last until sunrise.

In the early days of expat life, I spent most of my off hours in the Silom with two other foreigners. Ray, a Canadian acquaintance from Vancouver, was someone I'd known for years but never hung out with at home. Our friendship developed as the result of a chance meeting in the Club Vancouver baths, during the month I'd gone home before moving to Bangkok. Ray, on a leave of absence from a local non-profit organization, had completed the necessary qualifications for teaching English as a second language and was mulling his options for his next destination. He was thinking of Indonesia, where he'd gone to visit a friend, but was undecided. So I told him about Thailand. A month after my return to Bangkok, I got a phone call at work: it was Ray. He was in town, having secured a teaching position at Thammasat University. Robin, an English journalist, had been living in Bangkok for about a month and was working at *Metro*, an English-language entertainment magazine, when we met at Telephone Pub during the *Songkran* festival. Robin and I shared a beer upstairs and stayed dry as Wit, his money-boy friends, and others engaged in a massive water fight outside in *soi* 4. I was leaving town for Saigon in a couple of days, I told Robin, but I'd be back in six weeks to begin work at *The Nation*. He assigned me a short piece for *Metro* and, after my return to Bangkok, we became drinking buddies.

Meeting Robin or Ray in the Silom after work was a chore. *The Nation* towers were so far away from the city that it seemed more practical to live near them. So my first home was the Highway Inn, a hotel and condo tower located just off the Bangna-Trat highway about ten minutes from *The Nation* by bus. For most of my office colleagues, the Highway Inn was merely a stopgap, a place to hang one's hat for a few weeks before finding permanent lodgings. I stayed for three months – despite the fact that the Highway Inn was a Christian-owned hotel with a neon-lit cross and a giant "Jesus Loves You" slogan on its side. On Sundays, the outside patio at the Highway Inn was filled with earnest Thai voices warbling gospel music in broken English. But looks can be deceiving. Upstairs, on the eleventh floor, the Highway Inn's bland, antiseptic interiors gave my room a sense of impermanence that made it the perfect field laboratory for cross-cultural desire. While I was there, a smorgasbord of "types" passed through my door: a nineteen-year-old Superlek go-go boy, a twenty-year-old "student," a Qantas flight attendant, a muscleboy masseur from Hero sauna, a security guard from Sathorn, the "straight" doorman from Icon. And so on....

∞

Sex in the so-called "Third World" had opened my eyes to many realities – not the least of which was my own relationship to money. Whether picking up the tab at dinner or supporting a bar boy's gambling addiction, I now understood that it was the *farang*'s responsibility not to be "cheap" with the locals – especially when they earned less than a tenth of what we did. The fact that the maximum monthly salary for the national police chief was less than what I earned as a copy editor made no sense at all. And this was only one of myriad economic injustices that separated Thais from *farang*. Pity I hadn't thought of these things while I was on holiday – but now I was getting the message loud and clear.

Most of the guys I'd fucked as a tourist gave me the brush-off now that I was back as a resident. Wisut, Deuan, and Saen in Chiang Mai, Ut in Phuket, and Chai on Samui didn't reply to my e-mails (with Deuan, as I said, snubbing me one night when I spotted him in Silom *soi* 4). The lesson? I had been too greedy, trying to pack in as many adventures as possible but without giving my young male companions even a fraction of what they'd come to expect from their foreign flings. Now that I was living in the city and showing up at the same bars I'd visited as a tourist, I was about as welcome on their turf as a panhandler at Bloomingdale's.

There were two rather dubious exceptions. First, there was Wit. Since we'd said our goodbyes during *Songkhran* in April, his situation had changed. Next door to his apartment building on *soi* 52, a construction site that had been little more than a skeleton frame when I left town was now a completed Tesco-Lotus chain department store. Wit's landlord had jacked up the rent by 2,000 baht a month – forcing Wit and other low-income residents out of the building. So now he was staying on *soi* 81, back with his friend Bee in a room full of moneyboys. His plan was to go to Australia on a tourist visa, apply for a work permit, and get a job on a cruise ship. The plan seemed highly improbable.

Like many Isaan guys who had worked the scene for a few years, however, Wit knew how to attract sympathy – and cash – without the word "money" ever passing his lips. He got so good at this, in fact, that I happily bought him a new pair of running shoes and shelled out 4,000 baht toward the cost of his plane ticket – even though we were no longer having sex and he was becoming less "exotic" the longer I lived in Bangkok. The final 1,000 baht I simply handed over to him at DJ Station one night, without even taking him home. It would have been nice to receive an e-mail from him now and then. But when I didn't hear from him for several months, I understood. By the time he returned a year later, broke again, I figured we were about even. The ATM was now closed.

Then there was Toy, the first beautiful Thai guy I'd slept with. Our actual fling had lasted less than twenty-four hours, but we had kept in touch periodically; he sent me the occasional e-mail to imply continued interest. Of course, we both knew it was all a big tease. Toy, after all, had provided the earliest lesson of what I would experience again and again in Thailand: the sense that things are not as they seem, that words don't mean what you think they should, and that a strong belief in the fundamental goodness of others is no excuse for gullibility.

Now that I was living in Bangkok, it seemed like I was running into Toy almost every time I was in the Silom *soi* 4 or *soi* 2. By this point I knew that he was a one-man Welcome Wagon for all the gay *farang* of Bangkok: Ray and Robin, my two best expat friends, had also been with him. Several times I approached him in *soi* 4, grabbing his arm to talk just as he had once grabbed mine. He was always superficially friendly, flashing the same smile as before. But now he seemed preoccupied, as if I were cramping his style. I didn't hold it against him. I understood that I had been too dazzled by his beauty when we first met to realize what was going on. For a time – once he was assured I no longer expected a freebie – it seemed possible to be his friend. One night at DJ Station, he handed me an invitation to his twenty-first birthday party.

It was the oddest birthday party I've ever attended. Most of the guests were foreigners, but few of us knew each other. Gradually it emerged that we had one thing in common: we had all fucked Toy at least once. At times, the party had the air of a mutual support group. One fellow from England told me how Toy was constantly harassing him for money; he had given it willingly, only to be disappointed later when Toy wouldn't have sex with him. Later, Toy's mother arrived and was warmly applauded by all her son's lovers. She even joined the group photo, wide-eyed in amazement at Toy's popularity.

Whenever I saw him afterward, Toy would express his weariness with the Silom treadmill: the endless string of bar nights, the smooth-talking rich *farang*, the unkept promises, the discarded phone numbers. For all his sweet-talking, and even his putting out, he still couldn't afford to go to school.

"How about modeling?" I asked.

"I can't get the work," he said. Thai advertising was racist and only hired "white" *look kreung* Thais, people of mixed Thai-western heritage. He had a point. But times were changing, I said; exceptions were made. I gave him the names and numbers of three modeling agencies and offered to do his portfolio. But he never followed it up. The last time I saw him, standing outside DJ Station, he was scrounging for 200 baht to get in the door. I gave it to him.

XVI
Houseboy Blues

AFTER THREE MONTHS AT THE HIGHWAY INN, it was time to move into my own apartment. The Bang Phli district of Samut Prakan province was just south of the Bangkok city boundary along the Bangna-Trat highway, not far from the *Nation* towers. The Suan Thon condominiums were part of a local franchise of gated complexes, each with its own large crew of security guards and groundskeepers. Situated at the end of a long, badly paved road off Sri Nakarin, a main thoroughfare running north to Bang Kapi, my new abode was a fully furnished, ground level, two-bedroom condo with a back garden and fish pond.

With a shared outdoor swimming pool included, the place was a bargain at 8,000 baht a month. Just outside the *soi* on Sri Nakarin, there was a Makro department store and a Carrefour supermarket, but not much else. With a bicycle I could get to work in twenty minutes via Sri Nakarin/Banga or a back road that ran through a swamp-filled junkyard and a barren plot of farmland run by the local temple. During the rainy season, the road was reduced to a thick, goopy mudbath of ruts more than half a metre deep. Using this route during the dry season, I was sometimes blocked by a herd of water buffalo.

It wasn't the ideal recipe for a busy social life. Given the distance, few guys I picked up at the bars were willing to visit my condo a second time – the thirty-kilometre taxi ride from the Silom a rather major inconvenience when one has to be on the opposite side of town the next morning. But one young man did want to visit the Suan Thon more than once: Tong, a twenty-three-year-old Isaan native of Buri Ram I had met one night at DJ Station while out with Robin, my English drinking buddy. Tong and I had spent a couple of nights together and a weekend in Pattaya a couple of months earlier. When we met again at DJ after I moved to Suan Thon, I took him home.

Tong was not considered beautiful by Bangkok Thai standards. Many Central Thais hold a classist/racist view of northeasterners that sees light skin as a sign of wealth or nobility and rust-coloured skin like Tong's as indicative of the peasant class. (Tong's round face, as well, was considered "too Lao" for Central Thais who preferred the more angular, Rattanakosin look.) But to me, Tong's sparkling eyes, porcelain lips, and perfect white teeth fit all the objective criteria for "beauty." His shy laugh was irresistible, and the fact he was great in bed made me want to keep on seeing him – despite knowing very little about him or where he came from.

Tong's home province had been a centre of the Khmer empire in Thailand during the Angkor period. Eight centuries later, the fields and roadsides of Buri Ram were still littered with piles of bricks from the old ruins. Tong had moved to Bangkok after finishing high school with vague plans to go to college and work in tourism. As for his family, he said very little. He didn't say what his father did for a living, only that he had beaten him as a child. All he said about his mother was that she still ran the same noodle stall she'd been running since he was a young boy. I didn't read this as a warning sign for our relationship, nor did it concern me that we'd met in a bar, or that Tong didn't seem in much of a hurry to get a job.

The morning after his second visit to Suan Thon, Tong asked if he could spend the day at the condo while I was at work. I paused just long enough to decide if I trusted him, then said yes. When I got home from the office that night, Tong greeted me at the door wearing string bikini underwear. Wafting through the doorway was the sweet spicy aroma of *massaman gai*, one of my favourite curried chicken dishes. When I walked in and dropped my bag, Tong wrapped his arms and legs around me and gave me a big, wet kiss. The next morning I peered through the bathroom door to find him, again in his underwear, sitting in the bathtub with a bucket of foamy water. He was hand washing my socks.

This is how western men lose their heads in Thailand. For the heteros, it's nostalgia for a pre-feminist, Ozzie and Harriet domestic world; for the homos, it's the houseboy/sex slave fantasy. Having Tong stark naked in the condo every day, ready to hop into bed at a moment's notice, was intoxicating – rather like gorging on a plateful of chocolate-covered strawberries. Until the day he finally asked, rather sheepishly, why I hadn't cut him his own set of keys, I had truly thought of him as "just visiting" – even though, on each "visit," he would bring another bag of his belongings from Bang Kapi. Soon there was nothing left to bring and he had filled the entire guestroom closet.

I never did ask Tong what was so bad about his own home that he had to move into Suan Thon. But the night we took a taxi to his sister-in-law's restaurant, on a dusty old *soi* in Bang Kapi, I got a pretty good idea. For the final half-kilometre, our taxi was surrounded as people rushed out of their corrugated tin-roofed shacks to witness our arrival. Tong, laughing playfully, tried to push me to the floor so I wouldn't see the squalor of the surroundings. Some wealthier *farang* had dumped him after visiting this place; he was worried that I would do the same. Finally, we arrived at his sister-in-law's restaurant. It was typical of the *som tam* shops one finds all over Thailand: a roadside diner with plastic patio furniture, a display case, and a menu featuring pork and seafood noodle soup, some fried noodle dishes, and spicy papaya salad.

The locals were all thrilled that Tong had brought home a new *farang*. All, that is, except for his best friend Jep. Before this occasion, the only other place I'd seen Jep was in the Silom bar district. There, he was always decked out in glittery nightclub attire, his hair gelled and his skin reeking of cologne. Here, as a short order chef at a country-style noodle stall, he might as well have been naked for me to "catch" him like this: sweating over a steaming wok wearing flip-flops, a sleeveless blue gym shirt, and cut-off jeans. A few nights earlier, in the crowded Telephone pub, two *farang* had fought over him; now, all he had were two filthy *soi* cats at his feet, fighting over scraps of pork fat. Jep lived here with Tong in an upstairs room. He didn't know that Tong had told me this, and he was unprepared for the shock of being seen by a *farang* outside the gay tourist ghetto. He seemed surprised that I'd be interested in visiting – as if there were no other place for me but the Silom and the suburban confines of my gated condo existence.

Jep loosened up when I sat down and ordered some noodles. Soon he was horsing around with Tong, trading gossip, and finally sitting down to join us for a beer and some noodles. Then Tong led me around the *soi* and introduced me to three different grocers, making sure I bought a couple of large bottles of beer from each one so that everyone would benefit from my visit. Mae, Tong's sister-in-law, was pleased. *Farang* so seldom came to this *soi* that the mere fact of my sitting in her restaurant had doubled her usual Sunday night business: people were flocking to her stall to find out who I was and why I was there, and then sitting down to talk about it over noodles. When the night was over, Tong and I walked down the *soi* and headed to the highway through a maze of clapboard houses at the edge of a *khlong*. I never did get to see his room.

∞

As with many First World/Third World romances, things with Tong were good in the beginning. We went to the movies at Seacon Square. We went to fresh markets together. We spent long afternoons lounging by the pool and entire evenings in the condo. Tong was happy to cook and clean or watch TV while I read or wrote. We also spent a lot of time entertaining friends: my English pal Robin spent a couple of nights in the guestroom, as did Jep and Seni, an old school chum of Tong's from Buri Ram, and Tong's cousin. Over five months, there were meals in the back garden or in the courtyard among the rubber trees and tiger lilies. I wasn't thinking much about the future, about where all this was going or how little money I was saving. Expat life was still novel, and things were cozy in the short term. Who cared if Tong wasn't working?

Tong pushed a lot of buttons that others couldn't reach, tapping my emotions in a way that became his greatest source of leverage. A smile on his face could brighten my day; when he was in a blue funk, I would do anything to snap him out of it. One thing we shared was a fondness for cats. There were half a dozen of them in my wing of Suan Thon, all owned by the staff. The condo kitties would creep into the garden when I was outside, slithering between my legs under the table as I sipped my morning coffee. After Tong moved in, they were always there, lounging on the deck and waiting for his next delicacy.

One day, he brought home a pet Siamese that another *farang* lover had given him and which he'd kept in the room at Bang Kapi. It was a purebred, more exotic than the condo kitties, and it wouldn't settle down in its new surroundings. On the first night it constantly pawed the window and wouldn't stop meowing until we let it outside. The next morning, it was gone. Two days later, one of the security guards handed Tong his pet's collar with the little bell attached. Frightened by the condo kitties, the Siamese had wandered toward the front gate where it was attacked and torn apart by a pack of *soi* dogs. The guards had found the corpse, removed the collar, and sent the remains away to be destroyed. That cat was one of the few things that Tong treasured; it was something he had wanted to share with me as a sign of his love. So its loss was pathetic, filling me with a sadness out of all proportion to the event itself.

Sadness was never far from the surface with Tong. His sleep was troubled by nightmares, and I sometimes had to startle him awake. He never said much about the dreams, only that someone – he wouldn't say who – was trying to hurt him. During our first trip to Koh Samet, he broke out with a skin rash that got worse by the hour. At the hospital in Bangkok, I had a panic attack as I was paying for his medicine: *This is the slippery slope. Tong will lapse into chronic health problems; there will be an endless pile of hospital bills. I will go broke caring for him.*

It was while Tong was recuperating in Bang Kapi, where his mother was visiting, that I went to Toy's birthday party and met Ahn. Ahn was twenty, tall and beautiful, with flowing long hair, the cheekbones of a model, and a sexy, baritone laugh. His English was excellent, and he had lots to say. He was from a middle-class family with enough money that his interest in western men was motivated by attraction rather than need. We hit it off right away. Before long, we were necking on Toy's balcony while everyone else was inside. After the party, I took him home. In bed that night, and again the next morning, there was an urgency about our lovemaking that disturbed me. I was head over heels with Ahn, but I also felt guilty. Was I not already in a live-in "relationship" with Tong? Ahn was hot for me as well, but he was also attached – to a twenty-five-year-old Israeli he'd met three years earlier. Ahn was due back in Tel Aviv in a few weeks and didn't know when he'd return to Bangkok. It was all a big mess.

The fling with Ahn prompted a serious reassessment of my relationship with Tong. What kind of future could I possibly build with someone I'd met in a disco and supported ever since? What plans could I make with an Isaan bar boy who insisted I stop using condoms after I praised that first decadent dish of crab curry he'd prepared for me? What prospects for nuptial bliss were there with someone who made no secret of his continued e-mail correspondence with several of the foreign tourists he'd met in Bangkok – a few of whom still professed their love, sent him money, and had no idea of each others' existence, nor mine? I knew three of Tong's Japanese lovers by name, and there were others from Singapore, Australia, England, and

Belgium (the latter with whom I would end up going halfers to buy a cell phone for Tong – despite never meeting the man). Tong had contacted all of these men using my computer. I wasn't shocked when he told me, but I didn't like the idea of his deceiving so many different suitors while living under my roof. On the other hand, I didn't feel I had any right to insist he sever his ties with them. Another part of me was hoping they'd send as much money as possible to take some of the burden off me. This was illogical, for it ignored the possibility that Tong might *not* have been contacting all these men if I were rich enough to satisfy his every consumer need. And that showed just how twisted our relationship had been at the core, from the very beginning.

While Tong was recovering from his skin rash in Bang Kapi, I began to contemplate an exit strategy. First, to dispel the guilt, I needed to rationalize dumping him. How would I feel if one of his sugar daddies arrived in Bangkok and snapped him up for a week in Phuket? Or a month in Europe? Had Tong taken it for granted that he would always be "taken care of" – if not by me, then by a succession of Mr Japans or Mr Singapores? All of these men were well off. Would Tong dump me for one of them the moment we had a big fight? Was this perhaps why he hadn't bothered looking for a job the whole time we were together? I thought about all this while two-timing with Ahn, who wanted to keep seeing me before he flew back to Tel Aviv.

When Tong returned to Suan Thon after his recovery from the skin rash, things went quickly downhill. He wouldn't stop asking if I'd brought someone home to the condo while he was away, and when I finally fessed up he grew morose. Reminding him of his sugar daddies didn't make any difference: he had a right to be with them, he said; I didn't have a right to be with other Thai guys. I felt trapped. I hadn't been looking for a live-in boyfriend, but I had gone all the way with Tong and now he was being possessive. While he had a friend from Buri Ram to visit, I ran off to a sauna and met an athletic, middle-class closet case named Than. We fucked for hours, then traded phone numbers.

Two early attempts to dump Tong were unsuccessful. The first time, he left in a huff when I phoned Than, in front of him, to arrange a date. But fifteen minutes after setting off on foot with no umbrella in the middle of a rainstorm, he was back. Looking like one of the condo kitties after a dunking in the fishpond, he looked me straight in the eye.

"I no want to leave you," he said. I embraced him.

But about a month later on a Sunday morning, I woke up, gathered all his clothes in a pile, and told him we were finished. At this he slumped in the couch, buried his face in his hands, and burst into tears, his body trembling and shaking with loud sobs.

"You no love me," he cried. "You have no heart!"

I said nothing as his tears began to flow. But my resolve was weakening.

"I have nowhere to go," he whimpered. "My sister-in-law, she break up with my brother, she have to leave restaurant. What can I do? Please, I love you so. I just jealous you, but I try to be better. Please, please, don't let me go...."

As he repeated these words over and over again, I thought only of the good things about Tong, and of all the little things he had done for me. Tong wasn't running off to live in Japan or Singapore or Australia or Belgium with those other guys. He was here, in Samut Prakan, living with me. And what had I done? I had panicked at the first sign of trouble and, while he was recovering from an illness, taken Ahn home for sex. Then it was one little fight and I was running off to a sauna with Than. *What an asshole*. As Tong lay trembling in my arms, I cast off every argument for dumping him and changed my mind. Again.

In a short-lived attempt to be faithful to Tong, I stopped seeing Than for a while. But having won me back a second time, Tong then set the stage for our final breakup with a series of moody episodes designed to humiliate me in public. During these episodes, Tong became demonic when friends were around. At the worst possible moment, a strange, previously unexpressed hostility would rise to the surface, and he would cloud the atmosphere by refusing to be introduced to a friend, storming out of a restaurant because of something I'd said, or threatening to leave a social gathering without me. Tong had five such episodes before I finally put the brakes on our relationship.

The end came in Chiang Mai, on my first trip to the north since the "noodle soup" adventure the previous year. We had travelled there with Edmund, my visiting Irish friend, and were staying at the Diamond Riverside, a hotel tower overlooking the Ping River a short walk from the Night Bazaar. Tong's mood shifted constantly throughout the three-day trip. He was happy when I took him to meet a Canadian woman and her Burmese husband who had led me to a story about the Shan. Happy when I took him to the Mae Rim waterfalls. Happy when we fucked three times on our last day in the city. But on the two occasions I took him to the Night Bazaar with Edmund, a cloud would fall over him and he'd sulk for the rest of the night.

I wasn't entirely blameless in all this. The Night Bazaar, after all, was where I had met several of my holiday flings the previous year. And sure enough, several of them were there when Tong and I passed through with Edmund. On the first night, I spotted Deuan mixing drinks at one of the bars. The last time I'd seen him, at the Bangkok Gay Festival, he had barely acknowledged me in the street. (This was a few weeks after the sneering incident at Balcony.) But now, seeking my business in his hometown, he flashed his best welcome-back-to-Chiang Mai smile. "I came with my boyfriend," I said, presenting Tong and then Edmund. Tong and Deuan smiled and exchanged pleasantries in Thai.

Deuan was looking good. He had bulked up in the gym and was sporting a brush-cut hairstyle that gave him the Japanese look of a Yukio Mishima military stud fantasy. Sitting with a customer was his roommate Saen, who recognized me immediately, jumped up, and gave me a kiss – my "butterfly wings" apparently forgotten. Also in the room was the beefy gym guy I'd played with in the shower on my first visit to the House of Male. Sitting Tong and Edmund down at a table, I introduced Tong to Saen and continued chatting with Deuan. I thought this was enough stimulation for one evening … until Chai walked in.

Chai was the delectable sex god I'd met at the House of Male on my last night in town, the one with whom Deuan and Saen had caught me frolicking in the pool.

"Hello," he smiled, when he caught me staring at him. "What's your name?"

"Don't you remember me?" I said. (Dumb question, really, given how many *farang* pass through Chiang Mai in a single year.) I leaned closer to him.

"You fucked me at the House of Male last year," I whispered in his ear.

Chai smiled: "Was I good?"

"You were fantastic. But that's my boyfriend sitting behind you."

"Phone me later," he said. "We can arrange to meet when he's busy."

"Sorry, Chai," I said, "not possible." Then I introduced the two of them. This seemed the smart thing to do, since Tong had clearly not enjoyed witnessing my conversation with Chai – the third such intimate conference he'd seen me enjoy with a different Chiang Mai guy in the space of five minutes.

Two nights later – the night before our flight back to Bangkok – we returned to Deuan and Saen's bar after shopping for Edmund in the Night Bazaar. The same cast of characters was there, with an added surprise: Phan, the master of metaphor who had likened Chiang Mai to "noodle soup," was back in town with an American lover he'd met a few months earlier and gone travelling with. Phan told me they were moving to Canada to live together and open a restaurant. I told this to Tong, but got no reaction: Tong and Phan disliked each other immediately. From then on, Tong slid into a deep, dark funk and eventually returned to the hotel alone, leaving me at the bar with Edmund.

When I got back to the hotel room, Tong was asleep but the light was on. Then I remembered something he had said just before leaving the bar: "Do you know where your passport is?" When I picked up my bag and reached into the pocket, the passport wasn't there. I searched the rest of the bag, but no luck. Then I looked through my books, a pile of clothes, and Tong's bag. Nothing. So I nudged him awake.

"Tong, where's my passport?"

He didn't move. I nudged him again. Suddenly he turned around.

"I threw it in the Ping River!" he snapped, before covering himself.

"No you didn't, Tong. Now, don't be stupid. Where's my passport?"

"I no have to tell you anything!"

"Shut up, Tong!" I said. "It's three o'clock in the morning. People are asleep."

"Shut up! You shut up, you fuck! I don't care! I can wake up anyone, I can say anything, you shut up!"

"Tong, please. I just want to know where you've put the passport. I'm sorry. If you're pissed off, we can talk in the morning. Where's my passport?"

"I tell you already! I threw it in the river! You no listen to me! You never listen to me! Now you go to bar and you fuck boy, you fuck-fuck-*fuck*!!!"

I lunged at him, pushing him back down on the bed and struggling to pin his arms while he continued shouting at the top of his lungs: "You no love me! You hate me! You hate me!"

With one hand, I grabbed a pillow and shoved it in his face. He tore it away and threw it off the bed, still screaming. When I put my hand over his mouth, he clamped his jaws down on my thumb – hard enough to tear into it. Pulling it from his grip, I got off the bed and backed away from him. My blood was all over his teeth and chin. I ran to the door, turning to look before opening it. Tong was balancing a heavy lounge chair above his head, preparing to heave it at me. I ran back and grabbed hold of it, bringing it gently to the floor after a struggle. Then I ran to the door again. The last thing I saw before entering the hallway was Tong, trying to rip the television set out of the wall.

Recovering in Edmund's room from the shock, I wrapped my bleeding thumb in a towel and lay down on the bed. A few minutes later, Tong came to the door and began knocking repeatedly, asking my forgiveness. Edmund turned him away. Then the phone started ringing; Edmund picked up and told Tong to go to sleep. In the morning, there was a scene at the front desk where I had to threaten to call the tourist police before Tong finally returned my passport, wallet, keys, and money. Tong seemed to realize that things had gone bad, and apologized repeatedly. But I insisted that we sit apart on the return flight to Bangkok. From Don Muang, I sent him to Bang Kapi in a separate taxi. The next day, I put all of his belongings in a box, met him outside Central Bangna department store, and sent him on his way.

The eleventh full moon of the year is *Loy Krathong* night in Thailand, an annual ritual of spiritual cleansing. Families gather by the country's riversides at night with their *krathongs* – tiny, lotus-shaped baskets made of banana leaves containing flowers, incense, candles, and money. Then, after lighting the candles, they send their *krathongs* down the river. By doing so, they purge all the bad karma of the previous year from their lives, pray for good luck in the coming year, and turn the river into a thing of glowing beauty. My father and stepmother happened to be visiting during the festival, so I met them at their hotel. Together we walked down to the banks of the Chao Phraya to launch our own *krathongs* amid a crowd of local Thais. On my way home, I stopped at DJ Station for a drink. There, for the first time in eight months, I saw Tong.

It had taken almost that long to get over him. After I'd sent him packing my emotions had wavered between concern for his welfare and disgust at my own stupidity for having allowed things to go as far as they had. Despite the violence that had ended our relationship, I missed the sound of Tong's voice, his nervous laugh, his smile, and the taste and smell of his body. Now here he was at DJ, standing upstairs with Jep and gazing down at the crowded dance floor. His face lit up when I approached. After consulting briefly with Jep, he invited me to the new apartment they were sharing in Phra Kanong. I still felt a slight throbbing in my thumb all these months later, but I accepted.

Back home, such a decision would have been unthinkable. But this was Thailand, and it was *Loy Krathong*. I was in a mood for forgiveness: I wanted to show Tong that I didn't consider him a bad person just because things had ended so badly between us. Tong, for his part, wanted to prove that he wasn't a rabid monster who would try to bite off one of my digits every time we met. But arriving at this stage had not been easy for either of us. In the days following the split, we had spoken a few times on the phone. I had called Tong to arrange for delivery of a few items he'd left at the condo; he had called to ask me to take him back. ("I just jealous you," he said, explaining his outburst in Chiang Mai; withholding my possessions had been an act of desperation.) It was hard. Tong didn't understand that we were wrong for each other, that his earnest appeals for forgiveness only made my decision to dump him all the more agonizing. I finally had to insist that we cease all contact. This time, to his credit, he made it easier for me by not bursting into tears.

The most difficult part of dumping Tong was knowing that I truly loved him, even though our relationship was doomed from the start. Our connection was defined by a client/patron dynamic in which I had to make all the decisions and pay for everything. After consenting to do things this way – by allowing him to move in and assume the "houseboy" role – I had then confused Tong by resisting the dynamic. The more I pressured him to get a job, the more he complained that I was not being enough of a "leader" – and that was about the same time his moody episodes began to flare up in public. Now, eight months later in a strange apartment, I was once again naked with Tong, inhaling the familiar scent of his smooth warm body. Just as we were about to fuck, he rolled out from under me, turned around, and took me in his mouth. I had a momentary vision of his jaws clamping down on my cock, but the vision passed as we brought each other off. All was forgiven.

In the morning, Tong opened the kitchen cupboards to get some glasses.

Inside were several large blue and white boxes. They were vitamins, he said. After I'd sent him away, he had stopped eating and was briefly hospitalized with a calcium deficiency. One of his Japanese lovers had come to the rescue – paying for his hospital care, the lease of this apartment, and an expensive vitamin supplement. Tong handed me a glass of orange juice. When I sat down to drink it, he stood behind me and began gently brushing my hair. Then my tears began to flow, and wouldn't stop.

Tong got me some tissue and asked what was wrong. "I don't know," I said, grasping for words. I wanted him to believe that I still cared about him; that I still loved him. But that was also the *last* thing I wanted him to know. Unless I was prepared to take him back, which I wasn't, such declarations would only hurt him. So I was mourning the fact that we could never be "just friends" once we were no longer lovers: this was where I finally had to let him go. After meeting one more time for lunch and a movie, we never saw each other again.

XVII
Purification Rites

WITH TONG OUT OF THE PICTURE, I couldn't stand being alone in the Suan Thon condo. The idea of living in the suburbs close to the office was no longer appealing: after a year in Thailand, it was time to move to the city. My new apartment, in Bangkok's Wattana district, was located halfway between *The Nation* and the Silom bar district, a short ride by motorbike taxi from Thonglor station on the Sukhumvit skytrain line of the Bangkok Transit System (BTS). The Thonglor Tower apartments were on *soi* 18 of Thong Lor Avenue, or Sukhumvit *soi* 55, one of Bangkok's trendier streets. The sidewalks were cluttered with noodle stalls and looked as though they'd been through a few earthquakes, but the condos were mostly high end. And the strip was filled with expensive Japanese restaurants, Singaporean teahouses, car dealers, nightclubs, a couple of Starbucks outlets, and heaps of wedding boutiques.

Thonglor was known as the "wedding *soi*," which in Bangkok was a sign of hipness: flashy weddings offered status-conscious "hi-so" families a chance to flaunt their conspicuous wealth. A few of the Thonglor wedding shops were quaint little mom-and-pop storefronts with modest window displays of bride and groom drag. But several others were garish, Greco-Roman "love shops" festooned with towering white pillars, plaster garden gnomes of Cupid playing the harp, and other kitsch Valentinia. Two or three of the latter variety, with names like "Viva Forever" and "Jardin de l'Amour," were housed in large, cream-coloured buildings that took up half-blocks and were advertised at night by giant floodlights. Every other day, it seemed, a camera crew would set up on the sidewalk to capture yet another happy Thai couple – or professional models, posing as a couple – in their fitting session.

The notion of renting an apartment in Bangkok's "wedding *soi*" was ironic, given that marriage was the last thing on my mind most days. But just having an urban life again was a relief after Samut Prakan, where my presence was a novelty. In Thonglor, people didn't stare at *farang*; foreigners were just part of the scenery. Not long after moving, I signed up for Thai lessons at a language school near the skytrain station and took out a membership at the Nielson Hays library, housed in a nineteenth-century mansion on Surawong Road. I also joined the Flying Farang, a group of expat ice hockey players who, along with a small collection of Thais, met every Sunday morning at a shopping mall in Lat Phrao to hold scrimmages in a fourth-floor ice rink. After my shift at *The Nation*, I began a habit of stopping for late-night snacks at *Ha-sip-ha Pochana* ("55"), a busy Sino-Thai grill on the corner of Sukhumvit Road that stayed open late and served the best beef and black pepper sauce in town. Or *Thon Krueng* ("Main Ingredient"), a family-style diner that served all my favourite Thai dishes: spicy *som tam* papaya salad, shrimp curry, stir-fried chicken with cashew nuts, and *Tom Yam Goong* served in a large earthenware pot. *Thon Krueng* also featured an endless parade of handsome waiters wearing orange coats – one of whom visited my apartment a couple of times when his shift was over.

Obelisk: a tall pillar, usually with four sides and a tapering
top, set up as a monument or landmark.
– *Oxford English Dictionary*

Another reason I decided on a Thonglor address was its proximity to The Obelisks, an eleven-story bathhouse on Sukhumvit *soi* 53. The Obelisks didn't have a tapering top, and calling it a landmark would be overstating things. But it was something of a monument for the men who gathered there. Among the five or six gay bathhouses situated along the Sukhumvit skytrain route, this one stood out for its opulent touches. Like Babylon, The Obelisks gave new meaning to the term "fuck palace." Eric Allyn's *The Men of Thailand* described it as "an elegant (almost piss-elegant) facility," with a décor that seemed more appropriate for a luxury hotel or an upscale art gallery than a place to have sex. Its "piss elegance" lay in its attention to detail, which implied a touch of class not necessarily indicative of the clientele.

Entering the sauna's front courtyard, which was lit by vertical beams of black designer floodlights, the visitor passed through a garden filled with coconut trees, mangroves, tiger lilies, orchids and bougainvillea, and then crossed a small wooden bridge over a tropical fish pond and water fountain. The sauna's large, oak front doors opened up to a foyer with smooth, black marble floors and a twenty-foot ceiling that exposed the second-floor restaurant. There, couples sat in their towels, checking out the new arrivals while munching on plates of spicy chicken basil and rice. After paying the

200-baht entry fee, the visitor passed through a turnstile and took an elevator to the locker room.

One of the reasons I preferred The Obelisks to the more touristy Babylon was its comparative lack of foreigners. The Obelisks was mainly a place for Thais who preferred other Thais. Even on nights when there wasn't a lot of action sex-wise, the entertainment that took place – intended or otherwise – was worth the price of admission. In the changing room, one could often find six or seven Thai men bumping elbows at the make-up mirrors, competing for the next available hairdryer. Above the restaurant and bar, there was a fully equipped weight room and gym, as well as a karaoke lounge. Here, picture two men – perfect strangers until a few minutes earlier, when they'd brought each other off in an upstairs cabin – gazing into each other's eyes, laughing hysterically as they warble through a ghastly duet of "My Heart Will Go On."

The sixth floor, the main gathering area, contained a dry sauna, steam room, cold water Jacuzzi, three shower rooms, and two seating areas from which to view the passing traffic – one near a large, open-air window that offered an expansive view of the city below. On the seventh floor was a massage room, where for an extra fee you could get loosened up by one of the staff. The eighth to tenth floors were reserved for sex. Each floor had two rows of private cabins containing a single-sized bed with a thin vinyl mattress, a side table with tissue paper and a container of lubricant, and a dimmer switch. One of these floors contained a porn cinema – an actual mini-theatre with half a dozen rows of seats. Another featured a maze, a dimly lit network of narrow pathways that swallowed you up within seconds of entering the labyrinth. (The appeal of this maze lay in the thrill of discovery. Now and then, while wandering through it, I would bump into someone attractive and we'd go find a room. But more often than not, I'd be rebuffed by some beauty I'd later find deep-throating another Thai guy, or stalked by someone undesirable as I struggled to find the exit.) On the eleventh and final floor, The Obelisks opened up to the Bangkok sky with a rooftop bar and a garden Jacuzzi flanked by two glass-walled steam rooms that overlooked the city.

Before moving to Thonglor, I had visited The Obelisks several times, even taking hour-long taxi rides to get there while I was living in Samut Prakan. But now that my favourite Thai sauna was less than two minutes away by motorbike, I planned on becoming a regular. Sadly, I wouldn't enjoy the privilege for very long: the Thai police shut down The Obelisks three months after I moved to Thonglor, and I was there on the night it happened. I'd been wandering through the maze when a sudden hush in the main hallway – followed by flashlight beams and the clicking of boot heels on cement – signaled that a police raid was in progress. Finally, a city-wide clampdown on nightlife had arrived in my neighbourhood.

∞

The police raid, part of an anti-vice campaign by the federal government, was ordered by the country's new interior minister, a pokerfaced authoritarian named Purachai Piumsombun. In recent months, Purachai had launched an all-out offensive on the sex trade – in the broadest definition of the term. Thailand had wallowed long enough in the gutter of prostitution, drugs, and low-life tourists, said the minister: it was time to clean up the country's image and attract "better quality" foreigners – by which he meant church-going CEOs who didn't like going out at night. It didn't matter that, according to every survey ever held, the majority of prostitution's clientele were Thai men.

Purachai made no secret of his resentment for what he saw as the corrupting influence of western culture. He longed for simpler times, when the Kingdom was impervious to foreign encroachment – a time before US marines on R&R during the Vietnam War turned Patpong and Pattaya into what too many regarded as the whorehouse capitals of Southeast Asia. Moralizing Thai politicians were nothing new. What made Purachai different was that he actually followed through on his threats: in a far-reaching "new social order" campaign that took the capital by storm, his crackdown on city bars and restaurants would eventually spread though the Kingdom. Soon, expats had a nickname for the interior minister: Purachai the Purifier.

The minister's methods of attaining a "new social order" ranged from cutting off liquor sales at midnight to anti-drug bar raids with random urine tests. Police checked tourist ID cards, booked teenagers for underage drinking, arrested sex trade workers, and raided massage parlours. Clubs that stayed open past two a.m. had their licences revoked; police officers who failed to enforce the law were reassigned to inactive posts. Purachai himself played celebrity cop by showing up at many of the bar raids. "This is going to be a prolonged war, and whoever is more tenacious will win," he said. (I was working on the news desk at *The Nation* the night he made this com-ment, and I edited the story in which he was quoted. Purachai's triumphalist, gunslinger posturing with the media seemed oddly familiar. When our Thai reporter asked how far he was prepared to clamp down on civil liberties to achieve his "new social order," his response – translated roughly as "You can see what I will do if you do not believe me" – recalled memories of Canadian Prime Minister Pierre Trudeau, facing down a CBC reporter during the 1970 October Crisis. So I reduced the clunky translation of Purachai's answer to three words: "Just watch me.")

Months later, Purachai would try to revive a 1972 curfew law used by the military junta of the day. The law, if applied, would prevent anyone under the age of eighteen from leaving their homes after ten p.m. and punish the parents of any minor who broke the law. The proposal didn't go anywhere, but that didn't stop Purachai from proposing an even more bizarre amendment: in a bid to curb prostitution, he wanted to make it illegal for single women to visit entertainment districts unaccompanied by a chaperone. The amendment failed.

As one of the first major policy initiatives of the Thai Rak Thai administra-tion, the "new social order" campaign revealed the Thaksin government's true colours as a *farang*-bashing force for xenophobic patriotism. In both spirit and execution, the campaign typified a new wave of Occidentalism in Thailand: the equation of modernity with the corruption of morals, which in turn is equated with the West. The underlying assumption of Occidental-ism, as practiced in the Far East, is that certain values of the West need to be purged in order to preserve the "Asian spirit" – roughly defined as "self-sac-rifice, discipline, austerity, individual submission to the common good, wor-ship of divine leadership, and a deep faith in the superiority of instinct over reason."[1] The evil western traits include liberalism, individualism, decadence, and moral laxity.

Occidentalism is based on four specific tropes that define western deca-dence: the City, the Bourgeois, Reason, and Feminism. The first has special resonance in the context of Purachai's "new social order":

1. Ian Buruma and Avishai Margalit, "Occidentalism," *New York Review of Books*, January 17, 2002.

> Anti-liberal revolts almost invariably contain a deep ha-
> tred of the City, that is to say, everything represented by
> urban civilization: commerce, mixed populations, artistic
> freedom, sexual license, scientific pursuits, leisure, per-
> sonal safety, wealth, and its usual concomitant, power.[2]

Ian Buruma touches on this phenomenon in an earlier essay about Thailand in particular.[3] As the country emerged from the ashes of absolute monarchy in 1932, a struggle began for its soul, a struggle defined by the fear of western colonialism, the loathing of Sino-Thai financial dominance, and the spread of Thai nationalism and patriotism. That struggle, writes Buruma, was symbolized by the ideological split between two modern men, "both educated in France, one a soldier and the other a civilian." Luang Phibunsongkhram, or "Phibun" (born Plaek Khittasangkha), was a right-wing populist and ultranationalist who was fond of Adolf Hitler and appealed to the military and conservative elite. Pridi Phanomyong, a left-wing intellectual democrat, was fond of Karl Marx and appealed to the civilian bureaucratic, professional, and educated elite.

For all their differences, both men were fiercely patriotic: Phibun promoted a "Thailand for Thais" policy while Pridi was a major force behind the "Free Thai" movement. (Both, ironically, were later ostracized for appearing to undermine Thai independence – Phibun for throwing his lot in with the Japanese during the war and Pridi for his anti-monarchist and Communist leanings.) But it was Phibun, who ruled Thailand for all but four years between 1938 and 1957, whose nationalist vision won out. This vision was part of a classic Oriental trope in which The Village symbolized all that was "pure Thai" and The City all that was alien. During the late 1930s, the evils of The City were symbolized by the Chinese; more than six decades later, it was the West.

Thailand's politicians were not alone in blaming the West for the corruption of morals and the decay of traditional Asian values since World War II. Malaysia's Mahathir Mohamad and Singapore's Lee Kuan Yew were both

---

2. *Ibid.*

3. Ian Buruma, *God's Dust: A Modern Asian Journey* (New York: Farrar, Strauss, Giroux, 1989).

staunch cultural nationalists who blamed the West for decadence and vice in their countries' main cities. "The promoters of Asian values today are doing what missionaries, whether 'Asian' or 'Japanese' or 'Christian', have always done," Buruma wrote, in the introduction to *The Missionary and the Libertine*.[4] However: "What the likes of Lee Kuan Yew call Asian values are more or less the values they were taught by their colonial schoolmasters in the days when Kuan Yew was still called Harry. The white man's burden has been covered with a Confucian sauce." The same might be said of Purachai Piumsombun – who, like Lee Kuan Yew and Phibun, was educated in the West.

While the majority of rural Thais supported Purachai's "new social order" campaign, urban Thais were divided. And for foreign residents, the sudden shift in government policy was a rude awakening. Many *farang* who had chosen to live in Thailand were drawn by the Kingdom's relaxed social mores and spirit of *sanuk*, or fun. "Amazing Thailand" was supposed to conjure visions of warm welcomes, first-rate hospitality, and unexpected pleasures – not puritanical echoes of bygone dictatorships. The spectre of police raids was ominous in a country whose last military coup was only a decade earlier. So when the men in brown suits and leather boots start showing up at gay men's saunas, sphincters tend to constrict – as mine did, that final night at The Obelisks.

Half an hour before the cops arrived, I had been sitting in the rooftop garden bar with my Canadian friend Ray, lamenting Purachai's campaign. A few days earlier, police had raided Telephone Pub and Balcony, two popular beer bars in Silom *soi* 4, as well as two bathhouses: Chakran, frequented mostly by Thai men, and Babylon, the city's most successful gay sauna. (During a subsequent raid at the latter, police turned on the dark room lights, tore the doors off private cubicles, ripped containers of lubricant off the walls, and posted signs that read "New Moral and Social Order.")

Ray and I had separated and I was coming out of the maze when two police officers entered the hallway and ordered everyone out. As one officer walked past, I stared down at his polished leather boots. He and his partner were strutting down the hall, altering the physical power dynamic in that

4. Buruma, *The Missionary and the Libertine* (London: Faber and Faber, 1996; revised edition 2002).

space by virtue of their uniforms. Without speaking to anyone, they simply used body language to direct us to the exits. Watching in silence as dozens of semi-naked Thai guys filed out of the cruising area without requiring so much as a barked order, I felt depressingly impotent. I was caught between my western sense of political outrage – the ACT-UP part that wanted to say *Fuck the police – this is our space!* – and my growing awareness of how things worked in Thailand, the part that knew resistance was futile and confrontation would make things worse.

The greatest leverage the cops had with the Thai customers was the knowledge that nobody wanted their presence at The Obelisks to reach the ears of parents, employers, wives, or girlfriends. As for me, Ray, and the few other westerners present, the cops were indifferent: harassing "liberated" foreigners wasn't worth the trouble. When Ray was asked to show his passport and instead presented his university professor's ID card, the police officer *wai*-ed him in respect. The cops were confident that *farang* customers wouldn't intervene on behalf of any arrested Thais, because we knew it wasn't our place to do so. But I only felt diminished by this knowledge, as if my so-called "liberation" was illusory. Suddenly my favourite sauna – with its "piss elegant" faux crystal chandelier hanging over the lobby, its marble floors, its padded wooden furniture, and its lush rooftop greenery – seemed like a mirage.

Although the "New Social Order" campaign eventually wound down and the bar raids stopped, The Obelisks closed its doors for good that night. Thanks to the scores of young men under the age of twenty-one found on the premises, the sauna lost its licence, and the owner couldn't bribe his way out of a large fine. What Ray and I found most striking was the Thai customers' indifference to the invasion of the state in private activities that complied with state regulations. Deference to authority was an instinct so deeply ingrained in Thai society that it trumped everything – fun included.

XVIII
Corruption of the Heart

THE FIRST TIME I VISITED BANGKOK, one of the city's more disturbing aspects was the disproportionate number of overweight, post-middle-aged western men walking around hand in hand with young Thai companions. It wasn't so much the age difference that shocked, or the fact that prostitution was involved; it was the disparity in pulchritude. Too often, the foreigner had the florid complexion and grizzled, beaten-up features of a chronic alcoholic who had staggered into the traffic once too often. The Thai companion, by contrast, seemed too attractive to have to settle – customer or not – for such a *farang kee nok*.[1] Part of me wondered how the white guys could be such jackasses, parading around Bangkok at age sixty wearing heavy metal T-shirts with dayglo surfing shorts. But the other part understood that Bangkok was the tourist capital of arrested development – a magnet for sad souls trying to recapture some vision of lost youth. I sympathized with such men, but I didn't want to *become* one of them.

Gazing into the mirror at age thirty-eight, I could see that I was no longer the svelte twenty-eight-year-old who, at the beginning of our story, gazed into a mirror looking for traces of his long-dead grandfather. Now, I'd begun to look like him: two years of Bangkok life had left bags under the eyes and a Michelin tire around the waist. On some days, I lost my breath running to catch a bus or a taxi. Unlike in Vancouver, where I rode a ten-speed all over the city, Bangkok was bicycle hell. In Vancouver, I was self-employed and constantly on the move; in Bangkok, I spent five days in an office where I seldom got out of my chair. In Vancouver, beer was an expensive luxury; in Bangkok, it was as cheap as bottled water back home. Presto: middle age had arrived.

Emotionally, I was holding it together. Getting an apartment in the city had been a smart move. In Thonglor, I found I could go without sex for up to two weeks at a stretch – although longer than that was difficult. Most days I

1. Literally translates as "birdshit foreigner," a most disparaging insult denoting a westerner who is cheap, unpresentable, or dresses and behaves poorly.

was happy to be on my own and had even learned to say "no" when a cute guy phoned to ask for a date. After Tong, I wasn't in a big hurry to get involved again. If anything, I was reconciled to the fate of living out the rest of my stay in Thailand without finding a steady lover. Friendship was what mattered most, with a reliable stable of "fuck buddies" coming a close second. I still had the hots for Ahn, the precocious twenty-year-old I had brought home from Toy's birthday party while I was with Tong. But two years later, Ahn was still in Tel Aviv, living out another episode in what was by then a five-year ball-and-chain with a possessive Israeli. Other than that hopeless infatuation, I wasn't looking.

My only romantic interest by the end of Year Two was Joe, a twenty-six-year-old tour guide from Chiang Mai. I'd met Joe through my English friend Robin, who'd had a short fling with him. We first hooked up a couple of months after the Tong disaster, when I had taken another trip up north to work on a story about displaced Shan people from Burma. When he came to pick me up at the Chiang Mai train station at nine o'clock one Monday morning, Joe was dressed all in black with a gold necklace, his spiky black hair rinsed with blond streaks. After taking me home on the back of his motorbike, he introduced me to his sisters, his brother, and his five-year-old nephew. He took me out drinking with friends, to the local sports complex to go swimming, and took me sightseeing around Chiang Mai. He showed me country-style Thai restaurants rarely frequented by *farang*, found me a decent guesthouse, and came along on my trip to Fang, near the Burmese border, to translate my interviews with Shan migrants. Throughout all this, he rode me like a horse.

Joe and I spent almost as much time in bed as out of it. We couldn't get enough of each other. When he came down to Bangkok to meet me at the airport after a three-week visit to Canada, he camped out at Thonglor Tower for the next week and showed no signs of leaving. When he greeted me at the door stark naked one night, I began to panic. After Tong, I was so paranoid that I found myself humming a new mantra: "Do *not* give him a set of keys …he is *not* moving in…." When I told him I needed to live alone, Joe said he understood: he wouldn't be happy living in Bangkok and was too much of a northern boy to leave Chiang Mai. But his ardor never cooled completely, and neither did mine. From then on, I would call Joe every time I returned to Chiang Mai, and he would visit my guesthouse – or take me to a "short-time room"[2] – where we'd enjoy yet another lusty session. Even after he was drafted, and I visited his army base in rural Phayao province, he got his commanding officer's permission to spend an hour and a half in my hotel room – yet another example of Thai hospitality, above and beyond the call of duty, that never ceased to amaze.

∞

After two years in Thailand, I was hardly a candidate for the monkhood. But I felt as though I was finally reaching some degree of sanity around my obsession with Asian male beauty – a task made more challenging by voracious Thai cuties like Joe. The truth was, I *had* to keep it together. History and literature were rife with stories of unfortunate western explorers who, in going native, tragically succumbed to the whims of their dicks. My own favourite example was Sir Roger Casement, the roving explorer and Irish Protestant turned nationalist. Six years after being knighted for his investigative reports on imperialist atrocities in the Belgian Congo and the Amazon, Casement was convicted of treason and executed for his role in the 1916 Easter Uprising. Several character witnesses had testified on his behalf: Arthur Conan Doyle and George Bernard Shaw had lobbied vigorously for a pardon. But Casement was doomed by the disclosure of his travel journals.

The Black Diaries had revealed a litany of sodomitical escapades with the young and well-hung natives of Britain's colonial outposts. Casement's couplings with exotic young ephebes such as Agostinho ("kissed many times"); Pepe ("bought cigarettes"); Gabriel Ramos ("X Deep to hilt" and ending "in very deep thrusts"); or Ramon ("Splendid erections. 10" at least") hardly ranked with the Marquis de Sade – or even *The Canterbury Tales* – for shock value. But only two decades after Oscar Wilde's undoing, *The Black Diaries* had explosive impact, as the following report to the British Cabinet indicated:

> Casement's diaries and his ledger entries … show that he
> has for years been addicted to the grossest sodomitical
> practices. Of late years he seems to have completed the

2. Mini, hotel-style bedrooms, often located in converted suburban Chiang Mai garages, that are rented out by the hour for sex.

> full cycle of sexual degeneracy and from a pervert he has
> become an invert – a woman or pathic who derives his
> satisfaction from attracting men and inducing them to
> use him.[3]

"The obvious implication," one writer has noted, "was that instead of Casement fucking the Africans and the Amazon Indians they had begun to fuck him. The British Cabinet at the time would have realised that this was not in keeping with the aims of the Empire."[4] Yes, in 1916, the vision of an officer of the Empire being ploughed in the ass by a dark-skinned colonial – and enjoying it! – would have been, to say the least, "disillusioning to admirers of Casement's humanitarian work."[5]

If Casement is a sympathetic historical figure, the same cannot be said for the fictional character Rene Gallimard, the closeted Rice Queen protagonist of David Henry Hwang's *M. Butterfly*. Gallimard, a French diplomat, subscribes to all the classic fetishes of the unreconstructed neocolonial. A bourgeois careerist and prisoner of his own desires, Gallimard's "Butterfly" is an impossible realization of the passive, inscrutable, mysterious lotus blossom stereotype. Bound by the collegial code of macho posturing among his colleagues, Gallimard is too blind to see Song Li Ling's true male identity – nor the fact he's being used politically by Communist China. In the end, Gallimard finds himself in an actual prison cell as the dupe in a Cold War espionage caper.

Perhaps an even more tragic literary figure of neocolonial lust is the heterosexual protagonist of *Burmese Days*, George Orwell's 1934 novel about racism and moral decay in Burma under British colonial rule in the years surrounding World War I. When we first meet Flory, a thirty-five-year-old white timber merchant, he's a shadow of the teenager who arrived in Rangoon so full of enthusiasm for his exotic new life. Despite acclimatizing to the harsh Burmese climate, he suffers nagging health problems in his mid-twenties and spends his twenty-seventh birthday in the hospital, "covered in

---

3. Memo by the legal adviser to the Home Office, cited in Colm Toibin, *Love in A Dark Time: Gay Lives from Wilde to Almodovar* (London: Picador, 2001).

4. Colm Toibin, *Love in a Dark Time.*

5. *Ibid.* This quote is from the preface of *Roger Casement's Diaries, 1910: The Black and the White*, edited by Roger Sawyer (New York: Random House, 1997), quoted by Toibin.

mud sores" that pockmark his skin. "Quite suddenly," we're told, "he had begun to look and feel very much older. His youth was finished. Eight years of Eastern life, fever, loneliness and intermittent drinking, had set their mark on him...."[6]

Like most newly arrived expatriates, Flory thrives in his first six months in Rangoon. At nineteen, he's still young enough to have a sense of awe about his new surroundings; still earnest enough to look up to the old hands of the firm, who invite him on their hunting and fishing trips – and on their whoring adventures in Rangoon. For the first year or two, he has too much fun to bother learning the local ways of life – burying himself in British novels and dining on specially imported beefsteak. "Too young to realise what life [is] preparing for him," he does "not see the years stretching out ahead, lonely, eventless, corrupting." He dodges service in World War I because "the East ha[s] already corrupted him, and he [does] not want to exchange his whiskey, his servants and his Burmese girls for the boredom of the parade ground and the strain of cruel marches."[7]

But after his hospital stay, Flory opens his eyes. He finally understands the illusion he has been living on behalf of the white man's burden and begins to find that each passing year is lonelier than the one before it. For a period, he takes a more active interest in the lives of the locals. But all the while he remains powerless to change his situation – either to rise above the Darwinian racist outlook of his compatriots or to become a self-actualizing, autonomous man in harmony with his surroundings. He had never returned to England; he tried to once, but his voyage ended at Colombo when he learned that three colleagues in Burma had died of blackwater fever and that he was needed back in Rangoon. In the end, he goes back to Burma for good – but in a state of spiritual inertia. Caught between dependence on his Burmese concubine and a hopeless infatuation with a British debutante who sees him as a sad figure, Flory becomes the epitome of the drunken, self-loathing, self-deluding expat.

The spiritual and political malaise from which Flory suffers is a symptom of

6. George Orwell, *Burmese Days* (New York: Time Inc., 1962).

7. *Ibid.*

an internal conflict between two competing impulses: those of the missionary and the libertine. Drawing from Edward Said's notion of Orientalism as a discourse of binary essentialisms (in which the West is always "rational" and the East is always "sensual"), Ian Buruma's *The Missionary and the Libertine* examines some of the peculiar motivations of westerners who choose to live in the Far East because of its romantic or sensual appeal. "It is a mark of the romantic that he or she seeks the unreal," writes Buruma. "The point of going East is not to find oneself, as so many hippy seekers thought, but to get rid of oneself – or at least those aspects of oneself one does not like."[8]

The "missionary" position, as it were, is that of crusading moralizer: a westerner going east to convert the "savages," or an Asian leader accusing the west of corrupting local "traditional" values. The "libertine" is the western romantic adventurer who idealizes Asians as children of nature and guiltless eroticism, or the Asian who lives up to that image. For the westerner, writes Buruma, both reflexes are often interchangeable:

> Lotusland exacts its price, for seekers after guilt-free sex do not always manage to shed their own sense of guilt. After the sensual charms wear off, or are taken for granted, a peculiar censoriousness sometimes sets in, and the East is denounced for its lack of universal values, its frivolousness, its amorality. All of a sudden the libertine becomes the missionary; the moralism he thought he had shed is deflected on to his hosts.[9]

Those who remain stuck in the first phase of delight with their Asian Arcadia, writes Buruma, "are blind to the dark sides of their East, wherever it may be, for Arcadia, by definition, has no shadows." When George Orwell spoke of "corruption" in *Burmese Days*, it was this shadow side he was talking about: less political corruption than corruption of the heart, those little concessions we make to greed and moral relativity that chip away at our social conscience. When Orwell wrote that "the East had already corrupted" Flory, he was referring to the perks of expatriate life in Asia – cheap booze, servants, passive

---

8. Buruma, *The Missionary and the Libertine* (London: Faber and Faber, 1996; revised edition 2002).
9. *Ibid.*

women – that bloat the ego and distort one's sense of reality. Thailand is one of the easiest places in the world for a westerner to become so "corrupted."

First, it is very difficult – if not impossible – to completely resist the charms of Thai beauty. That's why moderation is the wisest approach, and better for everyone concerned. Adding up the notches on your bedpost might seem exotic to friends back home – and even then, they're more likely to tire of your stories and dismiss you as a walking boner. But for the Thai guys you meet, such behaviour only confirms their belief in the stereotypical foreign butterfly. It's also physically and spiritually draining. For apart from the tingling sensation in your body that can turn to numbness, serial copulation in Bangkok can also leave you feeling that you've lost control of your life and that – perhaps worse – the biggest impact you've made on Thailand is the emotional wreckage you've left behind. While most Thai guys remain friendly after you've dumped them, that's only their public face; chances are, more than a few probably wouldn't mind tossing you into one of Bangkok's filthier *khlongs*.

For the libertine Rice Queen with missionary tendencies, corruption of the heart goes hand in hand with disillusionment: that stripping away of the glittery illusions that attracted you to Thailand in the first place but mysteriously faded the moment the work permit came through. Disillusionment isn't always a bad thing. For those fortunate enough to experience nothing but magical moments on their first visit – quaint episodes of Thai generosity and *mai pen rai* folk wisdom, punctuated by lots of no-strings-attached sex – disillusionment during expat life becomes a necessary corrective; a sober recognition of the giant chasm in wealth and privilege between the Rice Queen and the average local.

That first rip-off by a taxi driver or scam artist charging a non-existent "farang price"; that frightening ride on a motorbike taxi with a driver peaking on *ya baa*; that first lover you regret giving your phone number to because he's always inventing new ways to drain your wallet: all these experiences remind you that you're in a real place, as opposed to the "Amazing Thailand" of the glossy brochures. It was only through disillusionment that I finally realized I had once been one of those very same *farang* I now complained about as a resident: the ones who traipse through the Kingdom indulging their boundless sense of entitlement without even knowing they're doing it.

There's also the disillusionment of cynicism bred by working at a daily newspaper. It's hard to take the "Amazing Thailand" campaigns without irony when you're constantly reminded of the country's harsher realities: the poor couples who abandon new-born babies or elderly parents on superhighway overpasses; the underpaid police officers who arrive at an accident scene and kick the victims to death so they can rob the corpses; the development projects that wipe out local economies and livelihoods with no impact assessment or public hearing; the temples plagued by greedy, lust-driven monks; the high school students who turn tricks so they can afford to buy a new cell phone (or stereo system, or automobile).

When one of the country's leading social critics, Sulak Sivaraksa, laments that shopping malls have replaced the temple as the central unifying force in Thai society, you can't help but feel at least partly responsible as a westerner. After all, there's a flip side to the fact Thailand has never been "colonized," "occupied," or otherwise "conquered" in the political sense: in the cultural and economic sense, virtually every corner of the country has been "colonized" by tourism, several of its military bases "occupied" by the US, and its youth all but "conquered" by global American monoculture.

And yet not even all this can sour you completely on the Kingdom. For even as the disillusioned part of you thinks it might be time to pack it in – to end the fantasy and accept your destiny as a cold-blooded native of the Northern Hemisphere – something happens to remind you why you are here. It might be a sunset in Ayutthaya you contemplate while sitting on an ancient royal viewing stand and watching a dozen mahouts cheerfully hose down their elephants. Or it might be those couple of days spent on the beach at Koh Samet – just a short bus ride away after a hard week at the office. It might be a sudden breakthrough in the Thai language, and the delight of the locals when you join their conversation as the only *farang*. Or it might be a smile on the street from a favourite lover you haven't seen in months. Like pleasure, no pain is permanent.

IXX
Coming Home

By late June of 2002, I had been living in Thailand for more than two years. By that point, I had been thinking about cross-cultural desire, and of what it means to be a Rice Queen, for more than a dozen. Having accumulated several hundred experiences – gathering impressions from three different continents and collecting enough stories to fill a book – my narrative was reaching its end. I was beginning to feel that I had achieved everything I had set out to do in order to answer questions I had posed when the journey began – long before I knew I would ever end up in Thailand. I had probed the mysteries of cross-cultural sex, followed my own desires to wherever they would lead, tried to make sense of them, and, in doing so, challenged my every assumption and stereotype about how the "Occident" relates to the "Orient," and vice-versa.

I could not have answered such questions exclusively from North American shores. When I first began exploring the meaning of Rice Queendom, my perspective was clouded by the privilege of cultural hegemony: as part of the dominant, white Euro culture that set all the rules in the place where I was born, grew up, and continued to live, my view was obscured by cultural blinders. Had I never gone to Southeast Asia – or, had I limited my exposure there to that first phase of "sensuous and sensual delight" – it is unlikely that my fundamental perceptions about ethnicity and culture would have changed to any significant degree. For from the time I began this journey until I moved to Thailand, I saw the journey itself in strictly anthropological terms. Even as the subject of a memoir about cross-cultural desire, I approached the idea of "Otherness" from the objective point of view of the victorious, rational, moneyed West. Had I stayed put in the West, my only duty here would have been to identify the fascination with Far East Asian beauty, record some of the more entertaining encounters, and conclude with some arch, liberal platitudes about the evils of racism – as if to imply that I, Your Narrator, were somehow above the fray.

Of course, my experiences in Southeast Asia pre-empted such an approach. Forced to confront my own capacity for racist behaviour – boundless greed and a myopic sense of entitlement being the main flaws – I had learned an important lesson that's not as obvious as it sounds: if you continue to treat an entire race of people as your own personal playpen, you run the risk of becoming the same stereotype you condemn. The Rice Queen, in essence, is a caricature. As with most caricatures, there's a grain of truth to the stereotype. The unreconstructed, non-self-critical Rice Queen is a furtive, guilt-ridden creature who prefers to go about his business undetected. To him, Asian boys are a secret habit to be enjoyed, like an illicit drug, without drawing attention to the habit. Like any illicit drug, Asian boys are addictive to the connoisseur. Once addiction sets in, can obsession be far behind?

Before moving to Thailand, I had wallowed in a few of my own obsessions. The first involved a Laotian student who first showed up at my door looking for sex even though I was nearly a decade older. This manipulative bad boy teased me for six years – occasionally offering a taste of his beautiful body, but never once hinting what was on his mind or in his heart. (Not surprisingly, he became an actor.) Another obsession, with a Korean clothing designer and part-time model, went nowhere because he was as much of a butterfly as I was. My final obsession, with another clothing designer – this one Japanese – was a hopeless infatuation. I'd met Shigeru at the Gay Games in Amsterdam, where I fell head over heels with him. But Shigeru was a popular disco bunny who had one long-term partner and a string of lovers all over the world, and was moving to Bangkok where he'd soon forget about me. After moving there myself, I bumped into him one night at Babylon. Two years of nightclubbing had taken their toll; he was a shadow of the lithesome twenty-year-old I had drooled over in 1998. Shigeru's last words to me were prophetic. "Don't get carried away with the boys here," he said, "you'll be ruined."

Two years later, I knew what he meant. I hadn't "obsessed" about any one person in Thailand, but that was only because there were too many hot and available boys to waste time fawning over one. The pursuit of sex itself had been an obsession, and in one case – with Tong – I *was* nearly "ruined." Having survived that ordeal, I had required several months to regain a sense of equilibrium. Once I did, things were easier out on the playing field. First, I reached a no-strings-attached agreement with Joe. Then I got over my infatuation with Ahn – who nonetheless agreed to meet me whenever he was back visiting from Israel. Finally, I even managed to establish that "reliable stable of fuck buddies" I had always wanted. Now happily single, I was finally free. It was time to turn my thoughts to what else I was doing in Thailand.

After two years at *The Nation*, I was not learning new skills. Back home, my currency as a freelance writer had long since dried up. I needed to think about new work. The NGO scene in Bangkok was appealing, but the likes of UNESCO weren't hiring copy editors with bachelor degrees. Outside of subbing, it seemed, all that was available was teaching English. I would have had to start from zero: first getting an ESL certificate and then doing some investigative grunt work to avoid ending up in some low-wage hellhole. Then there was Thai society. Since I'd learned to speak more of the language, doors had opened and people were friendlier. But not even the long-term expat who's fluently bilingual can claim to be part of Thai society if he has white skin.

Thai xenophobia was much kinder and gentler than the Japanese variety, but it still limited the *farang*'s relationship to the country at large. I was beginning to miss that part of being a citizen I enjoyed most about my own country: the part that took for granted things like participating in politics or speaking out on matters of national importance. I found myself repeating the words of film critic Donald Ritchie, one of Japan's most distinguished *gajin*: "If you need to belong," he told one interviewer, "you should not become an expatriate. No matter where you go there is still going to be a line that you cannot cross."[1] After my third trip back to Canada in the summer of 2002, I decided to spend one more year at *The Nation*, save some money, then cash in my chips and go home.

∞

Mae Sot
May 2003

The midday sun filters through cracks in the wall as I wake up on the hard wooden floor of a Karen "safe" house near the Burmese border. Just outside the door, amid the scattered howls of country dogs and a crowing rooster, I can hear voices chatting in an ancient dialect. A familiar laugh among them has woken me up, reminding me why I have come all this way: why I boarded

1. From an interview with Mary Kitson, *Kansai Time Out*, September 1996.

an all-night bus from Bangkok and took the day off work, passing through two police roadblocks to arrive in a designated migrant zone where Burmese people would rather live under a curfew and earn two dollars a day selling betel nuts at the local market than face the prospect of returning to their own country. The sound of that laugh reminds me that I have come here for one of these people – or, at least, for his belongings. I have come to deliver his cell phone and bring back to Bangkok the heavy bag of Burmese food, clothing, and other goodies that people on the other side have asked him to take to their refugee relatives. I can take this bag with me on the bus, but I cannot take *him*.

After three years in Thailand, more than a decade's exploration into the meaning of Rice Queendom, and hundreds of lovers from all over the Far East, the journey has come down to this: I have fallen in love, for the first time, with a Burmese migrant worker. That's right: after trolling through the bars and bathhouses of Bangkok, Pattaya, and Chiang Mai, bedding down with untold dozens of Thai boys and casting all of them aside in one way or another, I have been hit by Cupid's arrow. It has come from the bow of Lalune, a twenty-eight-year-old waiter from Burma's rebellious Karen state. Of all the candidates for long-term romance, I have chosen someone who – thanks to the world's most notorious pariah dictatorship – has missed out on a post-secondary education, someone who has spent the better part of his youth concealing his nationality from Thai people, avoiding the Thai police and working under the table to afford a life of wage slavery that is infinitely preferable to the Burmese alternative.

Like so much else that has happened to me in Thailand, Lalune's arrival in my life defies logic. I met him precisely at a time when I had given up on love and was no longer looking for a partner. I met him at a sauna, where – as with so many others – I thought nothing would come of our first meeting. He had a cherubic, almost doll-like face. His twinkling brown eyes regarded me with an inquisitiveness that was simple, uncomplicated, and earnest. Instead of calling me a few hours after leaving Thonglor Tower the morning after we spent the night together, he waited a few days. When we met again, I told him I was flying to Canada for a couple of weeks; he said he would wait for my return. Later, when I was back, he said he couldn't see me for three weeks because an older *farang* was staying with him; I said I would wait until the end of their visit and see him again. After that, we started going places together.

We went to Koh Samet a couple of times and Pattaya several more. We went to Kanchanaburi, where we hiked the trails at Erawan Falls Provincial Park and crossed the Bridge on the River Kwai. We went to Muang Boran "mini-Thai village" in Samut Prakan and Dusit Zoo in Bangkok. We went to restaurants, shopping malls, and movie cinemas. Over Christmas, I told him I was returning to Canada in less than a year. Would he like to come with me? He said yes. Then – two years after pledging never again to do such a thing – I asked Lalune to move in with me. Finally, after bringing all of his belongings to Thonglor Tower in one trip, he then crossed the border back into Burma so he could apply for the passport he would need to travel with me to Canada. Now he is back in Mae Sot and needs me to help him because he cannot legally return to Bangkok. After handing me his belongings and sending me back on the bus with them, he will have to sneak his way back to the capital by bribing a policeman the same way he'd done in Bangkok to get here the first time.

There will be many more hoops for Lalune to jump through. His first attempt to bribe a police officer to "courier" him back to Bangkok will end in disaster. The cop, after taking his money, will desert him and other Burmese migrants near Tak, where they will then be picked up by border police and brought back to a holding cell in Mae Sot. Lalune will be released earlier than the others, because he speaks Thai. Then, rather than trying his luck with another corrupt police officer who might exploit him like the previous one did, he will pay a chicken farmer to take him to Bangkok. Three nights later, he will call me on his cell phone from the back of the chicken farmer's pickup truck, where he's hiding, with other Burmese illegals, between bales of hay.

Once he has his passport and is legally admitted to Thailand on a tourist visa, he will then apply for a visitor's permit to Canada so he can join me on the plane back to Vancouver. But his application will be rejected on the grounds that he is an "overstay risk." A month later, I will leave the country without him. From that moment on, Lalune's status in Thailand will be in jeopardy. When he crosses the border into Laos to renew his tourist visa to Thailand – the country where he has lived for the past dozen years – he will be denied. Ordered by Laotian authorities to return to Burma – where his newly minted passport would be immediately confiscated, preventing him from ever flying to Canada – he will instead bribe a Laotian fisherman to take him across the Mekong River so he can return to Bangkok. Then, safely back in the city, he will return to the cheap apartment he moved into just before my departure, resume his traditional Thai massage course at Wat Pho, and call me on the phone to let me know that everything's all right.

For the next six months he will stay put, waiting for me to launch the immigration application that will one day reunite us. The following May, he will return to Laos illegally to pay off the US $750 he owes in "overstay" fees. He will then get an exit stamp – but not before Laotian customs officials try to shake him down for twice the amount he owes. Then he will fly to Burma, where he will be forced to bribe police officials US $375 for the privilege of processing his criminal record check certificates for both Rangoon and his hometown of Hpa-An, in Karen State. Finally, when asked by curious Thai embassy officials what he's been doing in Laos for the past six months, he will invent a story about how "a friend from the temple" in Vientiane needed help at the family restaurant while he cared for his ailing father. The embassy will grant Lalune a two-month tourist visa that will allow him to re-enter Thailand, obtain his Thai criminal record check (free of charge) and send it, along with all remaining documents, to the Canadian High Commission in Singapore.

A few weeks later, I will contemplate my fifteen-year journey of Rice Queendom – the places it has brought me and the lessons I have learned – as, standing in the waiting area at Vancouver International Airport, I finally set eyes on the face that can bring the entire mystery, and this story, to an end.

Acknowledgments

The Rice Queen Diaries is the product of more than a decade's reflection, reading, discussion, and revision. Thus I am indebted to several individuals and agencies on both sides of the Pacific.

I should first acknowledge the Canada Council of the Arts and the BC Arts Council, whose early financial assistance got me started when *RQD* was set exclusively in the West. Among the many friends and colleagues who provided encouragement, I am especially grateful to Stan Persky, who patiently nudged me toward a manuscript while sharing ideas, books, and lengthy critiques over lunch or evening drinks in Vancouver, Berlin and Bangkok. Kevin Griffin, Don Larventz, Warren O'Briain, and Walter Quan reviewed the manuscript while Brian Fawcett conducted a surgeon's line edit on two chapters and posted excerpts from an earlier draft of *RQD* on *www.dooneyscafe.com*. David Beers, Cindy Filipenko, and Gareth Kirkby published excerpts or related essays in the *Vancouver Sun* and *Xtra! West*. Thanks also to Daniel Collins, Lorenz von Fersen, Terry Glavin, Gordon Brent Ingram, Paul Isaacs, Salle Jafar, Simon Kwan, Rolf Maurer, Randall Roach, Doug Sanders, Bernard and Catherine von Schulmann, plus a couple of artists whose ideas have had a particular influence on this book: Nhan duc Nguyen, whose drawing graces its front cover, and video maker Wayne Yung, one of its earliest cheerleaders.

In Thailand, I am most grateful to colleagues at *The Nation* newspaper in Bangkok. Former deputy managing editor Frank Delfino offered me a job that kept me in the Kingdom, while chief sub editor Chris Burslem approved the leave of absence that allowed me to complete a first draft of *RQD*. Features sub editor Lucille Standley sat through several readings of the manuscript and offered helpful advice over dinner at Le Banyan, while deputy chief sub editor Brian Roddis provided sober perspective when I needed it most. Thai staffers Veena Thoopkrajae, Achara Deboonme, Phatarawadee Phataranawik, Nanitya Tangwisutijit, Paisarn Likhitpreechakul, and Kreangsak Suwanpantakul were always generous with their insights on Thai culture, society, and politics.

Pichai Bantuvachiraporn, Thammasat Sangsrijan, and Sattawat Wong-sirisak inspired me with their beauty, sweetness, and love, while expat confidantes "Ray" and Robin Newbold offered the reassuring companionship of the fellow traveller. Thanks as well to the friendly staff at the Nielson Hays Library and to Edmund Lynch, a visiting friend who donated a planeload of relevant texts on Asiana.

Special thanks must go to publisher Brian Lam for believing in *RQD*, and to his fabulous team at Arsenal Pulp Press: especially production manager Shyla Seller, co-marketing directors Tessa Vanderkop and Janice Beley, and proofreader Linda Field.

Final thanks must go to all the lovers, flings, obsessions, and boyfriends who made this book possible – but especially my partner Lune, to whom this book is dedicated, for having enough confidence in me to take the greatest leap of faith in his life.

DANIEL GAWTHROP is the author of three previous books, including *Affirmation: The AIDS Odyssey of Dr. Peter* (New Star) and *Vanishing Halo: Saving the Boreal Forest* (Greystone). He lives in Vancouver.